G20 Entrepreneurship Services Report

Jian Gao · Ruitao Jia · Qing Su

G20 Entrepreneurship Services Report

Jian Gao
School of Economics
and Management
Tsinghua University
Beijing, China

Ruitao Jia
Entrepreneurship Research
Center on G20 Economies
Tsinghua University
Beijing, China

Qing Su
Entrepreneurship Research
Center on G20 Economies
Tsinghua University
Beijing, China

ISBN 978-981-16-6786-2   ISBN 978-981-16-6787-9 (eBook)
https://doi.org/10.1007/978-981-16-6787-9

Jointly published with Tsinghua University Press

© Tsinghua University Press 2022
This work is subject to copyright. All rights are solely and exclusively licensed by the Publisher, whether the whole or part of the material is concerned, specifically the rights of translation, reprinting, reuse of illustrations, recitation, broadcasting, reproduction on microfilms or in any other physical way, and transmission or information storage and retrieval, electronic adaptation, computer software, or by similar or dissimilar methodology now known or hereafter developed.
The use of general descriptive names, registered names, trademarks, service marks, etc. in this publication does not imply, even in the absence of a specific statement, that such names are exempt from the relevant protective laws and regulations and therefore free for general use.
The publishers, the authors, and the editors are safe to assume that the advice and information in this book are believed to be true and accurate at the date of publication. Neither the publishers nor the authors or the editors give a warranty, express or implied, with respect to the material contained herein or for any errors or omissions that may have been made. The publishers remain neutral with regard to jurisdictional claims in published maps and institutional affiliations.

Cover credit: Marina Lohrbach_shutterstock.com

This Palgrave Macmillan imprint is published by the registered company Springer Nature Singapore Pte Ltd.
The registered company address is: 152 Beach Road, #21-01/04 Gateway East, Singapore 189721, Singapore

PREFACE

The world's economy is undergoing profound changes. While full of uncertainty and instability, it faces many challenges and opportunities. Since the G20 Entrepreneurship Action Plan was issued at the G20 Hangzhou Summit 2016, the G20 member states have responded to changing challenges and leveraged entrepreneurship to promote employment and economic growth.

Entrepreneurs need services, and sustainability is required for entrepreneurship. The provision of high-quality entrepreneurship services is a key element of the G20 Entrepreneurship Action Plan. Although all member states share these beliefs, entrepreneurship services which the governments provide varied in willingness, planning, richness, and effectiveness due to the difference in entrepreneurial environments and entrepreneur's abilities. It is concluded that entrepreneurship services involve a wide range of departments, a sophisticated structure and multi-party participation, and long-term persistence. In the report, we observe the entrepreneurship services of G20 members from the following aspects: government services, fiscal and financial supports, entrepreneur services, entrepreneurship education, and fair competition for SMEs. And we mainly focus on the new progresses of G20 members since 2016 and analyze the similarities and differences of measures taken in different aspects of entrepreneurship services. As for the measures before 2016, we analyze the significance and effects of these measures which have lasted up to date, in a bid to help G20 member states to provide high-quality entrepreneurship service.

Based on the observation and research of the G20 entrepreneurship services, we found that: integration of entrepreneurship into the national strategic plan would comprehensively promote the development of entrepreneurship; revising relevant laws and regulations in combination with the characteristics at different stages of economic developments is the important experience on ensuring and boosting entrepreneurship development; special government agencies for start-ups and SMEs are useful for the formation of an efficient network of entrepreneurship services; how to use and innovate finance, taxation and financial support methods is still a common challenge for all members under the downward pressure of economy and fiscal revenue; governmental efforts are still needed in strengthening investments, innovating service models and guiding involvement of all sectors to cultivate services for entrepreneurs in technology, information, market exploration, entrepreneurship incubation, exchange platform and entrepreneurship education, which are important steps to create beneficial entrepreneurial environments. And we can see that entrepreneurship developments in G20 member states remain unbalanced due to different national situations and demands, and members with better developments should continue the support for developing countries to improve their entrepreneurship service systems, enhance their quality of entrepreneurship services, and enable them to achieve sustainable developments. In addition, during the outbreak of COVID-19 in 2020, some G20 members took the impact of the Covid-19 on businesses as an opportunity to accelerate the digital transformation of SMEs by providing the digital transformation solution, digital skill training for employees, and amending the laws to support teleworking, which are not only the bailout measures, but also the long-term sustainable actions.

We have already carried out relevant research work on the fair competition for SMEs—especially anti-trust, but these reports do not include topics such as supporting entrepreneurs to fulfill their obligations as employers, making efforts to regularize their operations, providing proper social protection for entrepreneurs, and integrating their employees into the social security system. We look forward to carrying out research and summarizing best practices in this area together with G20 member states to contribute to the improvement on the rights and interests of entrepreneurs and enhancement of the protection on their rights and interests.

Although G20 members have adopted the measures in promoting innovation and entrepreneurship, there are still discrepancies in some specific measures due to the different national conditions. Therefore, we believe that in the process of promoting entrepreneurship development and improving the quality of entrepreneurship services, G20 members need to strengthen exchanges and cooperation in the future to enhance mutual learning. As the research team of these reports, we hope to strengthen communication and cooperation, and Entrepreneurship Research Center on G20 Economies would fulfill its mission to deepen information exchange and expand the platform for sharing good practices. We are willing to actively discuss with G20 members to exchange experiences and research results of entrepreneurship services. At the same time, we are looking forward to more involvement of the International Labor Organization, Organization for Economic Cooperation and Development, World Bank Group, and the International Monetary Fund to our work in a joint effort to strengthen research on the entrepreneurship development of G20 members and provide valuable new insights to members in various ways.

Beijing, China

Jian Gao
Ruitao Jia
Qing Su

Acknowledgments

The G20 entrepreneurship service report is the necessary work in the implementation of the G20 Entrepreneurship Action Plan. Through systematic research and the release of related reports on G20 entrepreneurship services, G20 members can gain a deeper understanding of the respective progress, existing problems, and best practices which can be used as a reference for their further implementation.

As this is the first report on entrepreneurship services of the G20 members, the research team has experienced various challenges in the process. Such exploration has gradually defined the direction of our future work, established the framework and research methods, and formed a more systematic theory context of understanding entrepreneurship services of G20 members in the world.

Here, we would like to express our deep appreciation to the colleagues of the Ministry of Human Resources and Social Security of China and especially those who have contributed a lot in our research: Mr. Hao Bin, director general of International Cooperation Department, Mr. LV Yulin, deputy director general of International Cooperation Department, Mr. Chai Haishan, deputy director general of Employment Promotion Department and Ms. Li Feixia, director in International Cooperation Department. In the process of completing the report on entrepreneurship services in Canada, Professor Lin Xiaohua of Canada's Ryerson University has given us valuable feedback and we thank him for his contribution.

Contents

General Introduction	1
I	2
Government Services	2
Fiscal and Financial Supports	3
Entrepreneur Services	3
Entrepreneurship Education	4
Fair Competition for SMEs	5
II	6
Government Services	7
Fiscal and Financial Support	10
Entrepreneur Services	15
Entrepreneurship Education	23
Fair Competition for SMEs	30
III	30
Argentina	33
Government Services	35
Fiscal and Financial Support	36
Entrepreneurial Services	40
Entrepreneurship Education	41
Australia	45
Government Services	47
Fiscal and Financial Support	48

Entrepreneur Services	50
Technical Services	50
Information Services	51
Market Support	51
Enterprise Incubation	52
Communication Platform	52
Digital Transformation Support	53
Entrepreneurship Education	53
Fair Competition for SMEs	56
Brazil	59
Government Services	61
Fiscal and Financial Support	62
Fiscal Support	62
Financial Support	63
Entrepreneur Services	64
Technical Services	65
Information Services	65
Enterprise Incubation	66
Communication Platform	66
Digital Transformation Support	66
Entrepreneurship Education	67
Canada	71
Government Services	73
Fiscal and Financial Support	73
Entrepreneur Services	74
Technical Services	74
Information Services	74
Market Support	75
Enterprise Incubation	75
Entrepreneurship Education	76
Fair Competition for SMEs	77
China	79
Government Services	82
Fiscal Support	86
Financial Support	87
Entrepreneur Services	91
Technical Services	91

Information Services	94
Enterprise Incubation	95
Communication Platform	96
Digital Transformation Support	99
Entrepreneurship Education	100
Protection of Entrepreneurs' Rights and Interests	105
Protection on Property Rights	105
Protect Entrepreneurs' Property Rights Under the Law	106
Protecting Entrepreneur's Innovation Rights and Interests Under the Law	107
Fair Competition for SMEs	108
Europe Union	111
Government Services	113
Fiscal and Financial Support	114
European Structure Funds	115
Progress Microfinance	116
European Investment Fund (EIF)	116
Market in Financial Instruments Directive (MiFID)	117
Entrepreneur Services	118
Information Services	118
Technical Services	119
Market Support	120
Enterprise Incubation	122
Digital Transformation Support	123
Entrepreneurship Education	123
Fair Competition for SMEs	126
France	127
Government Services	128
Fiscal and Financial Support	129
Entrepreneur Services	130
Technical Services	130
Market Support	130
Enterprise Incubation	131
Communication Platform	131
Digital Transformation Support	132
Entrepreneurship Education	132
Fair Competition for SMEs	133

Germany	135
Government Services	137
Fiscal and Financial Support	139
Financial Support	140
Entrepreneur Services	141
Technical Services	141
Information Services	142
Enterprise Incubation	143
Communication Platform	144
Digital Transformation Support	144
Entrepreneurship Education	145
Fair Competition for SMEs	149
India	151
Government Services	152
Fiscal and Financial Support	153
Entrepreneur Services	154
Information Services	154
Technical Services	154
Market Support	154
Enterprise Incubation	155
Digital Transformation Support	155
Entrepreneurship Education	156
Fair Competition for SMEs	157
Indonesia	159
Government Services	161
Fiscal and Financial Support	162
Entrepreneur Services	164
Technical Services	165
Enterprise Incubation	165
Communication Platform	166
Digital Transformation Support	167
Entrepreneurship Education	167
Fair Competition for SMEs	170
Italy	171
Government Services	173
Fiscal and Financial Support	174
Entrepreneur Services	176

Entrepreneurship Education	178
Fair Competition for SMEs	179
Japan	181
Government Services	183
Fiscal and Financial Support	183
Entrepreneur Services	185
Technical Services	185
Market Support	186
Enterprise Incubation	187
Communication Platform	187
Digital Transformation Support	187
Entrepreneurship Education	188
Fair Competition for SMEs	189
Korea	191
Government Services	193
Fiscal and Financial Support	194
Entrepreneur Services	196
Market Support	196
Communication Platform	200
Digital Transformation Support	201
Entrepreneurship Education	201
Fair Competition for SMEs	203
Mexico	205
Government Services	207
Fiscal and Financial Support	208
Entrepreneur Services	211
Entrepreneurship Education	214
Russia	219
Government Services	220
Fiscal and Financial Support	222
Entrepreneur Services	224
Technical Services	224
Market Support	224
Enterprise Incubation	225
Communication Platform	226
Digital Transformation Support	226

Entrepreneurship Education	227
Fair Competition for SMEs	231
Saudi Arabia	233
Government Services	234
Fiscal and Financial Support	236
Entrepreneur Services	236
Technical Services	236
Enterprise Incubation	237
Communication Platform	237
Digital Transformation Support	237
Entrepreneurship Education	238
South Africa	241
Government Services	243
Fiscal and Financial Support	245
Entrepreneur Services	247
Entrepreneurship Education	248
Turkey	253
Government Services	254
Fiscal and Financial Support	255
Entrepreneur Services	257
Market Support	257
Enterprise Incubation	257
Communication Platform	257
Digital Transformation Support	258
Entrepreneurship Education	259
Fair Competition for SMEs	261
United Kingdom	263
Government Services	265
Fiscal and Financial Support	266
Entrepreneur Services	268
Technical Services	268
Information Services	268
Market Support	269
Enterprise Incubation	270
Communication Platform	270
Digital Transformation Support	271

Entrepreneurship Education	271
Fair Competition for SMEs	273
United States	275
Government Services	277
Fiscal and Financial Support	280
Entrepreneur Services	283
Technical Services	283
Information Services	284
Market Support	285
Enterprise Incubation	286
Digital Transformation Support	287
Entrepreneurship Education	288
Fair Competition for SMEs	290
Index	293

List of Tables

China

Table 1	Tax preferential policies prior to 2016 (inclusive)	88
Table 2	Relevant government documents (preferential policies) on venture capital since 2017	92

General Introduction

The world's political economy is undergoing profound changes. While full of uncertainty and instability, it faces many challenges and opportunities. At present, the structural contradictions in the world economy are still prominent. The momentum of sustainable growth is still insufficient. However, the growth of emerging economies has brought broad markets and therefore new drivers to the world economy. Aging and rejuvenation of the population are taking place simultaneously in different countries and regions. Unemployment rate, especially among the youths, remains high, yet demographic changes and migration are shifting the landscape of global resource allocation and industrial supply chain. Technological innovation makes the world closer, boosting resource allocation efficacy. As the prosperity and decline among regions and industries are in sharp contrast, new technologies and new markets bring more opportunities. The popularization of education and the new mode of communication has enabled more people to have equal access to educational resources, including entrepreneurship education.

Since the G20 Entrepreneurship Action Plan was issued at the G20 Hangzhou Summit 2016, the G20 member states have responded to changing challenges and leveraged entrepreneurship to promote employment and growth. In addition, they have improved legal frameworks, systems and policy methods, formulated economic, financial, labor and social policies, and actively exchanged knowledge and experience. Moreover, they have collaborated and endeavored to continuously improve business services in the areas of government services, fiscal and financial supports, entrepreneur services, entrepreneurship education, and fair competition for SMEs.

I

The provision of quality entrepreneurship services is a key element of the G20 Entrepreneurship Action Plan. Entrepreneurship services are constant topics of the four pillars in the action plan. Entrepreneurs need services, and sustainability is required for entrepreneurship. While all member states share these beliefs, the governments provide entrepreneurship services varied in willingness, planning, richness, and effectiveness. In addition, entrepreneurial environments and entrepreneur's abilities are diverse. Entrepreneurship services involve a wide range of departments, a sophisticated structure and multi-party participation, and take long-term persistence. G20 member states are expected to nurture innovations and make persistent efforts to improve entrepreneurial services.

Entrepreneurial services mainly include government services, fiscal and financial supports, entrepreneurs' services, entrepreneurial education, and fair competition for SMEs.

Government Services

Governmental entrepreneurship services include: formulating supportive strategic plans, laws, and regulations; setting up functional departments responsible for entrepreneurship developments; allocating government resources and removing obstacles for entrepreneurial activities; and creating a conducive policy environment and a social and cultural atmosphere for entrepreneurship.

Public policies and government measures are needed in an entrepreneurial society in that entrepreneurship should have a clear purpose and entrepreneurs need sound management. At the same time, it is also necessary to minimize the possible administrative burdens on startups and entrepreneurs, reduce both time and social costs of starting a business, and mitigate the market, financial, and personnel risks in starting a business. Public service agencies should have motivation and incentives to constantly explore and find more effective and specified policies and practices.

Fiscal and Financial Supports

Entrepreneurs need encouraging fiscal and financial policies that can promote capital formation and alleviate their most pressing financial problem, namely, cash shortage.

Fiscal and taxation supports for entrepreneurial services take various forms. The central government may arrange a special fund in the budget to support the public service system and financing system of entrepreneurship through subsidies, government purchase of services, and incentives. The member states have set up venture funds to guide and drive domestic and international funds to support start-ups. In terms of tax support, the tax burden of start-ups and entrepreneurs is alleviated by deferment, reduction, and exemption of corporate income tax and value-added tax, or simplified tax collection and management procedures. In addition, administrative charges are decreased or exempted to help start-up survive and develop.

Financial supports involve monetary policy tools that encourage and guide financial institutions to increase credit supports to start-ups and entrepreneurs. The member states have utilized differentiated regulatory policies to promote and support inclusive finance to facilitate large state-owned commercial banks and small and medium-sized regional banks, who are incentivized to provide financial services for start-ups and entrepreneurs. Specialized financial service institutions are also set up for start-ups. The member states should improve the guarantee and financing system and the policy credit guarantee system to support the financing of start-ups. The capital market system, equity financing, and bond market should be developed to provide diversified financing channels for entrepreneurship.

Entrepreneur Services

We observed and studied entrepreneur services from the aspects of technical support, information support, market support, entrepreneurship incubation, and exchange platform in entrepreneurial processes. The governments need to encourage entrepreneurs to take the important opportunities brought by changes in the market and industry, bring convenience for technological innovation and technology transfer, and play a leading and guiding role through government procurement.

In the globalized market, it means fairness and efficiency for entrepreneurs to have an easy access to open and transparent information. Online platforms with low cost, convenience, and universality have played an irreplaceable and direct role for entrepreneurs to obtain and use information, which are prerequisite conditions for entrepreneurship services.

Entrepreneurs turn their creativity into services and products by establishing enterprises or even new large-scale and global industries, while entrepreneurship incubation may provide necessary resources and supports. The nature, content, and form of entrepreneurship incubation are changing. Entrepreneurship incubation is no longer limited to providing office premises and convenient services, but enters the borderless state with full value chain coverage. Companies, scientific research institutions, and universities have incorporated entrepreneurship incubation into their own development as an important force and platform for openness and innovation.

Through the exchange of experience, entrepreneurs can improve the predictability of decision-making and reduce information asymmetry. By sharing entrepreneurial experience and lessons, entrepreneurs may acquire knowledge by practice and draw on experience from failures. Technology exchange can improve the feasibility and technology commercialization, help protect intellectual property rights, improve entrepreneurs' business awareness, enhance trust among business partners, and discover the potentials of new technologies.

Starting a business is a process in which teams pursue opportunities without many resources. With a platform for exchange, resources can circulate efficiently to those with higher productivity, higher returns, and more efficient uses. So far, the exploration in this area has an ample room to grow.

Entrepreneurship Education

Entrepreneurship education runs through the whole education from primary school, secondary school, vocational education, higher education, to adult education and is included in the social training system. Entrepreneurship education and teaching at different levels of entrepreneurial spirit, recognition, and capability and with different emphases can be launched from primary schools to universities. In addition to the regular education system, other public and private organizations can also provide entrepreneurship education services, training programs, and projects.

Entrepreneurship education is different from the conventional class teaching and knowledge dissemination. It needs to deepen the understanding of the characteristics of entrepreneurship education, improve the concepts of entrepreneurship education, and redesign the curriculum system, teaching contents, and teaching methods.

More importantly, it is necessary to greatly improve teachers' educational abilities, explore the application of digital technologies and other innovative services in entrepreneurship education and training, and continuously expand the scale and scope.

In order to provide financial subsidies for entrepreneurship education and training, governments need to encourage enterprises, social partners, and other stakeholders to provide targeted entrepreneurship training during the life cycle of an enterprise from its establishment to its growth, and also strongly support specific groups, including women, immigrants, young people and the disabled, to receive entrepreneurship education and training.

Fair Competition for SMEs

On fair competition for SMEs, anti-trust is an important content. The protection of SMEs by anti-trust law can be divided into two levels: The first level is general protection. That is to say, by regulating monopoly agreements, prohibiting abuse of market dominance, concentration of operators, and administrative monopoly, we can ensure an effective competitive environment, so that SMEs will not participate in market competition fairly because of unfair competition behaviors of large enterprises, thus playing a protective role for SMEs. Another level is special protection. That is to say, in some aspects, it makes different regulations for SMEs and large enterprises, increases the regulations for large enterprises, relaxes the regulations for small enterprises, and directly protects the development of SMEs. Exemption from competition restriction agreements between SMEs is the special protection for SMEs.

II

This report focuses on the new progresses of G20 member states since 2016 and analyzes the similarities and differences of measures taken in different aspects of entrepreneurship services. As for the measures before 2016, we analyze the significance and effects of these measures to date, in a bid to help G20 member states to provide quality entrepreneurship services.

Based on the observation and research of the G20 entrepreneurial services, we found that:

- Incorporation of entrepreneurship into the national strategic plan would comprehensively promote the development of entrepreneurship;
- Revising relevant laws and regulations at different stages of economic developments in combination with the characteristics of entrepreneurial developments is an important piece of experience on ensuring and boosting entrepreneurship development;
- Special government agencies for start-ups and SMEs are conducive to the formation of an efficient service network system for start-ups and entrepreneurs;
- How to use and innovate finance, taxation and financial support methods is still a common challenge for all member states under the downward pressure of economy and fiscal revenue;
- Governmental efforts are still needed to strengthen investments, innovate service models, and guide the involvement of all sectors. More specifically, cultivating services for entrepreneurs in technology, information, market exploration, entrepreneurship incubation and exchange platform services, entrepreneurship education, and creating beneficial entrepreneurial environments; and
- Entrepreneurship developments in G20 member states vary due to different national situations and demands. Countries with better developments should continue to help developing countries build better entrepreneurial service systems, help them improve the quality of entrepreneurial services, and enable these countries to better achieve sustainable developments.

Government Services

Governments of G20 member states attach strategic importance to innovation and entrepreneurship and have issued national strategic plans to promote innovation and entrepreneurship.

In the strategic plans issued by the G20 member states, some plans promote entrepreneurship in an all-round way. For example, the Chinese government released the Opinions of the State Council Concerning Strengthening the Implementation of Innovation-Driven Development Strategy to Further Promote Mass Entrepreneurship and Mass Innovation. Premier Li Keqiang of China's State Council proposed in the 2018 government work report to promote mass entrepreneurship and mass innovation. The Chinese government will continue its supports for financing, taxation and talents to further stimulate enterprises' creativity. The Indian government initiated the "Start Up India", an innovation and entrepreneurship program in 2016, which aims to shore up the sustainable development of Indian economy by championing innovation and entrepreneurship. Mexico made strategic plans to promote entrepreneurship and strengthen the developments of small and medium enterprises (SMEs) in its National Development Plan 2013–2018, and proposed measures to promote innovation and entrepreneurship in its Special Plan for Science, Technology and Innovation 2014–2018. The Russian government adopted the SME Development Strategy until 2030 to determine the important position of SMEs in Russia's long-term stable economic growth at national level. In 2017, the South African government made the development of SMEs a priority in the National Development Plan (NDP). The British government released the Small Business, Enterprise and Employment (SBEE) Act 2015 to promote SME developments from financial supports, regulatory reforms, government procurement, education, etc. The US government launched the Global Entrepreneurship Program (GEP), seeking to promote entrepreneurship and stimulate innovation by coordinating government programs for the private sector and supporting entrepreneurs around the world.

Some plans to support entrepreneurship from the economic and financial aspects. For example, since 2017 the Indonesian government has implemented the 16th Economic Stimulation Plan, which is mainly aimed at improving and speeding up the processing of various investment licenses so as to improve the entrepreneurial environments and facilitate the administrative licensing of enterprises and businesses. In line with the national plan for industry 4.0, Italy launched the Refinancing of Smart & Start Italia in the 2017 Budget and start-up visa. With Saudi Vision 2030, the Saudi government has formulated a financial sector development plan for innovation and entrepreneurship, start-ups and SMEs, and the "Saudi Private Sector Stimulus Program".

Some plans focus on supporting R&D innovation, technology transfer, and commercialization. For example, Argentina has increased its investment in R&D in the 2020 National Innovation Plan, and plans to increase its investment in R&D to 1.65% of GDP by 2020. Australia's National Innovation and Science Agenda (NISA) encourages entrepreneurship and innovation by setting up special funds, reforming visa systems, and launching Entrepreneurs' Program. France's new edition of France-Europe 2020: National Research Strategy (France Europe 2020) attaches great importance to and supports the development of innovative technologies, the promotion of industry-university-research cooperation, and the transformation and transfer of scientific research achievements. At the end of 2016, the US passed the American Innovation and Competitiveness Act, encouraging private sector innovation, manufacturing innovation, and accelerating technology transfer and commercialization.

Some member states have made efforts to improve the efficiency of government services, simplify government procedures at all levels, simplify registration procedures, and reduce the administrative burdens of new ventures.

The Chinese government has continued to improve the market environment for fair competition and deepen the reform of the commercial system, greatly streamlining business-related licenses through measures such as three certificates in one, multi-certificates in one, tax and land tax joint operation, delegating or canceling administrative approvals in large numbers and lowering the threshold for entrepreneurship. In 2017, there were 19.249 million new market players nationwide, up to 16.6% year on year, with an average daily addition of 52.27 million. In 2016, the country's newly registered market players were 16.513 million, with an increased rate of 11.6%.

In 2017, the Brazilian government, in cooperation with Serviço-Brasileiro de Apoioàs Micro e PequenasEmpresas (SEBRAE) and Banco do Brasil, launched the Most Simple Entrepreneurship Program. Germany introduced the Cutting Bureaucracy Act in 2016 and 2017 to reduce the administrative burdens on small businesses and implemented SME Test in 2016. The Indonesian government announced in early 2018 that it would try its best to improve business regulations and give priority to improving business facilities. The Italian Decree-Law No. 3 of 24 January 2015 reformed the company registration process in terms of reducing registration fees, improving registration efficiency and online registration. At the beginning of 2017, the US government passed the Regulation Account Ability Act (2017), aiming at reducing the red tape of government departments, cutting unnecessary red tape regulations, and promoting employment, innovation, and economic growth.

Special small business service agencies and other institutions and organizations of some member states have formed service network systems featuring division of labor, cooperation, and efficient operation.

The practices of these countries are typical, such as Argentine Entrepreneur and SME Secretariat under the auspice of the Ministry of Production (SEPYME), the Brazilian SEBRAE, the Indian Ministry of Micro, Small and Medium Enterprises (MSME), the Indonesian Ministry of Cooperatives and SMEs, the Japanese Small and Medium Enterprise Agency, the Mexican National Entrepreneurship Institute (INADEM), the Russian Department for the Development of Small and Medium-Sized Businesses and Competition, the Turkish Small and Medium Industry Development Organization (KOSGEB), the US Small Business Administration (SBA), and the EU's SME-Envoy Network for which each member state nominates an envoy.

Some member states have streamlined, merged, or newly established specialized small business service departments that originally provided support to SMEs. For example, Saudi Arabia set up the Small and Medium Enterprises General Authority in 2016, to support the promotion of start-ups and SMEs. The South Korean government upgraded the Department of SMEs to the Ministry of SMEs and Startups, to promote the shift of the economic structure to entrepreneurship and SMEs.

Protecting and promoting entrepreneurship by legal means is an important piece of experience for member states to develop innovation and entrepreneurship.

Some member states have not only basic laws for the development of SMEs, but also special laws for all aspects of the operation of SMEs, such as laws on preventing large enterprises from merging SMEs to form industry monopoly, protecting invention patents of small enterprises, and encouraging and promoting the transfer of scientific and technological achievements to SMEs. Countries represented by Argentina, France,

Germany, Italy, Japan, South Korea, the UK, and the US have relatively comprehensive legal service systems. According to the requirements of different stages of economic development and the characteristics of entrepreneurship development, the governments of some member states revised the laws and policies related to entrepreneurship in time to maximize support for entrepreneurship development. The Chinese government revised the Law on Promotion of Small and Medium-Sized Enterprises in 2018. The new version of the SME law prescribes measures for promoting the development of start-ups and SMEs from multiple aspects, including fiscal and financial support, innovation and entrepreneurship support and services, market expansion, and protection on rights and interests. In 2017, the Argentine government promulgated the Entrepreneurs' Law, which is aimed at increasing Argentina's entrepreneurial and venture investment activities and simplifying business registration to improve the convenience of starting businesses in Argentina. Australia's 2017 Treasury Laws Amendment Bill adds provisions to avoid personal liability of managers due to bankruptcy. Japan's Act on Strengthening the Management of SMEs came into effect in 2016, which is the policy framework for the Japanese government to improve the productivity of SMEs. In 2016, the Saudi government released the new Companies Law, aiming to provide a better investment environment for investors, encourage businessmen from SMEs to invest in Saudi Arabia, and enhance its competitive advantages on the international market.

Fiscal and Financial Support

Fiscal and financial services for entrepreneurship are relatively special fields and are highly dependent on a country's economic development stage and degree of government supervision. Financing difficulties and high costs are common problems faced by start-ups and entrepreneurs. In the context of the complicated international situation, difficulties, and challenges, how to provide quality fiscal and financial services for start-ups and businesses according to their respective national conditions is a challenge for every G20 member state.

Since 2016, the member states have implemented various preferential policies such as tax relief for start-ups and entrepreneurs under the downward pressure of economy and fiscal revenue, continuously pushing forward tax reform, effectively reducing the burdens on start-ups and entrepreneurs, and encouraging enterprises to research and develop innovation.

Some member states have implemented measures including lowering the individual and corporate income tax rate, raising the upper limit of the operating revenue of small businesses, or raising the upper limit of the threshold of value-added tax or exemption from value-added tax, and lowering or reducing capital gains tax.

In 2018, China introduced seven tax cut measures, which are expected to reduce the tax burden on enterprises by about 9.18 billion US dollars in the whole year. In 2017, the annual taxable income limit for low-profit small enterprises will be raised, and the taxable income will be calculated in half and the corporate income tax will be paid at the preferential rate of 20%. Before that, Chinese government also introduced tax preferential measures for incubators, technology-based SMEs and supported enterprise research and development, and exempted SMEs within a certain range from value-added tax and business tax, and reduced or eliminated a number of administrative fees.

The French government reduced corporate income tax on SMEs in the 2018 government budget, explicitly reducing the corporate tax rate to 28% by 2022, and also subsidizing innovation and entrepreneurship through the Innovation Competition program.

In early 2018, the Indonesian government lowered the preferential income tax rate for SMEs from 1 to 0.5%. At the beginning of 2016, the Indonesian government reduced the number of taxes to be paid by SMEs from 54 to 10, all of which can be paid online.

In January 2018, the EU issued a law on value-added tax incentives for SMEs to reduce the tax burden on SMEs.

In early 2017, the Australian government began a three-year reform of the corporate tax system, raised the upper limit of the operating revenue of small businesses, and reduced the corporate tax rate for small enterprises to 27.5%.

India lowered the corporate tax rate of SMEs to 25% in 2017.

The Japanese government continues to implement tax cut and preferential policies for SMEs. The main measures include: reducing tax rates, increasing tax credits for employees' wages, and tax preferential treatment for depreciation of fixed assets. According to the 2017 Tax Reform Outline, the enterprise income tax rate of SMEs earning less than 70,000 US dollars will be reduced to 15% by March 2019.

In December 2017, the Saudi Small and Medium Enterprises General Authority announced to exempt new enterprises established from 2016 to 2021 from government taxes (in the form of disbursement) during their operation in the first three years.

The South Korean government has implemented tax cut and policy loan incentives for innovation and entrepreneurship and SMEs. The corporate tax of SMEs in South Korea can be reduced by 5–30%. In 2017, the South Korean government provided loans of 750 million US dollars for SMEs in the form of "SME Policy Grants" through the supplementary budget.

In 2016, the UK government announced that it would continue to implement phased tax cuts and plan to reduce the income tax rate of SMEs to 17% by 2020. At the beginning of 2017, the British government launched a 5-year tax cut plan with a total of 8.9 billion pounds, focusing on supporting SMEs, permanently doubling the reduction of income tax for SMEs, and adjusting the tax threshold to 12,000 pounds.

The US government introduced the Tax Cuts and Jobs Act at the end of 2017, which changed the eight progressive rates of federal corporate income tax (average rate of large companies is about 35%) to a single rate of 21%.

The Turkish government has taken initiatives to reduce fees and taxes for R&D, innovative enterprises, start-ups, and SMEs, focusing on supporting young entrepreneurs, private institutions engaged in R&D, educational institutions, and high-tech companies. Under the Law No. 6663 amended in January 2016, the income of young entrepreneurs under 19,800 US dollars shall be exempted from individual income tax for three years.

The South African government has continuously raised the small business income tax threshold since 2015, from 5948 US dollars in 2015 to 6359 US dollars at present.

In addition, some member states have reformed the tax collection and management system to reduce the tax burden and tax-related administrative burden on SMEs.

In 2016, the Argentine government set up a special tax system for SMEs. The significance of the special tax system is to further reduce the tax burden of SMEs through tax credits. In 2016, the Brazilian government raised the income standard of small and micro businesses included in the Simple National Tax Law, so that more enterprises may have the access to the tax benefits provided by the Simple National Tax Law. Brazil is one of the countries with heavy taxes in South America. Simplifying reforms in tax system in Brazil has reduced the tax burden on small and micro businesses and simplified the reporting and payment process. In 2016, Russia further simplified the tax payment for SMEs and raised the annual income standard for enterprises using the "simplified tax system".

At the same time, G20 member states have actively taken measures to promote the resolution of financing difficulties, especially for start-ups, expand direct financing channels, foster capital markets where direct financing can be developed, and provide diversified financing channels for start-ups and entrepreneurs. The most important problem facing the development of start-ups is the shortage of funds. Under normal conditions, it is difficult for start-ups to obtain bank loans. Therefore, the governments of member states regard helping start-ups obtain funds as the focus of supporting start-up development. Through the enactment of laws, they set up special financial institutions including SME banks, provide financing projects for start-ups, set up special loan guarantee funds, and establish credit guarantee systems to solve the financing problem of start-ups through multiple channels.

Member States have also taken measures to stimulate the development of venture capital, such as setting up venture capital funds, developing equity investment funds, developing second boards, improving the investment and withdrawal mechanism of venture capital, and encouraging and supporting potential venture enterprises to directly enter the capital market to obtain development funds.

The governments of member states attach importance to optimizing capital markets and enriching venture financing channels in order to support the financing of SMEs.

In 2018, the Brazilian government announced that it would allow Fintech companies with small loan business to obtain licenses and encourage Fintech companies to participate in the market. In 2016, Brazil promulgated the Angel Investment Law to stimulate the development of Brazilian venture capital.

Through the combination of central finance and nongovernmental capital, China set up a national SME development fund and focuses on supporting the growth of seed and growing SMEs. In addition, it launched preferential taxation policies on stimulating venture investment in 2017 and 2018.

The Argentine Development Strategy 2017 and Entrepreneurs' Law of 2017 launched series measures to stimulate venture investment, respectively.

In 2017, Canada launched the Strategic Innovation Fund to support the rapid development of innovative enterprises and launched a new Venture Capital Catalyst Initiative (VCCI) to stimulate venture capital development. In 2017, the Business Development Bank of Canada also introduced a series of measures to support small enterprises, innovation, and entrepreneurship in some special areas.

In 2017, Germany continued to implement the INVEST—Grant for Venture Capital, which helps start-ups find investment and encourages private investors to provide venture capital. In 2016, the German Federal Ministry of Economic Affairs and Energy, the ERP Special Fund, and the European Investment Fund (EIF) jointly set up the ERP/EIF-Wachstumsfazilität of 500 million euros.

In 2017, the Turkish government allowed its Ministry of Finance to directly invest in venture capital funds up to 2 billion Turkish lire (equivalent to 530 million US dollars) by the end of 2023. The Turkish Ministry of Finance promised to inject about 71.64 million Turkish lire into Turkish Growth and Innovation Fund.

In 2016, the Australian government set up a government-led fund to provide tax incentives for venture capital to develop venture capital. In 2017, it passed the Crowd-Sourced Equity Fund (CSEF) to promote venture capital's support for entrepreneurial innovation.

In 2016, the South African set up ZAR X Stock Exchange, which is the second stock exchange in South Africa after Johannesburg Stock Exchange (JES), and to which the first stock exchange license issued by the South African government in more than 100 years.

Member States increased their supports for entrepreneurship in the form of bank loans, guarantees, and other financial supports.

In 2017, the Russian central bank has eased bank regulation for SMEs in 2017. During 2017–2018, the Russian central bank launched the SME loan subsidies to implement the "loan program with interest rate at 6.5%". Besides, the guarantee system with the Russian Federal SME Corporation as the core has expanded the financial channels. The South Korean government provided loans of 750 million US dollars for SMEs in the form of "SME Policy Grants" through the supplementary budget. The Bank of Korea, the central bank of South Korea, increased the credit limit for SMEs in 2015 and 2017, respectively.

In a bid to facilitate SMEs to get loans, Germany prescribed standardized guarantee conditions in 2017 to reduce procedural burdens on SMEs and simplify loan application procedures. Since 2016, the Chinese government has expanded the scope of business guarantee loans, provided discount interest on business guarantee loans to help start-ups and SMEs solve their financing problems.

Entrepreneur Services

Entrepreneurship requires a good environment for entrepreneurship and innovation. Since 2016, the member states have committed themselves to fostering and providing a supportive environment for entrepreneurship and innovation, including technology, information, market development, entrepreneurship incubation, and platform services.

Governments of member states formulated attractive policies and measures to provide financial subsidies and tax incentives for technological innovation of start-ups. They promote new technology research and development. Cooperation is encouraged between institutions of higher education, research institutions and start-ups, and SMEs. The member states also promote technology transfer and marketization, and improve the product quality and level of start-ups.

Some member states provided financial and technical supports for innovation and entrepreneurship through the establishment of funds or projects.

In 2018, the Brazilian government revised the Innovation Law which introduces a framework for cooperation between public and private research sectors, constituting a new national innovation system. The revised law also encourages research and development activities of SMEs through tax incentives. The Chinese government proposed to set up a specialized technology transfer organization, a market-oriented socialized technology transfer organization, a hub-type technology trading market by 2020, to improve the quality and efficiency of technology trading, and provide guidance on improving the technology transfer mechanism and promoting the capitalization of scientific and technological achievements and industries. The Saudi government formulated the 2018–2020 Plan of the Public Investment Fund (PIF), which plans to invest 56 billion US dollars in international and domestic frontier scientific R&D by 2020 and will build the Neom City at the juncture of the Red Sea, Egypt, and Jordan.

In 2017, Canada 2017 Budget proposed to invest about 39.80 million US dollars to launch Innovative Solutions Canada. Germany released the five important action areas that encourage technology-based start-ups. German Digital Strategy 2025 (2016) proposed to invest 1 billion euros in launching the "Digital Investment Program for Small and Medium-Sized Enterprises" by 2018.

In 2016, the Australian Global Innovation Strategy: Helping Australia Compete Internationally set up the Global Connections Fund, which supports exchanges and cooperation between SMEs and researchers at home and abroad. The French government proposed measures to promote the transfer and transformation of scientific and technological achievements, emphasizing the importance of higher education institutions in France's innovation system as they are an important subject linking public scientific research and enterprises. The British government set up the National Productivity Investment Fund (NPIF) and the Industrial Strategy Challenge Fund (ISCF) to prioritize the technology innovation, speed up the conversion of research results, and encourage corporate innovation. In addition, it committed to continuing the incremental of R&D input to keep its advantages in technological innovation.

Providing efficient information channels and quality information for entrepreneurs is the key to promoting entrepreneurial development.

Since 2016, some member states, including Australia, China, India, Russia, the UK, and the EU, have taken concrete actions, such as improving the channels of public information and government services and promoting the popularization and sharing of information network resources, in order to help SMEs obtain quality information in a timely manner and participate in market competition fairly.

In 2017, the Australian government launched the Australian Small Business Advisory Services (ASBAS) to assist service providers in providing low-cost and high-quality digital advisory services and solutions for Australian small enterprises. In addition, it issued the National Business Simplification Initiative-Connecting Government Digital Business Services' Budget for 2017–2018 to implement the National Business Simplification Initiative launched by Australia in 2016.

The Chinese government authorities provide policy consultation and public information services for innovative start-ups and MSMEs through Internet platforms. In 2017, China Mobile, China Telecom, and China

Unicom jointly launched the special action of speeding up Internet speed and reducing fees to support the use of the Internet by SMEs.

Within the framework of the Russian Federation Information Society Development Strategy 2017–2030, the Russian government announced the Russian Federation's Digital Economy Plan in July 2017, planning to improve the availability and quality of public services and products through modern digital technology so as to create conditions for building an information society.

In 2016, the Indian Development (Furnishing of Information) Rules 2016 require all Indian SMEs to furnish their corporate information and help the government supervise and urge the implementation of SME development plans and programs.

In order to help SMEs get financed from other credit service providers through shared credit data and matched finance providers, the British government further specified the list of designated banks and financial platforms in the Small and Medium-Sized Business (Finance Platform) Regulations at the end of 2016.

The EU promotes the sharing of scientific research information among SMEs and the commercialization of research results by sharing public scientific research information and the incorporation of SMEs into the development of public pan-European information infrastructure.

In terms of market support, the governments of member states and small business service agencies give priority to start-ups and SMEs through government procurement. Measures are taken to ensure timely payment of government procurement to small enterprises, and to support market expansion of products and services of start-ups and small enterprises. Government procurement also plays the role of guiding enterprises to increase research and development investment and enhance innovation capability.

The governments of Australia, India, Japan, Russia, the UK, and the US have further improved their government procurement systems.

In 2017, the Australian government announced that it would improve the payment efficiency of SMEs providing services and commodities for the government and set up a digital marketplace, making it easier for start-ups and small enterprises to understand government procurement requirements, obtaining technical support from the government, and competing with large enterprises in a fair environment.

In 2017, the UK released the Developing a Modern Industrial Strategy: Green Paper, proposing to improve the government procurement system and giving full play to the government procurement in guiding business to increase research and development investment and enhancing innovation capability.

In 2017, the US passed the Clarity for America's Small Contractors Act of 2017, which emphasizes the openness and transparency of government procurement to ensure that small businesses can secure government procurement orders fairly. In addition, the Small Business Payment for Performance Act of 2017 (HR 2594) submitted by the Small Business Committee to the House of Representatives is to ensure the timely payment to small businesses in government procurement.

In 2016, India launched the National Scheduled Caste/Scheduled Tribe Hub program to support SMEs to become government public sector suppliers. The "MSME SAMADHAAN" website portal launched in 2017 in order to support the SMEs, the central government, and the provincial governments to jointly monitor payment to SMEs.

In 2016, Japan released the Basic Policies for Future-oriented Trade Practices, amended Act against Delay in Payment of Subcontracting Proceed, and began the "Subcontract G-men door-to-door investigation".

The Russian Federation's SMB Development Strategy until 2030 proposes to increase the share of SMEs in government procurement. In 2016, the Russian government determined the list of enterprises and instructed them to purchase innovative and high-tech products developed by SMEs in order to improve their technology and production capacity.

The technological development leading the market, the rapid localization, and the management system responding to the changes in the global market environment are the key factors that determine the fate of enterprises in the global market. After a period of growth, many companies, including start-ups, have stagnated in the domestic and foreign markets due to conceptual and technical reasons.

Canada, France, Japan, South Korea, the European Union, and other member states promote start-ups and small businesses to expand the global market and overcome growth stagnation.

In 2017, the Canadian government launched the Canada's CanExport Program and plans to set up a fund of about 39.8 million US dollars to provide financial support for SMEs to expand their overseas markets. France launched the "French Fab" campaign as a brand representing the overall image of French industry. The campaign reshaped the image of French industry at home and abroad, and expanded the international influence of French industry. Japan formulated the Strategy to Boost Export Power of Agriculture, Forestry, and Fisheries, which will bring huge overseas market opportunities for SMEs. South Korea started to implement the Online Reverse-Direct Purchase Store Project for Best SME Products, combining SMEs with large enterprises to expand overseas markets using the online platform of large enterprises.

The EU's COSME includes supporting SMEs to be international and enter the market, creating a favorable environment conducive to competition, and providing market support and services for SMEs.

Entrepreneurship incubation is an important part of the promotion of innovation and entrepreneurship among G20 member states.

Although countries have different names for this, it is essentially to provide support and services for enterprises to innovate and start businesses, which ensures that start-up companies can get the resources, information, and networks they need to turn their ideas into new industries of globalization and scale.

Entrepreneurship incubation is no longer limited to providing office premises and convenient services.

The Argentine Entrepreneurs' Law of 2017 provides measures to support start-up incubation as well as technical and fiscal assistance for 13 accelerators. In the next year, the government also plans to create 10 new accelerators with the private sector to help Argentine entrepreneurs.

The Australian government's Landing Pads program, which began in 2016, has set up five business centers in San Francisco, Berlin, Shanghai, Tel Aviv, and Singapore to provide resident incubation for Australian technology-based business enterprises to expand overseas markets.

The Innovation Superclusters Initiative proposed in the 2017 Canadian Federal Budget will pay a close eye on high-tech industries.

In 2017, Station F, the world's largest technology start-up incubator, began its operations in Paris. In addition to providing hardware services such as office space for entrepreneurs, Station F also has business incubation and acceleration projects, each of which is an independent incubator. These projects are aimed at global entrepreneurs and provided by Station F alone or jointly with global technology enterprises, covering various fields of digital ecosystem, including digital finance, Internet health, Internet e-commerce platform, and artificial intelligence.

In China, the Ministry of Finance, the Ministry of Industry and Information Technology, the Ministry of Science and Technology, the Ministry of Commerce, and the State Administration for Industry and Commerce jointly launched the "mass entrepreneurship and innovation base" to provide space for supporting innovation and entrepreneurship of micro and small businesses. Mass entrepreneurship and innovation space have expanded rapidly and its investment and financing capacity has been greatly improved.

Mexican 500 StartupMexico Incubator, part of the 500 Startup Global Incubator, was established in 2011 and has invested more than 100 enterprises so far, mainly in financial technology, transportation, tourism, education, e-commerce, civic technology, and healthcare. It provides incubators in Mexico City with a 16-week seed program, 47,500 US dollars in cash and service worth of 12,500 US dollars, as well as open investment courses for free.

The "Pitch@Palace", a program founded by Prince Andrew, Duke of York in 2014, has held a swathe of innovation and entrepreneurship competitions worldwide, with a profound significance.

The "Data Pitch" program, a startup accelerator funded by the European Commission, was officially launched in 2017. According to the envision of the European Commission, the project will better link existing enterprises and organizations in the region with start-ups through a large amount of data, and experienced enterprises can use the accumulated data to help start-ups conduct information analysis. The project aims to build a data-driven innovation ecosystem across the EU.

Companies, scientific research institutions, and universities have incorporated entrepreneurship incubation into their own development as an important force and platform for openness and innovation.

The Brazilian business incubators emphasize the transfer of scientific and technological achievements and the cooperation among start-ups, scientific research institutions, and social subjects. For example, the technology innovation business incubators managed by the Inova institution of the University of Campinas Marcelo, helps start-ups in emerging technologies. The Brazilian Abastartups also provides services such as business incubation, business operation guidance, and investment for entrepreneurs.

Some university incubators in Canada have been set up in combination with the characteristics of universities. For example, the digital media area of Ryerson University is an incubator with digital media incubation as its core. The TEC Edmonton Incubator is a representative of regional incubators and accelerators and provides services to emerging technology start-ups.

The Indian government's ASPIR plans to set up 100 incubators in India and launch the National Innovation Development and Governance Program (NIDHI) of the Indian Ministry of Science and Technology to build a new research institute in the fiscal year 2016–2017. In September 2017, ZDream Labs, the first China-India Internet incubator, was established in New Delhi.

Incubator service standards are standardized to guide business incubators to provide high-quality incubation services.

In April 2018, the Saudi Small and Medium Enterprises General Authority formulated and promulgated the business incubator regulations. The incubator needs to apply for a permit issued by the department, and the permit applicant must be a government enterprise company or association. Other application conditions include the feasibility study on opening the incubator by the administrative department and the hard conditions such as the incubator site. In 2017, the Chinese government released a service standard for mass entrepreneurship and innovation space and implemented the national measures for filing mass entrepreneurship and innovation space to guide sustainable and healthy development. The KOSGEB has set standards for incubator operation. Incubators that meet the evaluation criteria can use the logo of İŞ GEM®, and incubator leasing companies can obtain venture capital support.

Since 2016, the member states have also committed themselves to a number of activities. They created open and shared innovation platforms and built exchange platforms to service innovation and entrepreneurship. They also provided various services such as financial investment, technology transfer, exhibition display, and market matching. Various innovation and entrepreneurship competitions were held to gather and integrate diverse innovation and entrepreneurship elements such as talent, technology, capital, and market. They guided all sectors of the domestic and international communities to support their own innovation and entrepreneurship and the internationalization of start-ups.

With the advent of the digital economy era, advanced digital technologies provide more diversified options for entrepreneurship and SMEs. Given its great potential to stimulate economic growth and innovation, digital transformation is on the top priority of the national agenda in many G20 members. Several G20 members have launched the long-term national digital strategies or programs to support the digital transformation of SMEs.

Argentine government put forward the Digital Agenda 2030 to promote innovation and entrepreneurship, and great importance is attached to the digital transformation of SMEs, which includes digital payment methods of enterprises, and the development of platforms for digital financial services. The Australian Department of Employment, Skills, Small and Family Business launched the Small Business Digital Champion Program in 2018 that provides a comprehensive digital transformation program for 100 small businesses in Australia, which receive support of up to 18,500 Australian dollars ($14,393) and services from business partners. The EU launched "Digital Innovation Hubs (DIH)" in 2016, with the help of universities and research institutions, to provide a one-stop information platform for SMEs to understand relevant digital technologies, finance, market prospects, and resource docking. Germany's Federal Economics Affairs Ministry has founded "Go-Digital" program in 2017 to help SMEs and Startups on their way to the digital future. The UK government has issued the "Digital Economy Strategy (2015–2018)" with the primary goal of "developing the digital economy and improving the business environment" to develop the UK into the country most suitable for digital entrepreneurship.

During the outbreak of Covid-19 in 2020, as many SMEs found it difficult to adapt to teleworking, new marketing tools, and other digital solutions, most of the G20 member governments provided bailout measures to help them mitigate the impact of the epidemic, which included establishing the digital platform, giving access to special subsidies and financing for SMEs and start-ups to deal with their current difficulties in management.

The governments of Argentine, Brazil, Canada, Italy, South Africa, and Russia provided the guidebook, information, toolbox, and consultations through digital platform to facilitate digital management of SMEs, and the government of Brazil, India, Indonesia, Mexico, and Turkey established digital platforms to support the digital marketing and resource matching of SMEs.

Japanese government provided a special subsidy of 0.3–4.5 million yen (about $30–40 thousand) for SMEs which introduced IT equipment of telework during the epidemic. And the government of China, issued the Special Action Plan for Empowering SMEs with Digitalization, which encouraged the financial institutions to give priority support in loans at preferential interest rates to SMEs that promote digital transformation. Saudi Arabian government provided 2 billion Saudi riyals ($5.3 billion) to provide and activate teleworking tools as an alternative to the regular work environment. In Australia, the AUD 150 million ($116 million) National Broadband Network Rescue Fund was used to help businesses' remote work and facilitate their digitalization.

During the pandemic, some G20 members used the impact of the Covid-19 on businesses as an opportunity to accelerate digital transformation of SMEs providing the digital transformation solution, digital skill training for employees, and amending the laws to support teleworking, which are not only the bailout measures, but also the long-term sustainable actions.

China's National Development and Reform Commission (NDRC) and other 145 organizations, jointly launched the Digital Transformation Partner Action (2020), which firstly provided more than 500 service initiatives on solving the problems encountered by MSMEs in the digital transformation. In 2020, the EU SME Strategy for a Sustainable and Digital Europe came into force, supporting European SMEs and helping them benefit from digitalization to meet the challenges posed by the pandemic. In 2020, UK government issued an online training program of free, high-quality digital skill courses for employers to share with their employees.

It is worth noting that the French government amended the French Labor Code during the epidemic: employers can make it mandatory for employees to telework if their jobs permit which accelerated remote working during the epidemic and advanced the process of digital transformation.

Entrepreneurship Education

Everyone has the potential to innovate and start a business, and everyone should be given equal opportunities. Entrepreneurship education is an effective and necessary way to provide this kind of opportunity and ability for individuals. In addition, the popularization of entrepreneurship education and the improvement of its quality also reflect whether a country has a positive entrepreneurial culture and a good entrepreneurial environment.

Entrepreneurship education runs through the whole education from primary school, secondary school, vocational education, higher education, to adult education.

The Brazilian higher education institutions have a high penetration rate of entrepreneurship education. There are also entrepreneurship training programs for middle school students, such as the "Medio Tec Program". Among the higher education institutions offering entrepreneurship education courses, some emphasize international exchanges such as the University of São Paulo, while others place a priority on entrepreneurship culture such as the Catholic University of Rio de Janeiro, each with its own characteristics. The German entrepreneurship education runs through secondary, higher, and vocational education. Russian higher education institutions are mainly managed by the state, in which the entrepreneurship education has embedded.

South Korea's "Work-Study Dual System" has special training programs for students from high schools and higher vocational colleges. Since the Reconstruction and Development Program (1994) called for the inclusion of entrepreneurship training in the education system, the South African government has placed a high priority on the entrepreneurship education.

Some US higher education institutions have incorporated entrepreneurship education into compulsory curriculum. Increasing US universities are offering entrepreneurship education to students in all departments. The US has also incorporated entrepreneurship education into the basic education, and most states have drawn up a syllabus of entrepreneurship education in the K12 education system.

The British government introduced initiative and entrepreneurship into the school education system, incorporated the entrepreneurship education into core curriculum system of universities, and has now formed a relatively comprehensive entrepreneurship education system and characteristic curricula.

Improving the concept of entrepreneurship education and redesigning the curriculum system, teaching contents, and teaching methods.

The entrepreneurship education courses in Australian higher education institutions are generally offered in business schools. These higher education institutions not only launched bachelor's and master's degrees of entrepreneurship education-related disciplines, but also built entrepreneurship ecosystem with an emphasis on international cooperation and cooperation with industries.

Canada's federal and provincial governments attach great importance to entrepreneurship education and training. Not only have entrepreneurship-related courses increased significantly, some universities represented by the University of Waterloo have also included entrepreneurship education in their strategic planning and are committed to building an entrepreneurship ecosystem that includes entrepreneurship education, practice, and research. Taking Laurel University as a representative, its entrepreneurship education includes scientific entrepreneurship and social entrepreneurship, reflecting the interdisciplinary nature of entrepreneurship education and solving social or environmental problems.

The student entrepreneurship action plan launched by the French Ministry of Education integrates the teaching module of innovation and entrepreneurship into the entire university curriculum system. The entrepreneurship education is included in almost all education programs of higher education institutions, represented by French EMLYON Business School. In 2016, the Ecole Polytechnique, the ENSTA ParisTech, and the TélécomParisTech signed a double-degree cooperation agreement with Zhejiang University in China.

Japan's entrepreneurship education also reflects the trend and characteristics of international cooperation. The "Consortium for Next-Generation Entrepreneurship Education" led by Waseda University was established in 2017. New York University plans to open entrepreneurship skills classes in Japan in April 2018 to help Japanese students cope with the changing working environment.

Represented by the Monterey Institute of Technology (Instituto Tecnológicoy de EstudiosSuperiores de Monterrey), Mexican higher education institutions have incorporated entrepreneurship education into the curriculum system and set up the Network of Centers for Entrepreneurial Families in connection with family business issues. The university has also set up incubators and accelerators to help entrepreneurs start and develop businesses.

Saudi universities not only include entrepreneurship education in their curriculum, but also placed a priority on international exchanges and cooperation with foreign universities. In addition, the Innovation Ecosystem is also included in the entrepreneurship education of Saudi higher education institutions.

South Korean higher education institutions attach importance to cooperation in entrepreneurship education among themselves, jointly launching various campaigns and creating platforms for entrepreneurship.

Chinese higher education institutions have included innovation and entrepreneurship courses in their compulsory courses, and have supported and trained student entrepreneurship teams and enterprises through the means such as building incubators and accelerators and holding entrepreneurship contests, such as Tsinghua x-lab, Tsinghua Management Entrepreneur Accelerator, and Tsinghua University's "President Cup" Innovation Challenge.

Other public and private organizations can also provide entrepreneurship education services for entrepreneurs.

Japan's Startup School Accreditation Scheme began in the fiscal year 2017 to provide services for start-up schools that meet Japanese government's accreditation standards through private sector enterprises entrusted with this task.

The I-Corps and NoBI-U projects jointly launched by Mexico and the US focus on helping entrepreneurs understand the real market demand and commercialize technology.

China has established the Innovation and Entrepreneurship Education Alliance, whose members include not only higher education institutions but also many enterprises, featuring cooperation between higher education institutions and enterprises in China's entrepreneurship education.

It is necessary to greatly improve teachers' educational ability, explore the application of digital technology and other innovative services in entrepreneurship education and training, and continuously expand the scale and scope of entrepreneurship education.

The Argentine government provides both online and offline trainings for entrepreneurs or SMEs, most of which are free of charge, such as the entrepreneurship training program of Argentine National Institute of Industrial Technology. The "Entrepreneur University" run by the Mexican INADEM provides entrepreneurs with a platform for online learning of entrepreneurial knowledge, as well as training programs and courses specifically for young entrepreneurs. Increasing higher education institutions in Indonesia are carrying out entrepreneurship education, and they have also started projects aimed at providing entrepreneurship education for middle school teachers.

The governments provide financial subsidies for entrepreneurship education and training. In addition, the governments provide targeted entrepreneurship training during the life cycle of enterprises.

In 2017, the Canada's Innovation and Skills Plan launched by the Canadian government equipped Canadians with job seeking skills.

The Indian government promotes the development of entrepreneurship training in the form of direct subsidies and provides entrepreneurship training programs in cooperation with enterprises, especially multinational enterprises. For example, the Assistant to Training Institutions (ATI) program (2016) works with Samsung Electronics to provide training in maintenance techniques for Indian youth.

South Africa has programs to provide entrepreneurship training to high-growth enterprises. At the government level, South Korea has a number of entrepreneurship training programs, for instance in software. The KOSGEB has been implementing entrepreneurship training courses nationwide since 2000 and is an important factor in informal (school) entrepreneurship education and training.

The EU's Entrepreneurship 2020 Action Plan takes strengthening entrepreneurship education and training to support entrepreneurship and economic growth and reviving the European entrepreneurship culture to develop the next generation of entrepreneurs as its main tasks.

The governments strongly support specific groups, including women, immigrants, young people, and the disabled, to receive entrepreneurship education and training.

In Argentina, there are entrepreneurship training programs for young and women entrepreneurs such as "From the Idea to the Project", a youth entrepreneurship training program launched by the National Institute of Youth. CRAR is a non-profit organization in Argentina, which mainly provides entrepreneurship training and education for female entrepreneurs. In addition, it serves as a network of platforms for communication and mutual support.

The Australian government provides special entrepreneurship training for special groups such as the youth and women to help them start businesses. For example, Encouraging Entrepreneurship and Self-Employment Initiative launched at the end of 2016 aims to help the youth start their own businesses. The NSW Women Entrepreneurs Network—WON aims to provide a one-stop service for women who want to start a business. Many training programs for women entrepreneurs can be found on the platform.

The Brazilian entrepreneurial training programs for women and youth are more international in nature, such as CicloBrilhante, a free entrepreneurship program for women, and Junior Enterprises, a young entrepreneur organization.

French BNP Paribas Wealth Management and Martine Liautaud's Women Initiative Foundation jointly launched the Women Entrepreneur Program for female entrepreneurs of world's high-growth enterprises.

Also developed is German entrepreneurship education for specific groups such as refugees, young people, and women, including Start-up Your Future, Start-up Nights, and Guide programs, for example.

The Italian government promotes youth entrepreneurship through various policies and actions to create a culture of youth entrepreneurship. For example, the Italian government designed and implemented the National Youth Plans, set up the Department for Youth and the National Youth Agency, and cooperated with non-governmental agencies such as Confindustria.

Since 2017, Japan has launched a number of entrepreneurship training campaigns for young people and women, such as the Global Tech EDGE NEXT program and the Tokyo Women's Entrepreneurship Acceleration Program initiated by the Tokyo Municipal Government. Japan Finance Corporate organizes "High School Student Business Plan Grand Prix" every year for high school students to improve young people's entrepreneurial ability.

In Mexico, there are also special institutions to support women's entrepreneurship. For example, the Communities of Social Entrepreneurs mainly dedicated to helping women entrepreneurs or businesswomen improve their business ability.

In response to youth unemployment, the South African government, in cooperation with international organizations and non-governmental organizations, joined entrepreneurship education at the secondary level to improve the employment and entrepreneurship of young students. The entrepreneurship education program in South African higher learning institutions is also provided for disadvantaged youth groups without university diplomas. Caring about social entrepreneurship and system change is a new trend in entrepreneurship education in South African higher education institutions.

Indian higher education institutions, represented by the Entrepreneurship Development Institute of India (EDII) and Indian Institute of Technology (IIT), not only provide entrepreneurship education courses and programs by themselves, but also provide entrepreneurship trainings for specific groups such as young people, college students, and women by working in tandem with government agencies and businesses.

In Indonesia, international organizations and multinational companies have actively promoted local entrepreneurship education and training, and have set up different programs to provide entrepreneurship training for special groups such as youth and women and high-growth enterprises, including the Indonesia Green Entrepreneurship Program of the International Labor Organization (ILO) and the "Womenwill" program sponsored by Google, a campaign launched by US-based non-profit organizations in Indonesia, in 2016.

We are pleased to see that some member states have successfully made entrepreneurship education part of their compulsory courses, and entrepreneurship education is already being integrated into the higher education system. Some member states are gradually extending the guidance framework of entrepreneurial universities to various higher education institutions and integrating entrepreneurship education into the entire education system, including primary, secondary, vocational, higher, and adult education. However, more member states are required to take similar actions.

The cooperation between educational institutions and enterprises is also one of the trends in entrepreneurship education in recent years. In the process of cooperation with enterprises, educational institutions can inspire a stronger entrepreneurial spirit, develop and activate enterprise innovation culture, and finally achieve the goal of improving entrepreneurship education. In addition, entrepreneurship education should enter the life of entrepreneurs through practical experience and experience of real entrepreneurship. Practical entrepreneurship experience can also be acquired outside education. The member states also encourage young people to acquire entrepreneurial mindset and skills through informal education.

However, certain groups, including women, immigrants, young people, and persons with disabilities, still face difficulties in starting businesses. For example, the difficulties faced by women entrepreneurs are mainly manifested in financing channels, social networks, and the coordination of the relationship between entrepreneurship and family. How to effectively develop the entrepreneurial potential of migrant entrepreneurs and fully develop the entrepreneurial potential of young unemployed are also the problems that the member states have been trying to solve.

Fair Competition for SMEs

The anti-trust laws of G20 member countries also improve the external competitive environment for the development of SMEs by prohibiting monopoly agreements, abusing market dominance, and controlling business mergers.

Based on the protection of SMEs in anti-monopoly in various countries, the following points have guiding and reference significance: (1) Countries protect the development of SMEs by creating a fair market competition environment through anti-trust laws. For example, the US is the first country to legislate on anti-monopoly; (2) Countries have established special anti-trust law enforcement agencies, and stipulated their independent legal status and clear responsibilities; (3) Countries restrict large enterprises from entering the industrial fields exclusive to SMEs. For example, Japan stipulates the fields of SMEs that large enterprises are restricted from entering; (4) Countries clarified the exemption provisions for some behaviors of SMEs in the anti-trust law, such as the conditions required by the monopoly agreement that can be exempted according to the EU, which stipulates that the exemption basis is based on the consequences of the monopoly agreement, and specifically quantifies the market share of the subject of the monopoly agreement that can be exempted; and (5) There are special provisions for SMEs in government procurement. For example, Germany clearly stipulates that a part of the shares should be reserved for SMEs.

III

These reports do not include topics such as supporting entrepreneurs to fulfill their obligations as employers, making efforts to regularize their operations, providing proper social protection for entrepreneurs, and integrating their employees into the social security system. However, we have already carried out and promoted relevant research work. We look forward to carrying out research and summarizing best practices in this area together with G20 member states to contribute to the improvement on the rights and interests of entrepreneurs and enhancement of the protection on their rights and interests.

Based on the common belief, G20 member states have adopted common measures in promoting innovation and entrepreneurship, but there are still discrepancies in some specific measures due to their different national conditions. In recent years, despite the continuous improvement of global economic growth and employment prospects, the labor market still faces various challenges. There have still been great differences in the number and quality of entrepreneurs, the quality and ability of entrepreneurs need to be improved, and the entrepreneurial ecological environment also needs to be improved. At the same time, digitization and automation, globalization, demographic transition, migration, and changes in personal and social expectations for work and welfare have brought about a series of major changes. The government has the opportunity to create new policies, mechanisms, models, and funding channels in promoting entrepreneurship. Therefore, we believe that in promoting entrepreneurship development and improving the quality of entrepreneurship services in various countries, G20 member states will need to strengthen exchanges and cooperation in the future to enhance mutual learning.

Through this report, we provide the following recommendations:

- G20 member states enrich and optimize their own entrepreneurship development strategies and policies under the guidance of the principles of the entrepreneurship action plan according to their national conditions, include progress reports on entrepreneurship development in their national employment plan self-reports, and continue to promote the implementation of the G20 Entrepreneurship Action Plan.
- G20 member states cooperate with stakeholders and relevant government agencies and social partners to help developing countries improve their entrepreneurial environment and achieve sustainable development according to their national conditions and priorities.

As the research team of the report, we hope to strengthen communication and cooperation:

- Entrepreneurship Research Center on G20 Economies is committed to deepening information exchange and expanding the platform for sharing good practices, and is willing to actively discuss with G20 member states to exchange experiences and research results of entrepreneurial services;

- Entrepreneurship Research Center on G20 Economies is willing to actively cooperate with the International Labor Organization, OECD, World Bank, and the International Monetary Fund to strengthen research on the entrepreneurial development process of G20 member states and actively provide valuable new insights to member states in various ways.

Argentina

The Argentine government[1] put forward the National Innovation Plan 2020 in early 2013, explicitly stating that the government's R&D investment will account for 1.65% of GDP by 2020, and formulated a series of public policies to promote innovation and entrepreneurship and support the development of SMEs. The Argentine entrepreneur and SME Secretariat under the auspice of the Ministry of Production (SEPYME) is Argentina's specialized SME management organization.

The Argentine government launched two important initiatives of tax policies on support innovation, entrepreneurship, and micro, small and medium enterprises (MSMEs): the tax payment "Grace Plan" implemented in 2013 and the special taxation system set up under the Law 27264 effective from 2016. Within the framework of the National Innovation Plan 2020, the Argentine government has implemented the tax payment "Grace Plan" for SMEs since August 1, 2013, which is an important step for the Argentine government to stimulate the development of domestic SMEs through a preferential tax system. In the subsequent Law 27264 (which came into effect on August 10, 2016), the Argentine government set up a special taxation system for SMEs. The Argentine government's financial support for entrepreneurship and SMEs also

---

[1] According to the International Monetary Fund (IMF), Argentina defines SMEs by their operating revenues. Argentine SMEs are those with an annual revenue of less than 10 million pesos (equivalent to 400,000 US dollars).

© The Author(s), under exclusive license to Springer Nature Singapore Pte Ltd. 2022
J. Gao et al., *G20 Entrepreneurship Services Report*,
https://doi.org/10.1007/978-981-16-6787-9_2

includes financial subsidies for SMEs and high-tech start-ups, especially for high-tech fields such as information and communication technology (ICT) and biology and other key industrial sectors such as energy. For example, the FONSOFT Trust Fund supports projects for the development of Argentine ICT and projects to start or consolidate the export of software-based SMEs. In addition, Argentina's sectoral Argentina Fund (FONARSEC) provides subsidies of up to 2.5 million pesos (equivalent to 130,000 US dollars) to high-tech companies.

In 2018, the Argentine government launched the Comprehensive Stimulation Plan for SMEs to provide financial support for innovative enterprises, start-ups, and SMEs. The Argentine Development Strategy 2017 and the Entrepreneurs' Law (2017) also launched a series of measures to stimulate venture investment. The Argentine government's financing support for start-ups and SMEs has seen certain results. The outstanding loan balance of SMEs posted a year-on-year increase of 51% in 2017 (vs. 31% in 2016).

The Argentine government's support for entrepreneurs is also reflected in improving the entrepreneurial environment, such as the Entrepreneurs' Law (2017), simplifying the registration process to enable rapid and convenient establishment of start-ups, and the government subsidizes the development and establishment of start-up incubators and accelerators. The Argentine government's Online Platform for Science and Technology Demand and Technology Transfer integrates science and technology resources and provides technical support for entrepreneurs. In 2020, the lockout caused by the Covid-19 made it difficult for MSMEs to operate regularly. With this in mind, the Argentine government adopted digital platform to facilitate the development and the sustainable development of MSMEs.

The Argentine government has been placing a high priority on its entrepreneurship education and training. The Argentine government provides both online and offline trainings for entrepreneurs or SMEs, most of which are free of charge, such as the entrepreneurship training program of the Argentine National Institute of Industrial Technology. In Argentina, there are also entrepreneurship training programs for young and women entrepreneurs such as "From the Idea to the Project", a youth entrepreneurship training program launched by the National Institute of Youth. CRAR is a non-profit organization in Argentina, which mainly provides entrepreneurship training and education for female entrepreneurs. In addition, it serves as a network of platforms for communication and mutual support. Some Argentine universities represented by the University of Buenos Aires (UBA) have also set up incubators while launching entrepreneurship education. Some of these incubators focus on technology-based start-ups, while others specifically support agriculture-based start-ups, or focus on establishing and improving regional entrepreneurial ecology, or cooperate with large enterprises to promote technology commercialization, and work in tandem with international organizations to improve the internationalization of enterprises.

Government Services

Argentina has relevant legal service in supporting innovation, entrepreneurship, and the development of SMEs.

In 2017, the Argentine government promulgated the Entrepreneurs' Law (Ley de Emprendedores) aimed at increasing Argentina's entrepreneurial and venture capital activities, simplifying business registration to improve the convenience of starting businesses, and providing diversified financing channels for start-ups and SMEs. The law also focuses on introducing new incentives, including tax relief, to actively promote the development of Argentine venture capital.

Argentina's Law on Small and Medium Enterprises (1995) gives a general description of the definition, characteristics, composition, and tax policy of SMEs. The new Small and Medium-sized Enterprises Law (2000) made new adjustments to, and requirements for, supportive measures, established the principle of "SMEs First", and gave preferential conditions to SMEs in bidding for government procurement projects. In order to facilitate SMEs to obtain loans, the new Small Business Law (2000) also stipulates that if SMEs invest in areas where the economy is underdeveloped or the unemployment rate is higher than the national average, they will get more favorable loans. In addition, the federal government has established policies and measures conducive to the long-term development of SMEs from time to time. The Argentine government subsequently promulgated the Framework Law on Science, Technology and Innovation (2001). Years ago, it released the Law on Protection of Intellectual Property Rights (1981) and the Law on Technology Transfer (1981). Therefore, all of these laws constitute the legal system to promote innovation and entrepreneurship and the development of SMEs.

The Argentine government has included the promotion of innovation and entrepreneurship in its recent development strategy and has formulated corresponding support policies.

The Argentine government put forward the National Innovation Plan 2020 in early 2013. In the plan, the Argentine government expressed that investment in R&D centers accounted for 0.65% (vs. 1.65% by 2020 as planned by the government) of GDP in the year. In addition, the plan intends to improve the percentage of private investment in R&D to 50% in 2020 from 26% in 2013. The key areas are agriculture, environmental protection, social development, renewable energy, industry, and medical care. In addition, Argentina has formulated a series of public policies to promote innovation and entrepreneurship and to support the development of SMEs, such as the Preferential Interest Rate Mechanism for Loans to SMEs, the Financial Credit Mechanism for Training SMEs, the Start-up Capital Plan, the Demand Support Plan for Science and Technology and the Investment Support Plan for Science and Technology Entrepreneurs. In 2018, Argentine government put forward the Digital Agenda 2030 to promote innovation and entrepreneurship, the digital transformation of SMEs, digital payment methods of enterprises, and the development of private platforms for digital financial services.[2]

Fiscal and Financial Support

The Argentine government launched two important initiatives of tax policies to support innovation, entrepreneurship, and micro, small and medium enterprises (MSMEs): the tax payment "Grace Plan" implemented as from 2013 and the special taxation system set up under the Law 27264 effective as from 2016.

Within the framework of the National Innovation Plan 2020, the Argentine government has implemented the tax payment "Grace Plan" for SMEs since August 1, 2013, which is an important step for the Argentine government to stimulate the development of domestic start-ups and SMEs through preferential tax system. The plan allows SMEs to delay paying taxes up to a maximum of 20 million pesos (equivalent to 1.04 million US dollars), with a grace period of six months and an interest

---

[2] Assessment on the progress of G20 Entrepreneurship Action Plan, Entrepreneurship Research Center on G20 Economies, Oct 22, 2019.

rate of 1.35–3%. The plan includes all types of taxes such as value-added tax, business tax, and income tax. The applicant must have appropriate qualifications and a good historical record to ensure tax revenue.

In Law 27264 (effective in 2016), the Argentine government has established a special tax system for MSMEs to reduce their tax burdens: (1) From January 1, 2019, the minimum deemed income tax (MDIT) will be abolished; (2) Special treatment of value-added tax: For micro and small businesses, the deadline for submission of monthly tax returns and payment of tax balances was extended by one month; (3) A system was established for repaying outstanding VAT balances to taxpayers through the use of government bonds; (4) Micro businesses and small enterprises can use the valid tax on debits and credits in bank accounts (TDC) as a credit for income tax, and medium-sized enterprises can use the 50%[3] TDC as a tax credit; and (5) 10% of investment in infrastructure construction and capital goods of SMEs can be used as a credit for income tax.

By providing financial subsidies, the Argentine government has focused on supporting the development of innovative start-ups and SMEs in high-tech fields such as information and communication technology (ICT), biology, and energy.

The FONSOFT Trust Fund has set up a project to support the development of information and communication technology (ICT) in Argentina such as non-refundable contributions (Aportes No Reembolsables). It supports SMEs for technological innovations by subsidizing partial project cost. SMEs can get subsidies through two channels: (1) product quality certification, by which a subsidy of up to 1 million US dollars can be obtained; or (2) development of new products, services, and solutions, by which a subsidy of up to 3 million US dollars can be obtained. The FONSOFT international subsidy program provides funding support for SMEs in the field of ICT to transform production structure and improve innovation capacity. Under this program, a subsidy of up to 2.5 million US dollars may be obtained. The ANR

---

[3] The financial transaction tax, or tax on debits and credits on bank accounts, is imposed on personal and corporate debit and credit (deposit and withdrawal) accounts at prescribed tax rate. A certain proportion (between 17 and 34%) of the tax can be credited against income tax. On July 31, 2017, Argentina announced Decree No. 588 of 2017, amending the financial transaction tax to exempt financial transactions in bank accounts of financial leasing companies from tax as of July 31.

FONSOFT Training program trains talents in the field of software and computer department, develop talents in this field, and support innovation programs. The cost of training programs can be subsidized by up to 50%, with a total amount not exceeding 500,000 US dollars.

The Export Credit (CE) program under the fund provides loans to start or consolidate the export of SMEs engaged in the software industry. For example, it provides technical assistance and support for enterprises to develop new products or upgrade existing products; launch export-related business training for enterprises; help enterprises upgrade technology or quality standards when they encounter barriers to access the target market; make external business promotion, explore new export markets, and establish internal foreign trade department for SMEs. The loan provided by FONSOFT can cover 80% of the total project cost, up to a maximum of 3.5 million US dollars.

Argentine Sectorial Fund (FonarSec) supports the development of biotechnology, nanotechnology, energy, health, agricultural and industrial sectors. It provides subsidies of up to 2.5 million pesos (equivalent to 130,000 US dollars) to high-tech companies to expand business, export, and commercialize technology.

In 2018, the Argentine government launched the Comprehensive Stimulation Plan for SMEs to provide financial support for innovative enterprises, start-ups, and SMEs. The Argentine Development Strategy 2017 and the Entrepreneurs' Law (2017) also launched a series of measures to stimulate venture investment.

On June 13, 2018, the Ministry of Production of Argentina and the National Bank of Argentina (BNA) jointly announced the launch of the SMEs Stimulus Comprehensive Plan to provide financing support of 22 billion pesos (equivalent to 1.15 billion US dollars) for SMEs. The plan announced that the loan interest rate for SMEs will be entitled to a 3% discount, and the final interest rate for loans will be 29% instead of 32%. Another measure of the plan is to allocate 156 million US dollars to Argentine Guarantee Fund (FOGAR) to provide automatic and partial loan guarantees for SMEs. The plan also includes a measure of allocating about 273 million US dollars to be managed by Argentine Foreign Trade and Investment Bank (BICE) to provide loans for projects of SMEs related to energy efficiency, regional economic development, industrial park construction, and agricultural machinery purchase.

Before that, the Argentine government also released the Argentine Development Strategy 2017 (July 2017). In this strategy, the Argentine government decided to carry out policy reforms to the monetary authorities to support the financing of entrepreneurship and SMEs. The government will lift restrictions on foreign exchange transactions, remove the upper and lower interest rate limits in the financial system, control inflation below 5% by 2019 to attract people to save. In addition, it will require financial institutions to allocate a certain proportion of their funds to finance SMEs. In 2017, the Argentine Ministry of Finance and the European Investment Bank (EIB) signed a loan of 71 million US dollars to support SMEs.

The Argentine Development Strategy 2017 has introduced a series of policies to facilitate SMEs tap into the capital market to obtain financing. For example, it devised the SME Global Plan, simplified the requirements for SMEs to issue bonds, and improved the mechanism for inspection and supervision to improve transparency and fair pricing. In addition, it introduced digital images to speed up the approval process for enterprises' admission to the market. In addition, a series of measures were introduced, such as reforming the promissory note system, setting up a financial aid office, and increasing the maximum issue limit of negotiable debt regime.

The Entrepreneurs' Law (Ley de Emprenderers) (2017) allows public funds to make joint investments with private investors for the first time to help start-up projects. At the same time, the Fiduciary Fund for the Development of Venture Capital (FONDCE) will be set up, which can provide up to 40% of the total committed capital, if the investing institution of the start-up provides the corresponding amount of funds. The law also imposes tax cuts on venture capital institutions. According to the regulations, 75% of any investment in SAS and SAS-certified investment funds can be used to offset some investors' income. Corresponding tax cut is available to the investment in less developed regions. In addition, the law encourages crowd funding platforms to help entrepreneurs access various financing channels, including financing by selling equity and offering convertible notes online. Under the law, Argentina will also establish a registry of venture capital institutions as a platform for registering and sharing information among Argentine venture capital institutions and individuals, making information exchange and tracking easier.

Since 2017, the Argentine government has increased its financial support for start-ups and SMEs. The outstanding loan balance of SMEs was 1124.59 billion pesos (equivalent to 586 billion US dollars), up 31% year on year, as at the end of 2016, and 1701.21 billion pesos (equivalent to 887 billion US dollars) as at the end of 2017, up 51% year on year.

Entrepreneurial Services

The Argentine government's entrepreneur services are reflected in improving the entrepreneurial environment, such as simplifying the registration process to enable rapid and convenient establishment of start-ups. The government funded the development and establishment of start-up incubators and accelerators, and strengthened the integration of science and technology resources to provide technical support for entrepreneurs.

The Argentine government simplified the business registration process in the Entrepreneurs' Law (2017), allowing entrepreneurs to register a simplified business entity (SAS) within 24 hours online via the Internet, including opening bank accounts, digital accounts, and establishing CUIT (Identification Number). SAS allows Argentine companies to have only one owner, but if the founder wants to add another partner, he does not need to modify the registration type of the company. In addition, the company is also provided with a temporary address, which only requires the founder to change to a permanent registered address within six months to one year. At present, it takes six months to one year to start a business in Argentina. Simplifying the registration process will effectively shorten the registration duration and make it faster and more convenient for entrepreneurs to start businesses in Argentina.

In addition, the law introduced measures to support entrepreneurship incubation. For example, the Argentine government will provide technical and financial assistance for 13 accelerator projects, of which 10 are dedicated to technology and social entrepreneurship, and 3 are research-based venture investment projects—creating new seed fund programs. The financial assistance required for the plan will come from various channels, including soft loans, non-reimbursable contributions, and venture capital development funds (FONDCE). In the next year, the government also plans to create 10 new accelerators with the private sector to help Argentine entrepreneurs promote development.

Argentine Ministry of Science and Technology has created an "online platform for scientific and technological needs and technology transfer" for government departments, scientific research institutions, higher learning institutions, and enterprises, etc. It can release information on technological R&D achievements, technological needs and technology transfer by different industries and form a communication network to effectively synergize "production, learning and research".

In 2020, the lockout caused by the Covid-19 made it difficult for MSMEs to operate regularly. With this in mind, the Argentine government adopted digital platform to facilitate the development and the sustainable development of MSMEs. In April of 2020, the Ministry of Productive Development of Argentina developed the virtual platform Capacitor, through which it provides MSMEs with discussion salons, technical assistance, and advice, with the aim of promoting the professionalization of management teams and improving the entrepreneurial and managerial capacities of entrepreneurs and SMEs. And the Argentine Ministry of Productive Development launched the Digital Assistance Network, which provided users with a new section containing guidebooks, activities and tutorials, as well as a teleworking and e-commerce platform for private businesses. The platform supports teleworking in a bid to improve remote collaboration and digital management of the enterprise.[4]

Entrepreneurship Education

The Argentine government has different ways of providing entrepreneurship training for young and women entrepreneurs.

The Argentine government provides both online and offline trainings for entrepreneurs or SMEs, most of which are free of charge. The entrepreneurship training program of the National Institute of Industrial Technology of Argentina provides technical training in many industries, including food, electronics and metrology, materials, chemicals, natural resources, and the environment.

The National Institute of Youth under Argentine Ministry of Social Development launches entrepreneurship education on the youth. Take

---

[4] Evaluation and Prospect of G20 Members' Policies to Support Entrepreneurship in the Post-pandemic Era, Entrepreneurship Research Center on G20 Economies, Oct 22, 2020.

the "From the Idea to the Project" as an example, the National Institute of Youth provides a 2-month training for young entrepreneurs, guides them to complete their business plans, and provides them with relevant suggestions and technical support. After the completion of the training, trainees may apply for micro loans. After their applications are approved, they may receive another 2-month entrepreneurship mentoring services. This project is completely free for young people applying for training and currently has 85 branches in 8 provinces of Argentina.

CRAR is a non-profit organization in Argentina, which mainly provides entrepreneurship training and education for female entrepreneurs. In addition, it serves as a network of platforms for communication and mutual support. According to the establishment length of start-ups, entrepreneurs are organized for primary and advanced trainings, of which the primary training mainly includes fundamental knowledge and gatherings relating to entrepreneurship, while the advanced training is themed, such as series campaigns of WIMEN which is organized every month. CARIR has a virtual community where women entrepreneurs can communicate online, with more than 1600 members.

Some Argentine higher learning institutions have also set up various incubators while launching entrepreneurship education, including those focusing on technological entrepreneurship, those specifically supporting agricultural entrepreneurship, and those focusing on establishing and improving regional entrepreneurship ecology. In addition, incubators of Argentine higher learning institutions featured in cooperation with large enterprises and international organizations to promote the commercialization of technology and improve the internationalization of enterprises.

The UBA, for example, has set up different incubators according to different professional types of start-ups. Incubation is an incubator for technology-based start-ups and has fostered about 100 start-ups since its establishment in 2003. Incubation offers entrepreneurship courses, which are open to students, graduates, faculty and researchers, providing opportunities for exchange with experienced businessmen and cooperation with students of different majors. Incubation also cooperated with other organizations to hold entrepreneurship competitions, such as Redemprendia's SPIN (2016) Entrepreneurship Competition, for students, teachers, and researchers from Ibero-American University. Argentine agriculture is a dominant industry. The UBA has set up the IncUBAgro, an agricultural business incubator. Relying on the scientific research strength of the university, IncUBAgro enjoys leading agricultural technology achievements. IncUBAgro assists entrepreneurs to explore opportunities for cooperation with large agricultural companies and promote industrial development.

The Entrepreneurship Center of IAE Business School of Austral University (Universidad Austral) is dedicated to promoting the establishment and improvement of the entrepreneurial ecology in the region. The main work of the Entrepreneurship Center includes training students in entrepreneurship knowledge, skills, and attitude. Among them, Naves (Ships) Entrepreneurship Contest is a large-scale campaign to help entrepreneurs turn ideas into companies, develop and expand their companies, and also support the innovative projects of mature companies. The Entrepreneurial Support Network of the Entrepreneurship Center includes more than 450 alumni, college teachers, and related personnel in the entrepreneurial ecology. Through campaigns such as the Naves Entrepreneurship Contest, the Entrepreneurship Center has helped entrepreneurs set up more than 400 enterprises. The Entrepreneurship Center and Alumni Organization jointly set up Club Business Angels to provide further financial and experience support for entrepreneurs. The Entrepreneurship Center also cooperates with large companies to launch some projects to promote the development of start-ups. For example, CITES Startups sponsored by CITES, a company owned by SancorSeguros Group, supports high-tech start-ups, including biotechnology and nanotechnology. The Entrepreneurship Center is a partner of CITES. The selected start-up enterprises will receive a 4-month training, with the trainers being the top-notch experts in the industry. After the training, the start-up team will have the opportunity to get an investment of 500,000 US dollars and incubate in CITES, with more professional assistance from technical laboratories, markets, and finance. The Entrepreneurship Center also took over the work of GEM (Global Entrepreneurship Monitor) and GUEST (Global University Entrepreneurial Social Spirit Student's Survey) in Argentina.

The Development Center for Entrepreneurs and Exporters (CEDEX) of the University of Palermo (UP) is dedicated to promoting the international development of enterprises. The center has established contacts with many domestic and foreign organizations, including the United Nations Development Programme (UNDP), Inter-American Development Bank, several universities and R&D institutions, the Ministry of Commerce, funds, government agencies, etc. CEDEX also cooperated with government agencies to launch entrepreneurship education campaigns. For example, the Olympic Entrepreneurship Competition sponsored by the General Entrepreneurship Directorate of the Government is an inter-university competition that can be attended by undergraduate or graduate students and requires enterprises to be established for less than three years. CEDEX offers special training courses on business logistics and international trade for entrepreneurs and business executives, with teachers of practical and teaching experience. At the same time, the center also offers courses on basic knowledge of entrepreneurship to help those who want to start a business put their ideas into practice.

Australia

The Australian government[1] set up a government-led fund, provides tax incentives for venture capital, and helps start-ups and SMEs expand financing channels and solve financing problems by developing equity crowd funding. In 2016, the Australian government set up the CSIRO Innovation Fund, a government-led fund, and provided tax incentives for venture capital investment through the Tax Law Amendment (Tax Incentives for Innovation) Bill 2016. The Crowd-Sourced Equity Fund (CSEF) adopted by in 2017 to help SMEs with difficulties in financing through conventional channels to fill their funding gap, thereby promoting investment support for venture innovation.

In terms of serving entrepreneurs, the Australian government has set up an "Industrial Growth Center" to promote commercialization of scientific and technological achievements, provided simplified and high-quality digital services, and supported the market expansion of start-ups and small businesses through government procurement. In November 2016, the Australian Department of Innovation, Industry, Science and Research (DIISR) released the Global Innovation Strategy: Helping Australia compete internationally. In November

---

[1] According to the definition of Australian Bureau of Statistics (ABS), small businesses are those employing less than 20 employees. According to ABS's statistics, there were about 2.23 million SMEs in 2017, accounting for 99.5% of the total number of enterprises. Australian SMEs created 5.5 million jobs and generated 380 billion US dollars.

© The Author(s), under exclusive license to Springer Nature Singapore Pte Ltd. 2022
J. Gao et al., *G20 Entrepreneurship Services Report*,
https://doi.org/10.1007/978-981-16-6787-9_3

2017, the Australian Government launched Australian Small Business Advisory Services (ASBAS) Digital Solutions to assist service providers in providing low-cost, high-quality digital consulting services and solutions for Australian small businesses. In 2017, the Australian government announced that it would improve the payment efficiency of SMEs providing services and commodities for the government and set up a digital marketplace in the digital technology, making it easier for start-ups and small enterprises to understand government procurement requirements, obtaining technical support from the government, and competing with large enterprises in a fair environment. In terms of business incubation, the Australian government's Landing Pads program, which began in 2016, has set up five business centers in San Francisco, Berlin, Shanghai, Tel Aviv, and Singapore to provide resident incubation support for Australian technology-based business enterprises to expand overseas markets. At the end of 2017, four regional incubator facilitators were appointed to advise start-up companies. To support start-ups in their digital operations during the outbreak of Covid-19 in 2020, NBN Co Limited has announced the allocation of AUD 150 million ($116 million) for coronavirus rescue measures, and to help businesses' remote work and facilitate their digitalization.

The Australian government provides special entrepreneurship training for the youth and women to help them start businesses. For example, Encouraging Entrepreneurship and Self-Employment Initiative launched at the end of 2016 aims to help the youth start their own businesses. The NSW Women Entrepreneurs Network—WON aims to provide a one-stop service for women who want to start a business. Many training programs for female entrepreneurs can be found on the platform. Although interdisciplinary teaching is the trend of entrepreneurship education, the entrepreneurship education courses in Australian higher learning institutions are generally offered in business schools. These universities not only launched bachelor's and master's degrees of entrepreneurship education-related disciplines, but also built entrepreneurship ecosystem, while attaching great importance to the international cooperation and cooperation with industries.

The then-effect Australian anti-trust law is the Competition and Consumer Act 2010. The law includes the prohibition of abuse of market dominance, which is closely related to the protection of SMEs. In the enforcement of anti-abuse of market dominance, the Australian Competition and Consumer Commission is responsible for unified enforcement in a "pyramid" law enforcement model.

Government Services

In June 2017, Australia's Treasury Laws Amendment Bill was submitted to the House of Representatives for consideration. The main contents of the bill include reducing bankruptcy liquidation from three years to one year, setting up a safe harbor and avoiding personal responsibility of managers due to bankruptcy. In July 2015, the Australian government adjusted the Employee Share Scheme (ESS) so that employees of start-ups can get shares or stocks as part of their compensation, in order to share the achievements of start-ups and mitigate their cash pressure. At the same time, it was announced that from July 1, 2015, the equity or options held by employees will not be subject to tax until financial benefits are generated. Eligible start-ups can offer employees a certain discount of stock rights and options, with the stock rights discount partially exempted from tax, and the option discount will be deferred until the option is sold.

The National Innovation and Science Agenda (NISA, 2015) issued by the Australian government in December 2015 mainly includes the following four parts: (1) encouraging entrepreneurship and innovation through new tax incentives and the establishment of CSIRO Innovation Fund and Biomedical Translation Fund; (2) supporting the cooperative research and development between universities and industry; (3) promoting the education of online and digital courses and reforming the visa system to attract overseas researchers and entrepreneurs; and (4) improving the government services in terms of service mode and open access to data, and promoting innovative small businesses and entrepreneurs to sell technology and services to the government.

As part of NISA, 2015, the Australian government launched the Entrepreneurs' Program to help start-ups and SMEs develop in four ways: (1) helping entrepreneurs accelerate the commercialization of their products and services; (2) providing start-ups and SMEs with supports and services such as management consulting, supply chain management, potential customer development and providing business growth grant of up to 20,000 Australian dollars; (3) supporting the development of new and existing business incubators; and (4) helping start-ups and SMEs improve their R&D capabilities and providing up to 50,000 Australian dollars in funding.

The Australian government has set up the Innovation and Science Committee of Cabinet, which is chaired by the Australian Prime Minister and is responsible for guiding the nation's innovation work. The purpose of the Committee is to ensure that innovation and science are the center of the government's work and implement NISA, 2015.

In addition, the Australian government set up the Innovation and Science Australia (ISA) in October 2016. ISA, as an independent legal entity, is composed of entrepreneurs, innovators, scientists, and university professors who have influence in their respective fields and is responsible for providing strategic advice for the government on science, research, and innovation.

In 2016, the Australian government set up Australian Small Business and Family Enterprise Ombudsman (ASBFEO) to replace the previous Australian Small Business Commissioner. The main responsibility of the ASBFEO is to promote the development of small and family businesses in Australia, provide dispute resolution services and ensure that government policies are in line with the interests of small businesses.

The Australian Department of Jobs and Small Business is responsible for the release of Australian policy on small businesses. The Australian government has a special website https://www.business.gov.au/, which provides consulting services in various aspects such as enterprise incorporation, operation management, startup, and financial support. The service methods include video, online access, telephone, etc.

Fiscal and Financial Support

In May 2015, the Australian government released the Budget for 2015/2016. Promoting employment and small business development is one of the most fundamental contents of the new budget. In the budget, the Australian government introduced the Jobs and Small Business Package to provide SMEs with a total tax cut of 5 billion Australian dollars, reducing the applicable tax rate for small businesses with an annual revenue of less than 2 million Australian dollars from 30 to 28.5%, the lowest tax rate applicable to small businesses since 1967. At the beginning of 2017, the Australian government began a three-year reform of the corporate tax system, raising the upper limit of business revenue for small businesses from 2 million Australian dollars to 10 million Australian dollars, and reducing the applicable corporate tax rate for small businesses from 28.5 to 27.5% accordingly. In the fiscal year 2018–2019, the upper limit of business revenue for small businesses will be raised to 25 million Australian dollars.

Capital adequacy is particularly important for start-ups. The Australian government has been attaching great importance to the role of venture capital in promoting the development of start-ups. In addition, it actively promotes the support of venture capital for start-ups and innovations by setting up government-led funds and providing tax incentives for venture capital.

According to the NISA, 2015, the Australian government set up the CSIRO Innovation Fund, with a size of 200 million Australian dollars (equivalent to 140 million US dollars), to invest in new companies and support CSIRO Innovation Fund and other publicly funded research institutions and higher learning institutions in technology development. A Biomedical Translation Fund was set up to invest 250 million Australian dollars (equivalent to 180 million US dollars) with the private sector to promote the commercialization of Australian medical research. In 2015, Australia established the Medical Research Future Fund (MRFF), which is about to reach 20 billion Australian dollars by 2020–2021. The fund focuses on R&D and innovation in health and medicine.

In 2016, the Australian Parliament adopted the Tax Law Amendment (Tax Incentives for Innovation) Bill 2016, which revised the relevant regulations in the Income Tax Assessment Act 1997, the Income Tax Assessment Act 1936, and the Taxation Administration Act 1953. After such amendment, those who subscribe stocks newly issued by early stage innovation companies (ESICs) may be entitled to the non-refundable tax credit at 20% of the purchase or investment amount, but the upper limit may not exceed 200,000 Australian dollars (equivalent to 150,000 US dollars). Gains from transfer of ESICs in 1–10 years will be exempted from taxes. A 10% non-refundable tax credit is provided for the early stage venture capital limited partnerships (ESVCLPs) and the promised capital ceiling of the new ESVCLPs is raised from 100 million Australian dollars (equivalent to US $7794 million) to 200 million Australian dollars (equivalent to US $156 million).

In September 2017, the Australian government introduced the Crowd-Sourced Equity Fund (CSEF) Bill, which aims to help SMEs with difficulties in financing through conventional channels fill the funding gap. Australian unlisted companies with annual revenue and total assets of less than 25 million US dollars are eligible to raise up to 5 million US dollars a year through the Crowd-Sourced Equity Fund (CSF), and retail investors may invest 10,000 US dollars a year for each enterprise and get corresponding equity returns. The advantage of this bill is that (1) it helps small businesses obtain funds, and (2) it increases investment opportunities for retail investors and reduces investment risks through strict regulation of Internet-based crowd funding agencies.

Entrepreneur Services

Technical Services

On November 4, 2016, the Australian DIISR released the Global Innovation Strategy: Helping Australia compete internationally (the "Strategy"), consisting of the following four parts: (1) Global Connections Fund, which supports exchanges and cooperation between SMEs and researchers at home and abroad. The fund includes a start-up fund and a bridge fund; (2) Global Innovation Linkages, which provides a 4-year funding of up to 1 million Australian dollars for Australian enterprises and research institutions in cooperation with global partners; (3) Landing Pads. Australia has set up five business centers in the San Francisco, Berlin, Shanghai, Tel Aviv, and Singapore; and (4) Regional Collaborations Program, which promotes industry-university-research cooperation through Australian-led projects and multilateral forums.

It is pointed in the NISA 2015 that Australia' economic development mode relying on resources and trade has declined and needs to seek transformation and find new growth points through innovation, and accordingly put forward plans to build an industrial growth center: The Industrial Growth Center, a non-profit independent legal entity, was set up in areas with comparative advantages and strategic significance, and innovation and entrepreneurship were carried out in the form of "government-industry-university-research" cooperation to promote commercialization and industrialization of scientific and technological achievements. As of December 2016, Australia had set up industrial growth centers in six areas: (1) AMGC in advanced manufacturing; (2) FIAL in food and agriculture; (3) MTPConnect in medical technology and medicine; (4) METS Ignited in mining equipment; (5) NERA in oil, natural gas, and energy resources; and (6) ACSGN in network security. The industrial growth centers provide such services as funding support, solutions, peer cooperation network for its members. All enterprises, universities, and research institutions may apply to become members of the centers.

Information Services

In November 2017, the Australian government launched ASBAS Digital Solutions. The DIISR is responsible for the implementation and management of the program. ASBAS is an ongoing project that starts a new round of funding every three years to support service providers in providing low-cost, high-quality digital consulting services for Australian small businesses. The total financing of the current operation program is 18.02 million US dollars and will be implemented from July 2, 2018 to June 30, 2021.

Market Support

On May 9, 2017, the Australian government released the National Business Simplification Initiative—Connecting Government Digital Business Services 2017–2018 Budget. In 2017–2018, the government will invest 9.1 million US dollars (including 3.5 million US dollars in capital funds) to simplify business registration and licensing services of federal, state, and regional governments. This measure links the federal government's enterprise online registration and licensing services with state and regional online services. After that, enterprises may start the registration and licensing process at business.gov.au or on state or regional government websites and receive corresponding guidance.

In November 2017, the Australian government announced to improve the payment efficiency of SMEs providing services and commodities for the government. From July 2019, the government must pay to SMEs within 20 working days (vs. previous 30 working days) for accounts not exceeding 1 million Australian dollars.

The Australian government spends about 6 billion Australian dollars a year on ICT and data services to support start-ups and SMEs to obtain more orders in government procurement. The Australian government has set up a digital marketplace for ICT products and data services under the NISA 2015, so that start-ups and small enterprises can more easily understand government procurement requirements and obtain government technical support to compete with large enterprises in a fair environment.

The Australian government set up the Digital Transformation Office (DTO) in July 2015 to improve the e-government. Up to now, the DTO has developed and established several distinctive "public platforms", such as cloud.gov.au, an online platform, through which Australian governments at all levels may use cloud services to provide digital services.

Enterprise Incubation

The Australian government opines that the role of incubators in the innovation ecosystem is crucial to ensure that start-ups have access to the resources, information, and networks they need to turn their ideas into new global and large-scale industries. For this reason, the Australian government has launched the Landing Pads and set up five start-up centers in San Francisco, Berlin, Shanghai, Tel Aviv, and Singapore to provide 90-day operation support for Australian start-ups. Participants can accelerate the design and development of products and services by staying at these overseas bases for 90 days, quickly adjust their financing road shows, find suitable partners, customers, and investors, and take business opportunities in the rapidly developing global market.

At the end of 2017, the Australian state government appointed a Regional Incubator Facilitator in each of the four regions. These expert facilitators will provide advice for start-ups and help them develop professional networks in Australia and overseas. In addition, they will promote contacts among local enterprises, industries, universities, research institutions, and the government. The four regions are WA, Central and Northern NEW, Eastern SA and Western VIC, and Northern QLD to ensure that all applicants will have access to an expert facilitator. In addition, Incubator Support is a 23 million US dollar project of the Entrepreneurs' Program under the NISA 2015, providing matching funds (up to 500,000 US dollar) for Australian incubators and accelerators and supporting the development of new and existing business incubators and accelerators. Since its launch in September 2016, the project has funded 51 new and existing incubators for nearly 7.7 million US dollars.

Communication Platform

The Small Business Fix-it Squad Program launched by Australia in 2016 helps SMEs reduce their operating costs by 140 million US dollars a year by coordinating the efforts of SMEs, tax professionals, state and local governments, and intermediary agencies to jointly analyze and solve a series of problems that may be encountered by small enterprises, including helping the youth to start businesses and hire employees.

Digital Transformation Support

The Australian Department of Employment, Skills, Small and Family Business launched the Small Business Digital Champion Program in 2018 that provides a comprehensive digital transformation program for 100 small businesses in Australia, which received support of up to 18,500 Australian dollars ($14,393) and low-cost services from business partners.[2]

To support start-ups in their digital operations during the outbreak of Covid-19 in 2020, NBN Co Limited, an Australian state-owned company (broadband provider, responsible for designing and building the National Broadband Network), has announced the allocation of AUD 150 million ($116 million) for coronavirus rescue measures and the waiver of a monthly fee for internet providers, who were required to use the AUD 150 million National Broadband Network Rescue Fund to help businesses' remote work and facilitate their digitalization.[3]

ENTREPRENEURSHIP EDUCATION

The Australian government provides special entrepreneurship training for the youth and the female to help them start businesses.

The Australian Department of Jobs and Small Business launched Encouraging Entrepreneurship and Self-Employment Initiative in December 2016 to help the youth start their own business. There are four specific measures: (1) Entrepreneurship Facilitators. Such support as entrepreneurship trainings is provided by working in tandem with local organizations in three regions in Australia where have high unemployment rate for the youth to enhance the youth's awareness of entrepreneurship and encourage the youth to start their own business; (2) SelfStart

---

[2] Assessment on the progress of G20 Entrepreneurship Action Plan, Entrepreneurship Research Center on G20 Economies, Oct 22, 2019.

[3] Evaluation and Prospect of G20 Members' Policies to Support Entrepreneurship in the Post-pandemic Era, Entrepreneurship Research Center on G20 Economies, Oct 22, 2020.

Online Hub. The main purpose is to provide entrepreneurs with advice related to entrepreneurship and guide young entrepreneurs in designing business plans and finding resources in the early stage of entrepreneurship; (3) Expanding the New Enterprise Incentive Scheme (NEIS). The NEIS provides entrepreneurship training and mentoring for entrepreneurs, with a total of 21 training providers and 8600 venues to receive training each year; and (4) Exploring Being My Own Boss' Workshops. The two-week seminar helps young entrepreneurs to learn more about the problems they may encounter in starting a business and the skills of running a business.

The NSW Women Entrepreneurs Network—WON, sponsored by the NSW government, aims to provide one-stop services for women who want to start a business, including setting up communities, expanding interpersonal networks, and sharing information. Many training programs for entrepreneurs can be found on the WON platform. For example, TAFE NSW (Technical and Further Education, New South Wales), a leading vocational education and training institution in NSW offers 1200 training courses covering almost all specialties, and the institution enrolls 500,000 students nationwide every year, which is praised for its wide range of industry partners. 50:50 is a project run by the University of New South Wales to encourage young Australian women to pursue degrees and careers in science and technology.

Although interdisciplinary teaching is the trend of entrepreneurship education, the entrepreneurship education courses in Australian universities are generally offered in business schools. These universities not only launched bachelor's and master's degrees of entrepreneurship education-related disciplines, but also built entrepreneurship ecosystem, while attaching great importance to the international cooperation and cooperation with industries.

Australian National University (ANU) has a Master of Entrepreneurship and Innovation program for students from various departments, which is set up by business schools for two years to develop students' innovative thinking methods, teamwork ability, adaptability to uncertainty, and ability to apply specific knowledge and skills to entrepreneurship and innovation practice.

The Innovation Act (IACT) is the largest entrepreneurship project in Canberra initiated by ANU. It targets students, faculty, and graduates of all Canberra higher learning institutions and supports hundreds of entrepreneurs every year. The project lasts for 10 weeks, including seminars, entrepreneurship counseling from local entrepreneurs. Students are required to form teams to generate innovative business plans. The top 20 teams will be invited to participate in Pitch Night, where they will present to influential judges and innovators. The top team that wins at Pitch Night will receive a seed fund of 50,000 Australian dollars and other entrepreneurial supports.

The University of Sydney has a series of courses and projects in the field of entrepreneurship and innovation. Starting in 2018, each undergraduate course will include a research project related to entrepreneurship or industry. The school has a hub to help students innovate and start their own businesses and help students from various disciplines commercialize their ideas. Specific projects include Hatchlab, which provides a 12-month incubation period for start-ups; Springboard, which supports creative development; and a series of lectures on entrepreneurship. Students can get guidance from experts in the field of entrepreneurship, expand personal networks, participate in industry seminars, and obtain seed funds. Sydney Genesis is a project founded in 2008 to provide entrepreneurial support for multi-disciplinary students, which is specifically operated by the business school. So far, the project has supported more than 900 students and alumni to start their own businesses. The University of Sydney also has an online learning platform, Open Learning Environment (OLE), which has more than 100 courses, many of which are about entrepreneurial skills. Students can learn for free, such as how to program and manage projects.

The University of Queensland is committed to building an ecosystem of entrepreneurship and innovation, including entrepreneurial practice learning, entrepreneurial action, and entrepreneurial research. UQ Idea Hub is a pre-incubator project. Its main goal is to help students turn ideas into practical business plans. Students can learn some basic knowledge and skills of entrepreneurship, get guidance from experienced entrepreneurs, and also have office space. Startup Academy is a project that guides students to verify the feasibility of starting a business plan in the market after their creativity is formed, improves the business plan and increases the success rate of starting a business. UQ ilab is a more practical start-up incubation platform. Apart from providing training and coaching, it will also provide assistance for entrepreneurs in seed funds. The University of Queensland also established the HYPE UQ SPIN Accelerator Program in cooperation with HYPE Sporttech Innovation, the world's leading innovation and start-up platform in sports. The University of Queensland also has a master's program in entrepreneurship and innovation for a period of 1.5 years.

The Swinburne University of Technology restarted the Australian Graduate School of Entrepreneurship (AGSE) in 2017. The entrepreneurship course will focus on cooperation with industry. AGSE launched the Master of Entrepreneurship and Innovation program for 1.5 years (completing the same causes as full-time or part-time students). The course is divided into several modules, including opportunity identification, creativity, and design; project management of start-ups; enterprise planning; enterprise growth management.

FAIR COMPETITION FOR SMEs

The then-effect of Australian anti-trust law is the Competition and Consumer Act 2010. The law includes the prohibition of abuse of market dominance, which is closely related to the protection of SMEs.

When Australia determines the abuse of market dominance, it consists of the following three constitutive requirements: (1) the enterprise must have dominance in the market; (2) the enterprise gains benefits through its dominance in the market; and (3) the purpose of the enterprise's act in (2) above should comply with Section 46 (1) of the Competition and Consumer Act 2010. If these three requirements are met at the same time, the enterprise will be regarded as abusing its dominance in the market.[4]

As the abuse of market dominance is expressed in different ways, countries adopted different legislative technologies to regulate the market dominance. The forms of expression of market dominance in Australia are not enumerated by law, but rather by jurisprudence, including predatory pricing, tied selling, refusal to deal, etc. At the level of legal liability, Australia's legal liability for abusing its market dominance includes civil liability, administrative liability, and criminal liability.

In the enforcement of anti-abuse of market dominance, the Australian Competition and Consumer Commission is responsible for unified enforcement in a "pyramid" law enforcement model.[5] The order in this

---

[4] Ji, Pingping. On Australian Legislation of Abuse of Market Dominance. *Journal of Heilongjiang University of Technology* (Comprehensive Edition), 2019, 19 (3).

[5] Miller, Russell V. *Miller's Australian Competition and Consumer Law Annotated* [M]. Canberra: Thomson Reuters (Professional) Australia, 2014.

pattern is as follows: (1) education, advice, and persuasion; (2) self-discipline management of trade associations; (3) administrative penalties; (4) fines; and (5) litigation.

Brazil

The Brazilian[1] government has determined the core position of SMEs in the economy through legislation and implemented the Simple National Tax Law to reduce tax burdens. In 2017, the government launched the action plan of "reducing administrative procedures and increasing credit" to improve the e-government. It effectively reduces the administrative burdens on enterprises, and increase credit supports for small and micro businesses. SEBRAE, Brazil's small and micro-enterprise development organization, is an important organization that helps SMEs develop. The Brazilian Innovation Funding Agency (FINEP) is mainly responsible for financing the development and innovation of Brazilian science and technology, which is a subordinate department of Brazilian Ministry of Science and Technology Innovation (MCTI). State-owned banks such as Banco do Brasil and Apex-Brasil play an active role in providing loans for SMEs and promoting overseas marketing.

Brazil is one of the South American countries with heavy taxes. The reforms to simplify tax system have reduced the tax burdens on SMEs and shortened the reporting and payment process. In 2016, the Brazilian government introduced the Grow Without Fear Program to expand the

---

[1] According to the definition of Brazilian tax authority, micro business refers to an enterprise with annual revenue of 120,000 Brazil reais (equivalent to 33,000 US dollars) or less; small business refers to an enterprise with annual revenue of more than 120,000 Brazil reais and less than 1.2 million Brazil reais (equivalent to 330,000 US dollars).

© The Author(s), under exclusive license to Springer Nature Singapore Pte Ltd. 2022
J. Gao et al., *G20 Entrepreneurship Services Report*,
https://doi.org/10.1007/978-981-16-6787-9_4

scope of SMEs in the Simple National Tax Law, so that more enterprises may be eligible for tax concessions. The Simple National Tax Law was officially implemented in July 2007, which is a key step in tax system in Brazil's simplification reform. In 1996, the Brazilian government implemented the Simples Federal Plan to simplify the tax system and provide differential tax benefits for SMEs through the integration of tax and payment systems.

According to 2016 data, new business lending by Brazilian SMEs accounted for 50.03% of the new loans in the year, but the interest rate for SMEs is still 12.7 percentage points higher than that of large Brazilian enterprises, and the financing pressure on Brazilian SMEs is still huge. To this end, the Brazilian government has taken a series of measures to increase financing support for SMEs and start-ups. In 2018, the government announced that it would allow Fintech companies with small loan business to obtain licenses, and encourage Fintech companies to participate in the market. In October 2016, it was announced that more than 30 billion Brazil reals (equivalent to 9.06 billion US dollars) of credit would be provided for SMEs for investment, equipment procurement, and enterprise operation. Measures that have been taken include PNMPO, a national small business credit program launched in 2005, DNDES card issued by Brazil BNDES, and FAMPE, a Brazilian credit guarantee fund. In 2016, Brazil promulgated the Angel Investment Law to stimulate the development of Brazilian venture capital.

In support of research and innovation, the Brazilian government is committed to systematizing scientific research. It encourages enterprises to participate in research and innovation to strengthen the market orientation of academic research, and attaches importance to promoting enterprise innovation by adopting a tax incentive "no expenditure" support method. The Innovation Law revised in 2018 introduces a framework for cooperation between public and private research sectors, constituting a new national innovation system, and also encourages research and development activities of SMEs through tax incentives. In providing information services for start-ups and SMEs, Lattes platform, a Brazilian human resources bank mainly provides information on scientific research talents. The Brazilian business incubators attach importance to the transfer of scientific and technological achievements and the cooperation among start-ups, scientific research institutions, and social subjects. For example, the technology innovation business incubators managed by the Inova institution of the University of Campinas Marcelo, helps start-ups in emerging technologies. The Brazilian Abastartups also provides services such as business incubation, business operation guidance, and investment for entrepreneurs.

The Brazilian government provides various entrepreneurship training programs, such as "Friend of Entrepreneurs" and "Progress". The entrepreneurial training programs for women and youth are more international in nature, such as CicloBrilhante, a free entrepreneurship program for women, and Junior Enterprises, a young entrepreneur organization. Entrepreneurship education penetration rate is high in Brazil. There are also entrepreneurship training programs for middle school students, such as the "MediotEcpRogramme". Among the higher education institutions offering entrepreneurship education courses, some attach importance to international exchanges such as the University of São Paulo, while others place a priority on entrepreneurship culture such as the Catholic University of Rio de Janeiro, each with its own characteristics.

In order to promote the digitalization of SMEs during the outbreak of Covid-19, the Brazilian government developed digital business platform for SMEs to make online promotion, at the same time, SEBRAE provided one-to-one consulting services and solutions of digitalization for SMEs to cope with the crisis.

Government Services

Brazil's Microenterprise Statute (ESTATUTO DA Micro EMPRESA) (1984) supports SMEs in taxation, credit, and business development. On this basis, the new Federal Constitution (1988) recognizes SME's core position in the economy, and stipulates that governments at different levels should take preferential measures. The General Law for Micro and Small Enterprises (Lei Complementary 123/2006) of 2006 reduced the tax burden on SMEs and encouraged state-owned banks to strengthen loan support.

In September 2017, the Brazilian government, in cooperation with SEBRAE (see below for details) and Banco do Brasil, launched the Most Simple Entrepreneurship Program (EmpreenderMais Simples). According to the action plan, SEBRAE, a SME development organization, will invest 200 million Brazil reals (equivalent to 60.38 million US dollars) to upgrade 10 computer systems to achieve a more flexible and less regulated business environment, so as to improve the e-government and reduce the administrative burden on enterprises. Banco do Brasil plans to provide credit support of 8.2 billion Brazil reals (equivalent to 2.476 billion US dollars) to 40,000 small and micro business through Workers' Assistance Fund (FAT) in the next two years.

EMPRESAS is an important organization that helps SMEs develop. It was established by the Brazilian government in 1972 and became an independent non-profit organization in 1990. SEBRAE cooperates with the government and financial institutions to improve market access for SMEs by helping them expand financing channels, reduce bureaucracy and tax burdens, and promote the sustainable development and competitiveness. SEBRAE has more than 700 service centers around Brazil, mainly providing consulting services for local enterprises, entrepreneurs, and students, as well as online and offline training, including finance, entrepreneurship, Internet-based small businesses, customer service, sales skills, and human resources, mostly free of charge.

The Brazilian government changed the Ministry of Science and Technology to the Ministry of Science and Technology Innovation (MSTI) in 2011, reflecting the significance of innovation. The FINEP is its subordinate, which is mainly responsible for funding the development and innovation of science and technology in Brazil.

Brazil's state-owned banks such as Banco do Brasil and CaixaEconômica Federal have played an active role in promoting loans for SMEs. The APEX-Brasil is committed to promoting Brazilian products and services overseas and attracting foreign companies to invest in strategic industries in Brazil. In addition to headquartering in Brasilia, the APEX-Brasil has 10 business offices in key markets around the world to assist Brazilian enterprises in the internationalization process, explore business opportunities and provide services to attract foreign investments.

FISCAL AND FINANCIAL SUPPORT

Fiscal Support

In 2016, the Brazilian government introduced the Grow Without Fear Program to raise the SME income standard in the Simple National Tax Law, so that more enterprises may have the access to tax benefits.

As early as 1996, the Brazilian government began implementing the Simples Federal Program in Law 9317 (1996) to simplify the tax system and provide differential tax benefits for SMEs through the integration of tax and payment systems. The General Law for Micro and Small Enterprises (Lei Complex 123/2006) of 2006 was a key step in the tax simplification reform, and the plan to rename it as the Simple National Tax Law came into effect in July of the following year. The Simple National Tax Law is an optional tax plan, which realizes the unified collection of municipal tax, state tax, and federal tax. SMEs can also choose to pay various taxes separately, but the unified tax rate paid under the Simple National Tax Law is lower. The taxes that enterprises need to pay are calculated according to the company's monthly income. SMEs can complete the unified payment of taxes only by filling out a document for tax and payment (Documento de Arrecado de ReceptisFederais, DARF). Brazil is one of the South American countries with heavy taxes. Reforms in tax system in Brazil have reduced the tax burdens on SMEs and simplified the reporting and payment process.

Financial Support

In 2016, new business lending for Brazilian SMEs totaled at 408.988 billion Brazil reals (equivalent to 123,468 million US dollars), accounting for 50.03% of the new loans of the year. However, the loan interest rate for SMEs is 33.5%, which is 12.7 percentage points higher than the loan interest rate (20.8%) for large enterprises. Brazilian SMEs are still under a huge financing pressure.

The government announced in October 2016 that it will provide more than 30 billion Brazil reals (equivalent to 9.06 billion US dollars) of credit to SMEs for investment, equipment procurement, and business operations. 20 billion Brazil reals (equivalent to 6.04 billion US dollars) will be provided by state-owned banks: CaixaEconômica Federal and Banco do Brasil, while the remaining 10 billion Brazil reals will come from private banks: Bradesco, Itaú, and Santander. Previously, the Brazilian government has taken a series of measures to increase financing support for SMEs and start-ups.

In 2005, the Brazilian Ministry of Labor and Employment initiated the Programa Nacional de MicrocreditoProdutivoOrientado (PNMPO) under Law 11110/2005 and provided loans for small businesses through the Worker Support Fund and mandatorily allocated 2% of demand deposits. In 2003, the Brazilian government, adopted the Law 10735/2003, requiring all commercial banks and state-owned banks to provide loans for low-income people and small business entrepreneurs through the 2% of demand deposits. In the same year, Brazil launched BNDES Card to finance SMEs. BNDES Card is similar to a credit card in that it can obtain financing support without actual guarantee.

The Brazilian government provides credit guarantees for SMEs through the FAMPE (Fundo de Aval as Micro e PequenasEmpresas) in order to increase banks' financing. The FAMPE provides up to 80% loan guarantee for SMEs.

In 2018, Brazil's National Monetary Council (CMN) announced that Fintechs providing small loans may obtain business licenses, no longer requiring to use banks as intermediaries. The purpose is to encourage better market participation, stimulate innovation in the financial industry and enhance market competition. According to the resolution of Brazil's CMN, Fintech companies have two options: a direct credit platform (SCD) or a personal lending platform (SEP). SCD (Sociedade de CréditoDireto): This kind of company can use its own capital to conduct financial operations directly on the Internet electronic platform and no longer require banks as a third party. SEP (Sociedade de Empréstimo entre Pessoas): This kind of company is a P2P platform, and lending through the network platform is a bridge between depositors and borrowers, with each borrower receiving a loan ceiling of 15,000 Brazil reais (equivalent to 4528 US dollars) from the same lender.

The Brazilian government promulgated the Angel Investment Law (Lei Complementar 155/2016) in 2016 to promote venture capital development. Start-ups can obtain angel funds from individuals, enterprises, and investment institutions through the "participation agreement" (contrato de participacao). Funds invested through the "participation agreement" are not included in the share capital, so angel investors are not equity owners of the enterprise and do not have management right and voting right. This can protect angel investors from corporate debts. In 2016, Brazil had 7070 angel investors, with an angel investment of 852 million Brazil reals (equivalent to 257 million US dollars), a slight increase of 9% year on year.

Entrepreneur Services

Brazil provides innovative support for entrepreneurs, including special legislative and fiscal incentives to encourage and support innovative R&D by start-ups and SMEs. The business incubator, which is mainly set up in higher education institutions, not only provides business incubation services to entrepreneurs, but also promotes cooperation among start-ups, scientific research institutions, and social entities so as to promote the transformation of scientific and technological achievements.

Technical Services

In support of research and innovation, the Brazilian government is committed to systematizing scientific research and encouraging enterprises to participate in research and innovation to strengthen the market orientation of academic research. Brazil's Innovation Law was first introduced in 2004 to encourage technology investment and independent innovation. The law was updated in 2016 and 2018. The newly revised Innovation Law introduced a framework for cooperation between public and private research sectors, constituting a new national innovation system, authorizing higher education institutions (HEIs) and public research institutions (PRIs) to cooperate more freely with companies, promoting the issuance of visas for foreign R&D personnel and employment by private companies, etc. In addition, the Brazilian government also attaches great importance to promoting enterprise innovation, but focuses on promoting R&D and innovation through tax incentives. For example, the new legislation introduces tax incentives to encourage SMEs to purchase research equipment and exempts the cost of public bidding for research and development activities up to 80,000 Brazil reals (equivalent to 24,151 US dollars).

Information Services

In providing information services for start-ups and SMEs, Lattes platform, a Brazilian human resources bank, has its own characteristics, mainly providing information on scientific research talents. Named after Cesar Lattes, a Brazilian physicist, the platform is operated by the National Counsel of Scientific and Technological Development and is a resume database of scientific and technical personnel. Its original purpose is to support national scientific research management institutions. Lattes platform is composed of four parts: resumes, organization directory, team classification, and display analysis. It features assistant decision-making, big data resources, and two-way development.

Enterprise Incubation

The Brazilian business incubators attach importance to the transfer of scientific and technological achievements and the cooperation among start-ups, scientific research institutions, and social subjects. For example, the Inova (Innova Unicamp Innovation Agency) of the University of Campinas Marcelo is an institution for industrialization of scientific and technological achievements of HEIs, which mainly manages the connection of scientific research efforts of HEIs and various enterprises, scientific parks of universities, and incubation and training of innovation and entrepreneurship, to create the ecosystem of innovation and entrepreneurship. Inova manages a technology innovation business incubator and helps start-ups of emerging technology. Inova and Unicamp Venture Group (UV), which is one of its cooperative institutions and founded by alumni businessmen in 2006, provide mentoring service for start-ups, build social networks, and set up investment funds to give financial supports for start-ups.

Communication Platform

Brazilian industry organizations play a major role in promoting exchanges between start-ups and SMEs. For example, the Brazilian Abastartup was established in 2016, headquartered in Bahia, Brazil, to provide services such as business incubation, business operation guidance, and investment for entrepreneurs. In 2018, it sponsored the first Brazilian Start-up Ecosystem Forum (FórumBrasileiro de Ecossistemas de startups).

Digital Transformation Support

In order to promote the digitalization of SMEs during the outbreak of Covid-19, the Brazilian government developed digital business platform (www.mercadoazul.sebrae.com.br) for SMEs to make online promotion. SMEs can make advertisements and find suppliers and distribution channels for their products and services throughout the country, free of charge. SEBRAE provided one-to-one consulting services and solutions of digitalization for SMEs, including hundreds of remote working solutions for SMEs to cope with the crisis. More than 500,000 small businesses have sought the agency's services since the Covid-19 spread in Brazil in March 2020.

ENTREPRENEURSHIP EDUCATION

The Brazilian government provides various entrepreneurship training programs directly by itself or in cooperation with higher education institutions (HEIs). Brazilian HEIs have a high penetration rate of entrepreneurship education, with more than 70% of universities offering entrepreneurship education courses and entrepreneurship training programs for middle school students.

Some Brazilian HEIs attach importance to international exchanges such as the University of São Paulo, while others place a priority on entrepreneurship culture such as the Catholic University of Rio de Janeiro.

Founded in 1934, the University of São Paulo has a professional master in entrepreneurship, which requires applicants to have entrepreneurial experience. Auspin, the university's innovative institution, promotes entrepreneurship education through cooperation with domestic and international organizations. Auspin works in tandem with SEBRATE, Brazil's private institution for entrepreneurship education, launched the online question-and-answer platform "DisqueTecnologia" on entrepreneurship education to answer the technical questions of SMEs. One of the key points of SEBTRATE's 40-year-old business is to cooperate with Brazilian universities and research institutions to develop entrepreneurship education. The Spin-Off Lean Acceleration (SOLA) project, in which Auspin participates, is led by Redemprendia, with financial support from the EU Erasmus + project. Eight European and Latin American universities cooperate to improve the university entrepreneurship education and entrepreneurship training mechanism of incubators. Auspin also cooperates with Eli Lilly, an American pharmaceutical company, to set up a platform for university scientific research industrialization in the medical field.

The Catholic University of Rio de Janeiro, which was founded in 1940, set up the Institute of Origin (Instituto Gênesis) in 1997. Its principal objectives include promoting the development of entrepreneurial culture and assisting entrepreneurs in starting and developing enterprises. In terms of entrepreneurial culture, the association mainly trains students' entrepreneurial spirit and understandings of entrepreneurial knowledge through courses, workshops, speeches or lectures. The association has also launched a number of projects to foster a culture of entrepreneurship, such as the Academia Industry Training (AIT) jointly launched by the association and the Swissnex Brazil, which links entrepreneurs and researchers from Brazil and Switzerland to explore the commercialization of leading technologies. The PronatecEmpreendedor project provides an 18-month distance entrepreneurship education course for 200 Brazilian teachers engaged in vocational education. In helping to start a business, Germinator platform provides training and consultation for entrepreneurs. Entrepreneurs on the platform are not required to be students of PUC-Rio. The Institute of Origin also provided teacher training in entrepreneurship education to the Enterprise Service Agency and the Ministry of Education, and cooperated with three universities in Chile and Peru to provide teacher training in entrepreneurship education.

In 2017, the Brazilian government launched the Progredir (Progress) program. By encouraging low-income people to start their own businesses. The Brazilian government provides a total of 3 billion Brazil reals (equivalent to 900 million US dollars) of small and micro loans each year and, in addition to financial support, provides technical support, vocational training, digital and financial education.

Brazil's Ministry of Labor and Ministry of Education, public and private universities jointly launched the Friend of Entrepreneur Education Program in October 2016 to provide business management guidance and technical support for potential entrepreneurs. Participating universities will be awarded the title of Friend of Entrepreneurs Institution. Brazil's Federal Professional Associations of Business Administration and Accounting is responsible for monitoring and improving the quality of training. In order to increase young people's ability to find jobs and start businesses, the Brazilian government also launched the Intermediate Technology Program (Medio Tec Programme) for entrepreneurship training for middle school students in 2017. Students receive various technical training, including those for electronic, financial, virtual games, sugar and alcohol industries, and cinemas. The Brazilian government has allocated 512 million Brazil reals (equivalent to 155 million US dollars) to public schools, which plan to train 64,000 students, including 116 technical courses.

In Brazil, entrepreneurship training programs for women and youth are more international. Empower Women, an online learning platform co-sponsored by UN Women and Canada to improve women's economic development skills, has done a lot of work in women's entrepreneurship training. Unilever is one of the member organizations. The company has jointly launched a free training program CicloBrilhante in Brazil with two

NGO organizations (Escola de Você and AliançaEmpreendedora) and well-known media figures for women who want to start a business but lack entrepreneurial skills. Since its launch in May 2015, CicloBrilhante has trained more than 60,000 women. The estimated figure at the end of 2016 was 180,000.

Junior Enterprises is an international non-profit organization founded and managed by college students. The organization originated in France and its goal is to add work practice to college students to make up for the lack of theoretical study. Students in this organization are called junior entrepreneurs, and they will learn relevant entrepreneurial and management skills. The mission of young entrepreneurs' organizations is not only to expand the practical courses of university students, but to promote some of the outstanding university students to become entrepreneurs and contribute to the country's development.

Canada

Canada Business Corporations Act is a fundamental law in Canada. A new Innovation and Skills Plan was proposed in the 2017 Canadian Federal Budget, aiming to make Canada a world innovation center. The first Women Entrepreneurship Strategy was proposed in the 2018 Canadian Federal Budget, providing dedicated support for women entrepreneurs. Affairs of small and medium-sized enterprises (SMEs) are in the charge of Innovation, Science and Economic Development Canada (ISED). The National Research Council (NRC) is a branch of ISED, organizing and implementing the Industrial Research Assistance Program (IRAP) for SMEs.

The Canadian government supports start-ups and SMEs through various tax cut policies, such as the Scientific Research and Experimental Development (SR&ED) Investment Tax Credit Policy and the Lifetime Capital Gains Exemption (LCGE). The Canada Small Business Financing Program (CSBFP) supports small enterprises by providing guarantee for fixed asset loans. In 2017, the Canadian government launched a strategic innovation fund and a new Venture Capital Catalyst Initiative (VCCI) to support the rapid development of start-ups. In the same year, Business Development Bank of Canada (BDC) also announced a series of measures to help small firms and star-ups in certain special fields.

In technical, information, and market services, various institutions and programs have been involved. IRAP provides technical assistance for SMEs at different stages. Besides, jointly implemented by BDC, Export Development Corporation of Canada (EDC), NRC-IRAP, ISED, and Global Affairs Canada's Trade Commissioner Service (TCS), the Accelerated Growth Service provides financial support and information services for SMEs. Finally, in 2016, the Canadian government initiated the Canada's CanExport Program, which aimed to help SMEs expand the overseas market.

Canada's enterprise incubation also has distinctive features. Futurpreneur Canada provides financing and consulting services for young entrepreneurs aged 18–39. The Canadian government allotted fund to this organization in 2017 and 2018 consecutively. Universities also set up incubators based on their own strengths. For example, Ryerson University, with its advantage in the media research, established an incubator centered around the digital media industry. TEC Edmonton Incubator is the representative of regional incubators, providing services for technology start-ups.

In entrepreneurship education, a key element in the 2017 Canada's Innovation and Skills Plan was to improve vocational training. Both Canadian federal government and provincial governments place a priority on entrepreneurship education, greatly increasing entrepreneurship courses in curricula. The University of Waterloo, for example, recognizes entrepreneurship education as part of the university strategy. Enactus Canada, a student entrepreneurship development organization in Canada, not only hosts entrepreneurship contests and campaigns, but also creates significant social values.

The Canadian Competition Act clearly expresses the purpose of protecting SMEs. The Act regulates the abuse of market dominance. The Act also lists criminal offenses prohibiting such as bid rigging between competitors or potential competitors to reach agreements to fix or increase prices. In addition, the Canadian Parliament's Budget Enforcement Act (Bill C-10) made changes to the competition law regarding merger review by raising the pre-filing threshold.

Government Services

Canada Business Corporations[1] Act applies to all companies in Canada, whereas local corporate laws regulate businesses in different provinces.

At the end of March 2017, a new Innovation and Skills Plan was proposed in the 2017 Canadian Federal Budget. This plan aimed to make Canada a world innovation center. According to this plan, new strategic innovation funds would be established and a program named Innovative Solutions Canada would be launched.

The first Women Entrepreneurship Strategy was proposed in the 2018 Canadian Federal Budget. This strategy planned to invest 2 billion Canadian dollars (equivalent to 1.6 billion US dollars) to double women-led enterprises by 2025. By far, firms led by women account for less than 16% of Canadian SMEs.

ISED is mainly in charge of Canadian SME affairs. As a branch of ISED, NRC is mainly responsible for the organization and implementation of IRAP and provides small enterprises and entrepreneurs with technical consulting and financing services.

Fiscal and Financial Support

The SR&ED Investment Tax Credit Policy was issued in the 1980s and is still in effect. In 2016, the policy provided about US $ 2.7 billion in tax aid for Canadian enterprises. It is still Canada's largest federal plan to support business research and development in the industrial sector.

According to the LCGE, Canada's Economic Action Plan (EAP) 2013 raised the exemption threshold for the lifetime capital gains of eligible corporate businesses to 800,000 Canadian dollars (equivalent to 640,000 US dollars) from 750,000 Canadian dollars (equivalent to 600,000 US dollars). In 2017, the exemption threshold was at 835,716 Canadian dollars (equivalent to 660,000 US dollars).

CSBFP provides financial support for small enterprises. Under this program, small businesses can obtain loans up to 1 million Canadian dollars (equivalent to 800,000 US dollars), of which 350,000 Canadian dollars (equivalent to 280,000 US dollars) can be used for any purpose, except real estate investment.

---

[1] Adopted on Mar 12, 2009.

The 2017 Canadian Federal Budget proposed the establishment of a five-year strategic innovation fund of 1.26 billion Canadian dollars (equivalent to 1 billion US dollars). In July 2017, the Canadian government announced the launch of the fund. Not only does this fund support innovation activities and firms with high potential, but also it attempts to attract new investment for Canada which creates new job opportunities.

In 2017, the Canadian government launched a new VCCI to provide 400 million Canadian dollars (equivalent to 318 million US dollars) through BDC. This fund attempts to stimulate the development of ventral capital in Canada. Of this fund, 350 million Canadian dollars (equivalent to 278 million US dollars) were used to found the parent fund and the remaining 50 million Canadian dollars (equivalent to 39.8 million US dollars) were provided for investors in several special fields.

BDC is the most important bank for small enterprises in Canada. It provides loans, venture capital, and consulting service for small enterprises. In April 2017, BDC Capital, the BDC's investment branch, announced that it would provide about 2 billion Canadian dollars (equivalent to 1.6 billion US dollars) over the next five years to support Canadian SMEs with light assets and high growth. In November 2016, BDC Capital allotted 50 million Canadian dollars (equivalent to 39.8 million US dollars) to support women-led enterprises.

Entrepreneur Services

Technical Services

The IRAP of Canada has been a major program run by the NRC of Canada in the past 70 years. It provides technical assistance for SMEs at different stages and helps them commercialize innovative products and services. Armed with professional knowledge in technology and management, NRC-IRAP's industrial technology advisors (ITAs) provide consulting services to SMEs.

Information Services

The Accelerated Growth Service, jointly implemented by various departments of the Canadian government, provides financing support, information consulting, export advice, and innovation assistance for SMEs.

Involved in this program are BDC, EDC, NRC-IRAP, ISED, and Global Affairs Canada's TCS.

During the outbreak of Covid-19, the Canadian government and some organizations have also introduced supporting measures to optimize its services to SMEs and start-ups. The government, in conjunction with the Canadian Chamber of Commerce, has created a toolbox platform to help SMEs prepare for its reopening and digitalization.[2]

Market Support

In 2016, the Canadian government initiated the Canada's CanExport Program, which was managed by the TCS under Global Affairs Canada. The program planned to set up a fund of 50 million Canadian dollars (39.8 million Canadian dollars) in the next five years and provide financial support for SMEs to expand overseas markets. It aimed to support 10,000 SMEs every year.

Founded in 1944, EDC is Canada's state-owned financial institution. EDC has a cross-industry department which provides export credit insurance and foreign investment guarantee for small enterprises so as to promote export.

Enterprise Incubation

Futurpreneur Canada is a national non-profit organization in Canada, providing financing and consulting service for young entrepreneurs aged 18–39. Its START-UP program can provide entrepreneurs with financial support of up to 45,000 Canadian dollars (equivalent to 35,800 US dollars) and 2-year mentoring service. In 2017 and 2018, the Canadian government allocated 14 million Canadian dollars (equivalent to 11.14 million US dollars) to Futurpreneur Canada.

Using its advantages in the media research, Ryerson University established a digital media zone in April 2010. The experimental zone is located in the famous Central Street in downtown Toronto and has access to various resources around that area. It is a work zone focusing on the incubation of digital media businesses. TEC Edmonton Incubator is the

---

[2] Evaluation and Prospect of G20 Members' Policies to Support Entrepreneurship in the Post-pandemic Era, Entrepreneurship Research Center on G20 Economies, Oct 22, 2020.

largest incubator and accelerator in the Edmonton region. It boosts the development of companies in emerging technologies.

Entrepreneurship Education

The 2017 Canada's Innovation and Skills Plan was launched to equip Canadians with the skills they need to get good jobs. It is dedicated to advocating Canadian citizens' lifetime study, helping adults return to school for continuing education, helping the unemployed to get job trainings through unemployment insurance, helping students to gain work experience, and attracting talents from both home and abroad.

Education in Canada is administered by each province. The provincial education departments formulate their own educational systems, and the federal government provides partial education funds to the provinces. Both Canadian federal government and provincial governments place a priority on entrepreneurship education and trainings. Over the past two decades, entrepreneurship education has grown rapidly in Canada. In 1979, 72 entrepreneurship courses were available, compared to 446 courses today.

The University of Waterloo, for example, recognizes entrepreneurship education as part of the university strategy, with the goal of establishing an entrepreneurial ecosystem. The University of Waterloo has drawn up the 2013–2018 Entrepreneurial University Implementation Plan. The plan aims at enhancing students' awareness of entrepreneurial opportunities. Teaching programs range from developing entrepreneurial plans, incubating projects, to speeding up commercialization. It also provides students with opportunities to learn from companies in the real business world.

Enactus Canada is a student entrepreneurship development organization in Canada. It hosts entrepreneurship contests and campaigns. The organization has already launched campaigns in more than 70 Canadian universities, in which thousands of students participate every year. Student entrepreneurs can hire used-to-be drug addicts who are recovering. Through these campaigns, people who can hardly find any job will get the chance to be employed.

Fair Competition for SMEs

The Canadian Competition Act clearly expresses the purpose of protecting SMEs: "The purpose of this Act is to maintain and encourage competition in Canada in order to promote the efficiency and adaptability of the Canadian economy, in order to expand opportunities for Canadian participation in world markets while at the same time recognizing the role of foreign competition in Canada, in order to ensure that small and medium-sized enterprises have an equitable opportunity to participate in the Canadian economy and in order to provide consumers with competitive prices and product choices.[3]"

The Act regulates the abuse of market dominance and prohibits the following practices: (a) one or more persons substantially or completely control, throughout Canada or any area thereof, a class or species of business, (b) that person or those persons have engaged in or are engaging in a practice of anti-competitive acts, and (c) the practice has had, is having or is likely to have the effect of preventing or lessening competition substantially in a market.

The Act also lists criminal offenses, one of which is "conspiracy offence", that is, prohibiting bid rigging between competitors or potential competitors to reach agreements to fix or increase prices, allocate sales customer areas or markets, and fix or reduce production or supply of products is another major criminal offense under the Competition Act. These criminal offenses are prosecuted in regular criminal courts.[4]

In addition, the Canadian Parliament's Budget Enforcement Act (Bill C-10)[5] made changes to the competition law regarding merger review by raising the pre-filing threshold from $50 million to $70 million; adding a waiting period for additional responses to the review process; and shortening the time period for review authorities to challenge approved mergers and acquisitions from three years to one year. The original 3-year period was shortened to 1 year.[6]

---

[3] https://laws-lois.justice.gc.ca/eng/acts/C-34/page-1.html#h-87830.

[4] https://www.dwpv.com/en.

[5] Adopted on Mar 12, 2009.

[6] http://shangwutousu.mofcom.gov.cn/article/lbqz/lbzn/200909/20090906494122.html.

China

Premier Li Keqiang proposed in the 2018 government work report to promote public entrepreneurship and innovation. Since the "Mass Entrepreneurship and Innovation" strategy at the Summer World Economic Forum in 2014, the Chinese government has been committed to optimizing the environment for innovation and entrepreneurship at the policy level, and supporting the sustained and quality development. Since 2016, the Chinese government has also continued to improve the market environment for fair competition and deepen the commercial system reform. Measures are taken to greatly streamline business-related licenses, for instance, three certificates in one, multi-certificates in one, tax and land tax joint operation, decentralizing or canceling administrative approvals in large numbers and lowering the overall cost of entrepreneurship.

China's entrepreneurship service system is mainly composed of the executive meetings of the State Council, the State Council's Leading Group for Promoting the Development of SMEs, in addition to ministries, commissions and agencies directly under the State Council, local governments at all levels, as well as enterprises, banks, higher learning institutions and social organizations.

The Chinese government introduced tax reduction measures for SMEs in 2017 and 2018, respectively. Prior to that, it also introduced tax preferential measures for incubators, technology-based SMEs and supported enterprise R&D, and exempted SMEs within a certain range from value-added tax and business tax and reduced or eliminated a number of administrative fees.

The Chinese government attaches great importance to optimizing the capital market, constantly innovating bank supports, and enriching the financing channels for MSMEs. Through the combination of central finance and nongovernmental capital, China set up a national SME development fund in 2015 and focuses on supporting the growth of seed and growing SMEs. Since 2016, the government has expanded the scope of business guarantee loans, provided business guarantee loans with interest discounts. Preferential tax policies were introduced in 2017 and 2018 to stimulate venture capital and help start-ups and SMEs solve their financing problems. The development of Chinese venture capital has expanded financing channels for entrepreneurial innovation enterprises and MSMEs. The People's Bank of China has formulated a credit policy that favors SMEs, while commercial banks in various countries provide financing services for SMEs.

The Chinese government regards promoting the transfer and transformation of scientific and technological achievements as an important task in "mass entrepreneurship and innovation". Since 2016, specific action plans have been formulated to improve the technology transfer mechanism. The Chinese government has also set up a national fund to guide the transformation of scientific and technological achievements. The Chinese government authorities provide policy consultation and public information services for innovative start-ups and MSMEs through Internet platforms. China Mobile, China Telecom, and China Unicom jointly launched the special action of speeding up Internet speed and reducing fees in 2017 to support Internet usage.

The Ministry of Finance, the Ministry of Industry and Information Technology, the Ministry of Science and Technology, the Ministry of Commerce, and the State Administration for Industry and Commerce jointly launched the "mass entrepreneurship and innovation base" to provide a workspace for entrepreneurs, which has expanded rapidly. In 2017, the Chinese government released a service standard for incubator workspace and implemented the national filing measures in order to guide sustainable and healthy development. The Chinese government continues to hold the "mass entrepreneurship and innovation" campaign week by setting up a platform for the exchange of innovation and entrepreneurship services. It also holds the national innovation contests through awards instead of subsidies. Other departments such as the China Council for the Promotion of International Trade (CCPIT) have also actively promoted the development of exchange platforms for entrepreneurship and innovation. During the outbreak of Covid-19 in 2020, the Chinese government accelerated the digital transformation of SMEs in several ways, as the government's prevention and control measures required that digital operations and production shall become necessary tools for business development.

The Chinese government continues to deepen the innovation and entrepreneurship education reform in higher learning institutions. At the same time, the Chinese government has actively promoted the mass entrepreneurship and innovation education reform demonstration, played the guiding role of venture capital, and strengthened entrepreneurship education and training. Chinese higher learning institutions have included innovation and entrepreneurship compulsory courses and have supported and trained student entrepreneurship teams and enterprises. Such measures include building incubators and accelerators and holding entrepreneurship contests. Tsinghua x-lab, Tsinghua Management Entrepreneur Accelerator, and Tsinghua University's "President Cup" Innovation Challenge are typical examples. China has established the Innovation and Entrepreneurship Education Alliance, whose members include not only higher learning institutions but also many enterprises, featuring cooperation between higher learning institutions and enterprises. China's entrepreneurship trainings have also made great progress in terms of scale, faculty strength, and coverage of overseas students, migrant workers, and women. Institutions for high-growth entrepreneurs, such as Hundun University, Dark Horse University, and Hupan University are established. China's policy of "mass entrepreneurship and innovation" has a far-reaching impact on the entrepreneurial culture.

With the further development of "mass entrepreneurship and innovation", the growing group of entrepreneurs, especially private entrepreneurs, is playing an increasingly important role in promoting economic development, especially in establishing a socialist market economic system in China. At present, China's economy is in a critical period of transformation and upgrading. It is urgent to vigorously stimulate and protect entrepreneurship, protect the legitimate rights and interests of entrepreneurs, and encourage more social subjects to engage in innovation and entrepreneurship.

Government Services

The Chinese government has enacted and promulgated a special law on SMEs, and has clearly implemented a supportive policy to create more favorable conditions for SME development. Based on the Law of the People's Republic of China on the Promotion of Small and Medium-sized Enterprises of 2002, the first law on SMEs, the Chinese government released the new version after amendment in 2018.

The new version proposes that the State Council should formulate a policy on SME development, establish a coordination mechanism for SME promotion, and coordinate throughout the country. It prescribes measures including fiscal and financial support, innovation and entrepreneurship supports and services, market expansion, and protection on rights and interests. For example, the chapter of "Fiscal and Taxation Support" propose that the state should set up a SME development fund to guide and drive social funds to support SMEs in the start-up period and promote entrepreneurship and innovation; preferential tax policies for small and micro-enterprises should be implemented, measures such as deferment, reduction and exemption of corporate income tax and value-added tax should be made, and tax collection and management procedures should be simplified so as to reduce the tax burden on SMEs.

The chapter of "Financing Promotion" proposes to improve the capital market, promote equity financing, develop and standardize the bond market, and facilitate SMEs to directly raise funds by various means; the state should improve the guarantee financing system and support financial institutions to provide guarantee financing for SMEs with accounts receivable, intellectual property rights, inventories, machinery, and equipment, etc.

The chapter of "Entrepreneurship Support" proposes to support social funds to invest in SMEs and provide tax incentives for venture capital enterprises and individual investors to invest in science and technology innovation enterprises in their initial stage; optimize the business approval process, realize the convenience of administrative licensing for SMEs, and reduce the establishment cost of SMEs.

The chapter of "Innovation Support" proposes to encourage SMEs to participate in R&D of key common technologies, use fiscal funds to set up scientific research projects, encourage institutions and large enterprises to open their own experiment facilities to SMEs, carry out technology R&D and cooperation, and help SMEs develop new products and professionals.

The chapter of "Market Development" proposes to support large enterprises to establish cooperative relations with SMEs, drive and promote SME development, formulate relevant preferential policies on government procurement of SMEs, and increase the share of SMEs in government procurement.

The chapter of "Protection on Rights and Interests" proposes to protect the property rights and other legitimate rights and interests of SMEs and their investors.

Premier Li Keqiang of China's State Council proposed in the 2018 government work report to promote mass entrepreneurship and mass innovation. The Chinese government will continue its supports for financing, taxation, and talent to further stimulate enterprises' creativity. Since Premier Li put forward the "Mass Entrepreneurship and Innovation" strategy at the Summer World Economic Forum in 2014, the Chinese government has been committed to optimizing the environment for innovation and entrepreneurship at the policy level and supporting the sustained and quality development of innovation and entrepreneurship.

In 2015, the "mass entrepreneurship and innovation" strategy was officially written in the Government Work Report during the annual meetings of the National People's Congress (NPC) and the Chinese People's Political Consultative Conference (CPPCC). The central government and local governments released a series of documents relating to "mass entrepreneurship and innovation" after the Chinese government issued the Opinions of the State Council Concerning Several Policies on Vigorously Boosting Mass Entrepreneurship and Innovation (Guo Fa [2015] No. 32) in June 2015. Under the "mass entrepreneurship and innovation" strategy, the State Council has issued 49 policies; relevant departments and local governments have released 845 supporting measures; and local governments launched 588 supporting measures. In July 2017, the Chinese government issued the Opinions of the State Council on Strengthening the Implementation of Innovation-Driven Development Strategy to Further Promote the Development of Mass Entrepreneurship and Innovation (Guo Fa [2017] No. 37), continuing to promote mass entrepreneurship and innovation. In order to further implement the innovation-driven development strategy, the Chinese government launched comprehensive innovation reform experiments in eight regions, including Beijing-Tianjin-Hebei, Shanghai, Guangdong (the Pearl River Delta), Anhui (Hefei, Wuhu, and Bengbu), Sichuan (Chengdu, Deyang, and Mianyang), Wuhan, Xi'an, and Shenyang. In September 2017, it issued the Notice of the General Office of the State Council on Promoting and Supporting Innovation-related Reform Initiatives (Guo Ban Fa [2017] No. 80), formally extending the reform initiatives in eight pilot areas or across the country.

The Chinese government has also continued to improve the market environment for fair competition and deepen the reform of the commercial system. It has greatly streamlined business-related licenses through measures such as three certificates in one, multi-certificates in one, tax and land tax joint operation, delegating or canceling administrative approvals in large numbers and lowering the threshold for entrepreneurship. In 2017, there were 19.249 million new market players nationwide, up 16.6% year on year, with an average daily addition of 52.27 million. In 2016, the country's newly registered market was 16.513 million, with an increase rate of 11.6%.

The Opinions of the State Council Concerning Several Policies on Vigorously Boosting Mass Entrepreneurship and Innovation (Guo Fa [2015] No. 32) was released in 2015. Later in the same year, it launched the reform of the business system of "integrating the business license issued by the administration for industry and commerce, the organization code certificate issued by the quality and technology supervision, and the certificate of taxation registration issued by the taxation into one business license issued by the administration for industry and commerce". In 2017, the Chinese government issued the Opinions of the State Council on Strengthening the Implementation of Innovation-Driven Development Strategy to Further Promote the Development of Mass Entrepreneurship and Innovation (Guo Fa [2017] No. 37), which proposed to "further improve censorship mechanism to create a unified, open, and orderly market environment for innovation and entrepreneurship; promote the reform of multi-certificate in one registration system; and strengthen regulation and enhance regulation efficiency". In the same year, the Circular of the General Office of the State Council on Promoting and Supporting Innovation-Related Reforms (Guo Ban Fa [2017] No. 80) places a high priority on entrepreneurship policies from five aspects: (1) one-stop service of quick patent review, confirmation of rights, and protection on rights", (2) "strengthening the assessment and incentives for innovation-oriented state-owned enterprises", (3) "public institutions introducing scarce or high-end talents by flexible distribution methods such as annual wage, agreed-upon wage, or project-based wage", (4) "coordinate use of public institutions' staffing within province", and

(5) "joint administration by state and local taxations". In addition, the Chinese government canceled 90 administrative approval items and delegated 152 administrative approval items to local governments for implementation in 2015 and 2106, continuously pushing forward the reform of the administrative approval system and enhancing the simplification of governance and delegation of power.

China's entrepreneurship service system is mainly composed of the executive meetings of the State Council, the State Council's Leading Group for Promoting the Development of SMEs, in addition to ministries, commissions and agencies directly under the State Council, local governments at all levels, as well as enterprises, banks, higher learning institutions, and social organizations. During the term of the incumbent Chinese government, more than 50 issues were discussed at the executive meetings of the State Council on mass entrepreneurship and innovation. The State Council's Leading Group for Promoting the Development of SMEs (hereinafter referred to as the "Leading Group") is headed by Liu He, a member of the Political Bureau of the Central Committee and Vice Premier of the State Council, with Miao Xu, Minister of Industry and Information, Liu Kun, Minister of Finance, and Gao Yu, a member of the Party Group of the State Council, as deputy heads, and the other 19 deputy ministerial members. The group was set up mainly to strengthen organizational leadership and policy coordination for promoting the development of SMEs.

In August 2015, the State Council of China agreed to establish an inter-ministerial joint conference system led by the National Development and Reform Commission (NDRC) and involving 28 departments, which aims to strengthen the overall coordination of the central government, establish a long-term working mechanism, implement the national strategy, and promote the development of innovation and entrepreneurship. At the fourth inter-ministerial joint meeting to promote mass entrepreneurship and innovation in July 2017, the work of mass entrepreneurship and innovation since 2017 and the overall consideration of the 2017 National Mass Entrepreneurship and Innovation Week were briefed.

Fiscal Support

The executing meeting of the State Council in April 2018 introduced seven tax cut measures, which are expected to reduce the tax burden on enterprises by 60 billion yuan (equivalent to 9.18 billion US dollars) in the whole year. This is a further tax cut in addition to the 2017 tax cut. These seven measures include: From January 1, 2018 to December 31, 2020, the ceiling of the unit value of newly purchased R&D instruments and equipment for enterprises entitled to the one-time pre-tax deduction for the current year will be increased from 1 million yuan (equivalent to 150,000 US dollars) to 5 million yuan (equivalent to 760,000 US dollars and the annual taxable income limit of small and micro-enterprises covered by the preferential policy on halved corporate income tax will be increased from 500,000 yuan (equivalent to 76,000 US dollars) to 1 million yuan (150,000 US dollars). From January 1, 2018, it will lift the non-deductible restriction on overseas R&D expenses entrusted by enterprises; extend the loss carrying-forward period of high-tech enterprises and scientific and technological SME from 5 to 10 years; and raise the pre-tax deduction limit for employees' education funds of high-tech enterprises from 2.5 to 8%. From May 1, 2018, the stamp duty levied on the capital account books set up by taxpayers will be halved according to the total amount of paid-in capital and capital reserve. Other account books collected on a case-by-case basis will be exempted from the stamp duty. In addition, the preferential policy of 70% deduction of taxable income for venture capital enterprises and angel investors will be applicable to the whole country, instead of the current pilot program in the eight areas of comprehensive innovation reform and Suzhou Industrial Park that invest in seed and start-up science and technology enterprises.

In April 2017, the executive meeting of the State Council resolved to expand the scope of small enterprises with low profits covered by the preferential corporate income tax. From January 1, 2017, to December 31, 2019, the ceiling of taxable income of small enterprises with low profits should be increased from 300,000 yuan (equivalent to 46,000 US dollars) to 500,000 yuan (equivalent to 76,000 US dollars). Eligible small enterprises with low profits should calculate their taxable amounts on a halved basis and pay the corporate income tax at the preferential tax rate of 20%. The pre-tax deduction ratio of technology-based SMEs for their R&D expense should be increased. From January 1, 2017, to December 31, 2019, the pre-tax deduction ratio of R&D expenses actually incurred by technology-based SMEs in developing new technologies, new products, and new processes is increased from 50 to 75%.

Prior to the tax cuts in 2017 and 2018, the Chinese government had introduced tax incentives for incubators, small and medium-sized technology-based enterprises and supporting enterprise R&D, exempted small and micro-enterprises within a certain range from value-added tax and business tax, and reduced or canceled a number of administrative fees (Table 1).

Financial Support

At the policy level, the Chinese government emphasizes optimizing the capital market, innovating bank support methods, and enriching venture financing channels. In addition, it has set up a national SME development fund through the combination of central finance and private capital to focus on supporting the SMEs in seed and start-up phases. Moreover, it has taken measures such as venture guarantee loans, discount interest on venture guarantee loans, and stimulating venture capital to help start-ups and SMEs solve their financing problems.

In the Opinions of the State Council Concerning Several Policies on Vigorously Boosting Mass Entrepreneurship and Innovation (Guo Fa [2015] No. 32), the Chinese Government proposed the requirement of convenient financing for start-ups from three aspects: optimizing the capital market, innovating bank support methods, and enriching the new mode of financing for start-ups. In the Opinions of the State Council on Strengthening the Implementation of Innovation-Driven Development Strategy to Further Promote the Development of Mass Entrepreneurship and Innovation (Guo Fa [2017] No. 37) released in 2017, the Chinese government stressed that it will further promote inclusive financial services, grant credit authority to large banks and county branches, and support local corporate banks to set up small and micro branches and community branches in grass-roots areas; provide investment and financing services covering the whole life cycle for scientific and technological SMEs through financing service mechanisms such as creditor's rights and equity; and promote the establishment of venture capital sub-funds by the National Venture Capital Guidance Fund for Emerging Industries, the National Small and Medium-sized Enterprise Development Fund, and the National Science and Technology Achievement Transformation Guidance Fund. The Circular of the General Office of the

Table 1 Tax preferential policies prior to 2016 (inclusive)

Issuing authority of preferential policies (documents)	Contents and targets of preferential policies
Ministry of Finance and State Administration of Taxation: Notice on Tax Policy on Science and Technology Business Incubator (Cai Shui [2016] No. 89)	From January 1, 2016, to December 31, 2018, **incubators will be exempted from property tax and land use tax as well as business tax and value-added tax**
Ministry of Science and Technology, Ministry of Finance, and State Administration of Taxation: Administrative Measures for Identification of High-tech Enterprises (Guo Ke Fa Huo [2016] No. 32)	From January 1, 2016, the conditions for identifying SMEs will be eased, the scope of high and new technology will be expanded, and **preferential policies of 15% enterprise income tax for technology-based enterprises, especially SMEs, will be implemented**
Ministry of Finance: Notice on Improving the Policy on Pre-tax Accrual and Deduction of Research and Development Expenses (Cai Shui [2015] No. 119)	From January 1, 2016, the scope of R&D activities covered by the policy on accrual and deduction of R&D expenses will be expanded, the standards for R&D expenses will be eased, and management on examination and approval will be simplified to encourage enterprises to engage in innovation and entrepreneurship
State Administration of Taxation: Notice of the State Administration of Taxation on Further Supporting Value-Added Tax and Business Tax Policies for Small and Micro Enterprises (Cai Shui [2014] No. 71)	**The preferential tax policy for small and micro-enterprises** will continue until December 31, 2017. The preferential tax policy stipulates that small-scale taxpayers and business tax taxpayers (including individual industrial and commercial households, other individuals, enterprises, and non-enterprise units) with monthly sales or revenue not exceeding 30,000 yuan (inclusive) (equivalent to 4600 US dollars) may be entitled to the preferential tax **exemption from VAT and business tax**
State Administration of Taxation: Notice on Further Expanding the Scope of Preferential Policies on Income Tax for Small Enterprises with Low Profits (Cai Shui [2015] No. 99)	From October 1, 2015, to December 31, 2017, for of **small enterprises with low profits** whose annual taxable income is between 200,000 yuan (equivalent to 30,000 US dollars) and 300,000 yuan (inclusive) (equivalent to 46,000 US dollars), their income **will be calculated at 50% and included in the taxable income, and the enterprise income tax will be paid at the rate of 20%**

(continued)

Table 1 (continued)

Ministry of Finance and NDRC: Notice on Policies Concerning Cleaning up and Standardizing a Batch of Administrative Charges (2017)	Starting from April 1, 2017, 41 administrative fees set up by the central government have been canceled or suspended, and the trademark registration fee has been reduced by 50%

State Council on Promoting and Supporting Innovation-Related Reforms (Guo Ban Fa [2017] No. 80) announced that reform measures will be taken in the area of innovation in technology and finance, such as financing services pledged by accounts receivable, one-stop investment and financing information services for SMEs, and patent pledge financing services bundled with loans, insurance, and financial risk compensation.

At the executive meeting of the State Council in September 2015, the central government decided to invest 15 billion yuan (equivalent to 2.3 billion US dollars) through consolidated funds to attract private and state-owned enterprises, financial institutions, local governments, and other social capital to participate in the establishment of the National SME Development Fund of 60 billion yuan (equivalent to 9.2 billion US dollars), and focus on supporting the development of SMEs in seed and start-up stages through the establishment of parent funds, direct investment funds and so on. By the end of December 2017, the four entity funds under the National SME Development Fund had completed 130 investment projects with an investment amount of 3.824 billion yuan (equivalent to 585 million US dollars).

The Notice on Implementing Enterprise Guarantee Loan to Support Entrepreneurship and Employment (Yin Fa [2016] No. 202) jointly issued by the People's Bank of China, the Ministry of Finance, and the Ministry of Human Resources and Social Security expanded the scope of enterprise guarantee loan to include special groups such as persons with employment difficulties (including disabled persons), demobilized veterans, released prisoners, and university graduates, and identified women as key targets. The Notice specifies that the maximum amount of enterprise guarantee loan is 100,000 yuan (equivalent to 15,000 US dollars), the period of enterprise guarantee loan is adjusted from two years to three years, and the individual enterprise guarantee loan is subsidized by the financial departments according to relevant regulations.

As for the discount interest on business guarantee loans, the Ministry of Finance issued the Administrative Measures for Specific Funds of Inclusive Finance Development (Cai Jin [2016] No. 85) in September 2016. In the Chapter of "Discount Interest and Reward Policy for Business Guarantee Loans", it stipulates giving full discount interest to entrepreneurship guarantee loans to individuals from poverty-stricken areas. For individuals from other areas, the interest discount should be 100% for the first year, two-thirds for the second year, and one-third for the third year. For eligible SMEs, the discount interest should be 50% of the benchmark loan interest rate on the signing date of the loan contract.

In order to strengthen the management on financial discount interest funds and improve the efficiency of the use of funds, the Ministry of Finance, the Ministry of Human Resources and Social Security, and the People's Bank of China jointly issued the Notice on Further Ensuring the Financial Discount Interest for Business Guarantee Loans in April 2018 to strengthen policy support and optimize application procedures. In this initiative, rural self-employed farmers are included in the scope of support. At the same time, the applicants for SME loans are adjusted to "small and micro enterprises that newly recruit employees eligible for applying the entrepreneurship guarantee loan up to 25% (or 15% for enterprises having more than 100 employees) of the existing employees in the current year and executed labor contracts for more than 1 year with such new employees".

The Chinese government continues to implement incentive measures for venture capital to help SMEs solve their financing problems. The development of China's venture capital has opened up financing channels for start-ups, innovative enterprises, and SMEs.

In 2016, Chinese angel investment agencies raised more than 130 angel funds and the amount of disclosed cases totaled more than 12 billion yuan (equivalent to 1.8 billion US dollars). The number of newly raised venture investment funds has exceeded more than 600 and the amount of new investable capital of venture capital funds exceeds 350 billion yuan (equivalent to 53.56 billion US dollars). The venture capital market has invested more than 3500 times and disclosed investment transactions of more than 120 billion yuan (equivalent to 18.36 billion US dollars).

Since 2017, the Chinese government has issued a series of documents to implement preferential tax policies for corporate venture capital enterprises, partnership venture capital enterprises, and angel investors to invest directly in start-up science and technology enterprises such as seed and start-up science and technology enterprises by means of equity investment. For example, 70% of the investible amount may be used to offset corresponding taxable income amount, income amount, or operating income amount, and taxable income amount from equity transfer (Table 2).

In order to broaden the channels for SMEs to obtain funds, China's SME board was officially launched in May 2004. The growth enterprise market was officially launched in 2009, making up for the shortcomings of the SME board and further broadening the financing mode of SMEs. In December 2013, the new OTC market (National Equities Exchange and Quotations, NEEQ) was reformed to accept applications for listing nationwide, not limited to unlisted companies in Zhongguancun Science and Technology Park, Tianjin Binhai, Wuhan Donghu and Shanghai Zhangjiang. It is a national equity trading platform for unlisted companies, mainly targeting SMEs. As of May 2018, there were more than 11,000 companies listed on the NEEQ.

The People's Bank of China has formulated a credit policy that favors SMEs, requiring all state-owned commercial banks to set up SME credit departments, and established thousands of village or township banks to provide financing services for SMEs. By the end of 2017, the national loan balance of SMEs amounted to 30.74 trillion yuan (equivalent to 4.7 trillion US dollars), up 15.14% year on year, 2.67 percentage points higher than the average growth rate of various loans. The number of SMEs with loan balance was 15.2092 million, increased by 1.5982 million over the past year for the same period.

Entrepreneur Services

Technical Services

The Chinese government regards promoting the transfer and transformation of scientific and technological achievements as an important task in implementing the "mass entrepreneurship and innovation" strategy. In addition, it has formulated specific action plans to improve the technology transfer mechanism. Moreover, the Chinese government has also set up a national fund to guide the transformation of scientific and technological achievements to promote capitalization and industrialization.

Table 2 Relevant government documents (preferential policies) on venture capital since 2017

Issuing authority of preferential policies (documents)	Contents and targets of preferential policies
Ministry of Finance and State Administration of Taxation: Notice on Tax Policies Concerning Venture Capital Enterprises and Angel Investors (Cai Shui [2018] No. 55)	In the case of equity investment in seed and start-up science and technology enterprises (science and technology start-ups) for 2 years (24 months, hereinafter the same): In relation to **corporate venture investment enterprises**, 70% of investment amount can be used to offset the taxable income amount of the corporate venture investment enterprises in the year when the equity is held for 2 years; if it is insufficient to offset in the year, it may be carried forward to offset in the coming tax years In relation to **limited partnership venture capital enterprises**, corporate or individual partners may offset their operating incomes distributed from the limited partnership venture capital enterprises with 70% of their investment; if it is insufficient to offset in the year, it may be carried forward to offset in the coming tax years In relation to **angel investors**, 70% of their investment amount may be used to offset the taxable income amount gained from transferring equities of the science and technology start-ups; if it is insufficient to offset in the year, it may be offset when the angel investors obtain the taxable income amount gained from transferring equities of the science and technology start-ups
State Administration of Taxation: Announcement of the State Administration of Taxation on Issues Concerning the Pilot Tax Policy for Venture Capital Enterprises and Angel Investors (Announcement of the State Administration of Taxation [2017] No. 20)	

(continued)

Table 2 (continued)

Ministry of Finance and State Administration of Taxation: Notice on Pilot Tax Policies Concerning Venture Capital Enterprises and Angel Investors (Cai Shui [2017] No. 38)

In the Circular of the General Office of the State Council on Issuing the Action Plan for Promoting the Transfer and Transformation of Scientific and Technological Achievements (Guo Ban Fa [2016] No. 28), the Chinese government clearly identified the 20 key tasks and made progress arrangements. These 20 key tasks include releasing a number of science and technology achievement packages urgently needed for industrial transformation, upgrading and development, establishing a national information system for science and technology achievements, strengthening the exchange of information on science and technology achievements, and promoting an online registration exchange system for science and technology achievements, which will be implemented and completed by the Ministry of Science and Technology in conjunction with relevant departments.

In May 2018, the Ministry of Science and Technology issued the Notice of "Several Opinions on the Development of the Technology Market" (Guo Ke Fa Chuan [2018] No. 48) in support of the National Technology Transfer System Development Plan. The opinions include: develop 20 high-level specialized technology transfer agencies with demonstration and leading role and 600 market-oriented socialized technology transfer agencies; develop 3–5 key technology trading markets; train 10,000 technology managers and technology brokers with the transaction amount of the national technology contract reaching 2 trillion yuan (equivalent to 30.6 million US dollars) by 2020, thus significantly improving the quality and efficiency of technology transactions. In addition, it provides guidance on improving the technology transfer mechanism and promoting the capitalization of scientific and technological achievements and industries.

The national fund to guide the transformation of scientific and technological achievements (hereinafter referred to as the "transformation fund") was jointly set up by the Ministry of Science and Technology and the Ministry of finance in 2001. The goal is to leverage the guiding role of financial funds, drive financial capital and private investment to transform and gather scientific and technological achievements by means of venture capital sub-fund and loan risk supplement, and support the transfer and transformation of scientific and technological achievements. Up to now, nine sub-funds of the transformation fund have been set up, with the central government contributing 3.83 billion yuan (equivalent to 586 million US dollars) and the total size of the fund reaching 17.355 billion yuan (equivalent to 2.556 billion US dollars).

Information Services

The Chinese government authorities provide policy consultation and public information services for innovative start-ups and MSMEs through Internet platforms. China Mobile, China Telecom, and China Unicom jointly launched the special action of speeding up Internet speed and reducing fees in 2017 to support Internet usage.

In 2018, China's NDRC organized the National Information Center to launch the National Innovation and Entrepreneurship Policy Information Service Network (hereinafter referred to as the "Service Network") (http://sc.ndrc.gov.cn), a unified publishing platform for innovation and entrepreneurship policies at the national level, which helps innovative entrepreneurs to obtain authoritative policy information and interpretation comprehensively, quickly, and easily.

In 2018, the China Council for Promotion of International Trade renovated the China Trade and Investment Network. It serves the functions of posting business opportunities and event notification and adds new services such as China and global exhibition project inquiry and credit inquiry for Chinese and foreign enterprises.

China Mobile, China Telecom, and China Unicom jointly launched the special action of speeding up Internet speed and reducing fees in 2017 to support SMEs to develop, innovate, and start businesses. China Telecom has launched a nationwide campaign of "benefiting enterprises by speeding up Internet speed", increasing the average bandwidth of SMEs to 50Mbps for free, up to a maximum of 6x, and continuing to reduce Internet access charges to provide a rich smart enterprise solution. The campaign is expected to benefit 12.3 million SMEs. China Mobile increased the starting bandwidth of dedicated internet access from 2 M to 10 M, and increased the speed for customers with bandwidth less than 200 M within the agreement period for free. China Unicom has greatly reduced the access charges for SMEs for dedicated internet access, benefiting 10 million SMEs, and has set up cloud service platforms for SMEs in various provinces to provide big data, cloud computing, Internet of Things and other products for SMEs.

Enterprise Incubation

The full name of "Mass Entrepreneurship and Innovation Base" is Model Cities of Entrepreneurship and Innovation Base of SMEs. By the end of 2016, there were more than 560,000 new SMEs in the Mass Entrepreneurship and Innovation Base, up 25.6% year on year. The number of new market participants was 3.14 million, accounting for about 7.2% of the country. In addition, it created 4.61 million new urban jobs. The turnover of technical contracts was 76.9 billion yuan (equivalent to 11.76 billion US dollars), up 52% year on year, accounting for about 5.6% of the total. The bases were jointly launched by the Ministry of Finance, Ministry of Industry and Information Technology, Ministry of Science and Technology, Ministry of Commerce, and State Administration for Industry and Commerce in 2015. During the three-year demonstration period, the central government issued incentive funds to the model cities: total rewards for cities specifically designated in the state plan and provincial capitals amounted to 900 million yuan (equivalent to 137 million US dollars) and total rewards for ordinary cities, including districts and counties under the municipalities directly under the central government, amounted to 600 million yuan (equivalent to 92 million US dollars). Both funds were used to provide SMEs with entrepreneurial innovation workspace, improve their service capabilities, support public service improvement, and encourage local policies and measures such as subsidized loans, tax incentives, and technological innovation.

The list of Mass Entrepreneurship and Innovation Demonstration Bases was determined by the Implementation Opinions of the General Office of the State Council on the Development of the Second Batch of Mass Entrepreneurship and Innovation Bases (Guo Ban Fa [2017] No. 54) of 2017 (92 bases) and the Opinions of the General Office of the State Council on the Development of Mass Entrepreneurship and Innovation Bases (Guo Ban Fa [2016] No. 35) of 2016 (28 bases).

In China, the incubator workspace has expanded rapidly. Its investment and financing capacity has been improved. The Chinese government released a service standard implemented the national filing measures to guide the sustainable and healthy development of incubators.

In 2017, there were more than 5700 incubator workspaces nationwide, an increase of 33% year on year. The total area is over 25 million square meters. More than 1.05 million jobs were created, up 36% year on year. There were more than 410,000 start-up teams and enterprises in operation, up 52% year on year. There were more than 87,000 newly registered enterprises, up 22% year on year. The workspaces created 1.7 million jobs, of which more than 460,000 jobs were offered to college students who graduated within two years. In 2017, the workspaces helped more than 18,000 start-up teams and enterprises to obtain investment, totaling 67 billion yuan (equivalent to 10.25 billion US dollars). In turn, the workspaces were also supported by investment. By the end of 2017, a total of 1091 workspaces have received social capital investment.

The Torch Center of China's Ministry of Science and Technology issued Public Innovation Space Service Specification (Trial) and the Workspace (Joint Office) Service Standard in September 2017, targeting entrepreneurial teams, start-ups, and maker groups, stipulating that maker space's service functions include entrepreneurship counseling, financing, resource matching, and atmosphere creation.

In the spirit of the Guiding Opinions of the General Office of the State Council on Developing Maker Spaces to Promote Mass Innovation and Entrepreneurship (Guo Ban Fa [2015] No. 9) and the Notice of the Ministry of Science and Technology on the Issuance of the "Guidelines for Developing Maker Spaces" (Guo Ke Fa Huo [2015] No. 297), the Ministry of Science and Technology identified 639 workspaces as national filing public innovation spaces in 2017 and incorporated them into the management and service system of science and technology business incubators at the national level to guide the healthy development of mass innovation and entrepreneurship.

Communication Platform

The Chinese government continues to hold the "mass entrepreneurship and innovation" campaign week and set up a platform for the exchange of innovation and entrepreneurship services. It holds the national innovation contests through awards instead of subsidies.

The third National Mass Entrepreneurship and Innovation Week was held from September 15 to 21, 2017, themed "Mass Entrepreneurship and Innovation Promoting Upgrades and Enhancing New Momentum". The week set up a main venue in Shanghai, a venue in Beijing, and many sub-venues all over the country. In addition, it was held overseas for the first time.

China's Ministry of Science and Technology and Ministry of Finance jointly issued the Notice of the Ministry of Science and Technology and Ministry of Finance on Supporting China's Innovation and Entrepreneurship Competition (Guo Ke Fa Zi [2016] No. 186). The notice confirmed that the central government will provide guidance support for outstanding enterprises by awarding prizes instead of subsidies, and will guide local governments and financial institutions to increase their support to outstanding enterprises. The sixth competition was launched in Beijing in April 2017. The finals will be held in six different cities and six fields: (1) electronic information, (2) Internet and mobile Internet, (3) biomedicine, (4) advanced manufacturing, (5) new energy and energy conservation and environmental protection, and (6) new materials. A total of 34,341 enterprises and teams contested in the fifth competition in 2016, a record high, covering all provinces, autonomous regions, and municipalities in the country. According to incomplete statistics, the total amount of local financial support for outstanding enterprises and teams contested in the competition is nearly 2 billion yuan (equivalent to 300 million US dollars), which is 17 times the amount of central financial support. The contesting companies in the fifth competition have already obtained an equity investment of 4 billion yuan (equivalent to 612 million US dollars). China Merchants Bank granted credit support to 144 enterprises in the fifth competition, totaling 3.5 billion yuan (equivalent to 536 million US dollars).

The Maker in China 2017 organized by the Ministry of Industry and Information Technology held a total of 12 regional competitions and 12 special events, attracting 5275 high-quality projects, up 65% year on year.

The National Innovation Competition for Rural Entrepreneurship Projects (2017) organized by the Ministry of Agriculture contested by a total of more than 30,000 contestants and events from 27 provinces and cities.

The second edition of China (Shenzhen) Innovation and Entrepreneurship International Competition (2017) was attended by 34 venture investment institutions that created a venture investment pool of 20.9 billion yuan (equivalent to 3.2 billion US dollars) that make portfolio investment in outstanding projects.

The fourth China College Students' Entrepreneurship Competition (2017) was attended by more than 80,000 entrepreneurial projects and 300,000 entrepreneurial students, co-sponsored by the Central Committee of the Communist Youth League, the Cyberspace Administration, the Ministry of Industry and Information, the Ministry of Human Resources and Social Security, the former Ministry of Agriculture, the Ministry of Commerce and the State Council Leading Group of Poverty Alleviation and Development. In 2017, a total of 1237 entries from 76 central enterprises and other social innovators were collected for the Shining Star Innovation Competition of the Central Enterprises, with investment of 935 million yuan (equivalent to 143 million US dollars) from various investment institutions, and product orders of 521 million yuan (equivalent to 79.73 million US dollars) were signed.

The Innovation Competition for China is aimed at all kinds of groups, focusing on high-level talents, returned students, students (graduates) from universities and technical colleges, demobilized soldiers, and returning migrant workers. The special competition is aimed at special groups such as workers and disabled people. The competition is organized by the Ministry of Human Resources and Social Affairs in conjunction with the NDRC, the Ministry of Science and Technology, the Central Committee of the Communist Youth League, and the China Disabled Persons' Federation.

In addition, other departments such as the China Council for Promotion of International Trade (CCPIT) have also actively promoted the development of exchange platforms for entrepreneurship and innovation. The CCPIT launched the new trade promotion activity cloud in 2018, adding such functions as automatic matching and negotiation of enterprises. In addition, the CCPIT supports SMEs to cooperate with international organizations by introducing training programs such as strategic decision-making, trade maps, standard maps, and market analysis tools to help SMEs diagnose management problems and enhance their export competitiveness. On the other hand, the resource-sharing platform for innovation and entrepreneurship developed by the Chinese government is becoming increasingly practical. Take the DRC (Design Resource Center) jointly established by Beijing Municipal Science and Technology Commission and Xicheng District as an example, it renders equipment in industrial design worth tens of millions of dollars to entrepreneurs at low prices or even free of charge.

Digital Transformation Support

During the outbreak of Covid-19 in 2020, the Chinese government accelerated the digital transformation of SMEs in several ways, as the government's prevention and control measures required that digital operations and production shall become necessary tools for business development.

(1) Encouraging the SMEs to develop online working modes such as teleworking. On February 18, 2020, the Ministry of Industry and Information Technology (MIIT) issued the Notice on Using New Generation of Information Technology for Supporting the Prevention and Control of the COVID-19 Epidemic and the Resumption of Work and Production, which, in the face of the serious impact of the epidemic on the resumption of work and production of SMEs, encourages the use of cloud computing to vigorously promote enterprises to the cloud, and focuses on the implementation of online working modes including teleworking, working from home, video conferencing, online training, collaborative R&D, and e-commerce. The telecommunication operators are supported to provide free office services on the cloud, such as cloud video conferencing, for more than six months for SMEs seriously affected by the epidemic, while providing free E-surfing cloud services for three months for SMEs nationwide.

(2) Providing multifaceted support (including financial support) to the transformation of SMEs. On March 19, 2020, China's Ministry of Industry and Information Technology (MIIT) issued the Special Action Plan for Empowering SMEs with Digitalization, which encouraged financial institutions to give priority support in loans at preferential interest rates to SMEs that encounter temporary liquidity difficulties and have good development prospects, and that promote the resumption of work and digital transformation and upgrading.

(3) Offering solutions to the challenges faced by SMEs in the digital transformation. On May 13, 2020, the NDRC and other 145 organizations, through online means, jointly launched the Digital Transformation Partner Action (2020), which focuses on solving

the problems encountered by MSMEs that are "unguided, underfunded, and unambitious to get involved in the digital transformation", launched the first batch of more than 500 service initiatives for MSMEs, so as to provide an all-round and full-chain service.[1]

Entrepreneurship Education

In recent years, the Chinese government has been deepening the innovation and entrepreneurship education reform in higher learning institutions.

Reform measures include improving the curriculum system and promoting universities to start innovative and entrepreneurial courses; promoting the reform of the teaching management system, of which the Regulations on Student Management in Ordinary higher learning institutions allows students to drop out of school and start their own businesses; promoting the establishment of innovation and entrepreneurship credit accumulation, and conversion system in higher learning institutions; establishing a talent pool of 10,000 outstanding innovative and entrepreneurial mentors nationwide, and selecting more than 4600 mentors in the first batch; highlighting the demonstration and leading role, in which 19 universities such as Tsinghua University and Peking University were selected as the mass entrepreneurship and innovation demonstration bases of the State Council; identifying 200 model higher learning institutions to deepen innovation and entrepreneurship education reform and give financial support; and launching mass entrepreneurship and innovation education and training for 50,000 teachers in vocational schools and applied undergraduate colleges.

At the same time, the Chinese government has actively promoted the mass entrepreneurship and innovation education reform demonstration, which played the guiding role of venture capital and strengthened entrepreneurship education and training to promote employment.

The Ministry of Education issued Notice on the List of the First Batch of Model Universities for Deepening Innovation and Entrepreneurship Education Reform and the Notice on the List of the Second

---

[1] Evaluation and Prospect of G20 Members' Policies to Support Entrepreneurship in the Post-pandemic Era, Entrepreneurship Research Center on G20 Economies, Oct 22, 2020.

Batch of Model Universities for Deepening Innovation and Entrepreneurship Education Reform, successively identifying 200 universities such as Tsinghua University and Peking University as "national model universities for deepening innovation and entrepreneurship education reform".

The Notice of the Ministry of Education on Ensuring Employment and Entrepreneurship of National Ordinary College Graduates 2018 and the Notice of the Ministry of Human Resources and Social Affairs on Continuous Implementation of Employment Action for Unemployed Graduates required to strengthen the entrepreneurship and vocational training on graduates of higher learning institutions. At present, the proportion of graduates as entrepreneurs has increased from 1.6% in 2011 to 3.0%.

Since 2014, the Ministry of Education has implemented a collaborative education project between industry and education. In 2017, 89 enterprises have supported more than 4500 projects, with a total amount of 260 million yuan (equivalent to 39.79 million US dollars). The Chinese government has also set up a special fund for college students' innovation and entrepreneurship education. During the 13th Five-Year Plan, 50 million yuan (equivalent to 7.65 million US dollars) was allocated each year to support college students' innovation and entrepreneurship.

Chinese higher learning institutions have included compulsory innovation and entrepreneurship courses, and have supported and trained student entrepreneurship teams and enterprises through such means as building incubators and accelerators and holding entrepreneurship contests. China has established the Innovation and Entrepreneurship Education Alliance, whose members include not only higher learning institutions but also renowned enterprises. Cooperation between higher learning institutions and enterprises is a feature of China's entrepreneurship education.

According to the Ministry of Education Information Office, at the end of 2016, there were more than 1000 universities offering innovative and entrepreneurial education courses, of which more than 900 universities offered compulsory innovation and entrepreneurship courses. Nearly 14,000 practical platforms for innovation and entrepreneurship education were developed. China's Internet Plus University Student Innovation and Entrepreneurship Competition was held for three consecutive years, with 330,000 entries and over 1.5 million participants in 2017. 33,054 projects were launched in 2016, involving 134,000 students from more than 900 higher learning institutions, with nearly 600 million yuan (equivalent to 92 million US dollars) in project funding.

Tsinghua University has been offering entrepreneurship education-related courses for many years. It supports and trains entrepreneurial teams and enterprises by hosting the President Cup entrepreneurship contest, and setting up Tsinghua x-lab and entrepreneurs' accelerators. In 2013, x-lab, an education platform was set up for the discovery and development of creative talents for innovation and entrepreneurship. Strongly tied with the School of Economics and Management and jointly developed by 15 departments, including departments of science, engineering, arts, and medicine in Tsinghua University, it developed an ecosystem of creative innovation and entrepreneurship education, integrated teaching and entrepreneurship practice resources, and developed students' creative thinking as well as entrepreneurship and entrepreneurial skills. Tsinghua University organized the annual President Cup entrepreneurship contest, focusing on social progress entrepreneurship projects for all students, alumni, and teachers. Several well-known investors and businesspersons served as judges. Innovative products were presented in various fields such as artificial intelligence, 3D printing, biomedicine, new energy, education, and technology. Many outstanding entrepreneurship projects received subsequently financing. As of April 2017, x-lab hosted more than 1200 start-up teams. Strengthened by the advantageous Engineering School, Tsinghua University transformed its 15,000-square-meter engineering skill training center into the i-Center workspace in 2014. It created an international cross-disciplinary innovation and entrepreneurship platform and support 3000 students for innovation and entrepreneurship activities every year.

The Innovation and Entrepreneurship Education Alliance was established in Tsinghua University in June 2015. The first batch of alliance members included 137 universities such as Tsinghua University, Peking University, and Zhejiang University, as well as innovative enterprises such as Baidu, Alibaba, Tencent, Intel, and Microsoft, and other related units.

China's entrepreneurship trainings have also made great progress in terms of scale and faculty strength.

By the end of 2017, there were 35 training institutions for business incubators in 32 provinces, municipalities, and autonomous regions. The total number of participants in primary training increased from 1469 in 2012 to 5300 in 2017. In 2017, 2,192,000 government-subsidized entrepreneurship trainings were organized nationwide.

The faculty of entrepreneurship training is also growing. In 2017, more than 230 entrepreneurship teacher training courses were completed by various institutions, with 64.6 million entrepreneurship trainers dispatched. In 2017, the Ministry of Human Resources and Social Affairs organized a themed event for entrepreneurs and a national entrepreneurship training lecturer contest, in which thousands of lecturers from all over the country took part. In the development of entrepreneurship training courses, the Ministry of Human Resources and Social Security, in cooperation with the International Labor Organization, has developed entrepreneurship training courses such as Start and Improve Your Business (SIYB) and Generate Your Business Idea (GYB) to promote online training.

Progress has also been made in entrepreneurial training for overseas students, migrant workers, and women.

In 2017, the Ministry of Human Resources and Social Affairs deployed talent programs such as the Innovation and Entrepreneurship Start-up Support Plan and the Action Plan of Overseas Chinese to Serve the Country, with total funding of 28.47 million yuan (equivalent to 4.36 million US dollars). The national human resources and social security system has attracted 43,000 overseas talents to return to China and paired 33,000 projects with talents and funds. The service window of the 1000 Talents Plan has processed more than 900 person-times of visa, residence, settlement, and other procedures, and has provided more than 2500 times of consulting services.

In 2016, the Ministry of Human Resources and Social Security, in conjunction with other departments, began to implement entrepreneurship promotion programs such as the University Student Entrepreneurship Leading Program and the Migrant Workers' Entrepreneurship Program, focusing on supporting the entrepreneurship of key groups such as university graduates, rural workers and laid-off employees of enterprises. In 2017, there were 4.012 million young entrepreneurs registered for the first time, of whom 645,000 were university entrepreneurs, an increase of 57.3 and 79.9%, respectively, over 2013. In 2017, more than 7.4 million people returned to their hometowns to start businesses.

The All-China Women's Federation has been implementing the Women's Action for Innovation and Entrepreneurship since 2015. By May 2018, the program has won more than 110 billion yuan (equivalent to 16.8 billion US dollars) in guarantee loans for more than 1.3 million women and helped 640 million women start businesses or get jobs. In May 2018, the federation launched a series of activities for 100 outstanding women in innovation and entrepreneurship to enter higher learning institutions. Meanwhile, it held a training course to promote women's innovation and entrepreneurship. In addition, China Women's Innovation and Entrepreneurship Contest was held, and a number of outstanding women entrepreneurs emerged through the contest, setting a good example for women entrepreneurs. In September 2017, the first China Women's Entrepreneurial Innovation Competition was held in Hangzhou, Zhejiang. Nearly 600,000 women from all walks of life participated in the contest, and 30 projects that entered the finals received 1.25 billion yuan (equivalent to 190 million US dollars) of intended investment.

At the beginning of 2018, China's NDRC and other 15 departments issued the Opinions on Supporting Disabled Persons' Self-Employment and Entrepreneurship, which defined more than 20 supporting policies to promote disabled persons' self-employment and entrepreneurship. It includes providing priority care for persons with disabilities to start their own businesses. For example, when the governments and street offices set up relevant convenient service outlets, not less than 10% of which should be reserved for persons with disabilities. The personal income tax on labor income obtained by individuals with disabilities was reduced in accordance with the relevant provisions. For persons with disabilities who start their own businesses, fees such as management fees, registration fees and license fees were exempted. The opinions also clearly stated that by the end of 2018, each of the provinces, autonomous regions, municipalities, and cities specifically designated in the state plan will have at least one incubator for the disabled.

China has training institutions for high-growth entrepreneurs, such as Hundun University, Dark Horse University, and Hupan University. These organizations will invite some well-known successful entrepreneurs or investors to serve as mentors for entrepreneurs. They help analyze potential weaknesses in the process of starting a business, including personal characteristics, leadership, corporate culture development and management mechanism, marketing, investment, and financing, etc. Through such activities, they will also build extensive networks for entrepreneurs, helping exchange experiences and lessons, at the same time expanding their business. These institutions generally have higher screening criteria for the selected students. For example, income needs to reach a certain scale or start-ups should have obtained venture investment.

China's policy of "mass entrepreneurship and innovation" has a far-reaching impact on the entrepreneurial culture. On the one hand, the introduction of the policy has greatly promoted entrepreneurship activities, including entrepreneurship education and training throughout the country, awakened people's awareness of entrepreneurship, regarded entrepreneurship as a way of employment, and improved the country's economic and technological strength through innovation. Government policies and related support measures have made it easier to start a business from a procedural aspect, and the channels for obtaining financial support have also increased significantly. There are many successful start-ups in China. Excluding those that have successfully listed in the capital markets of China and the US, Chinese unicorn enterprises valued at over 1 billion US dollars account for 36% of the world's total. Successful start-ups have strong incentives for new entrepreneurs. On the other hand, successful entrepreneurs are, after all, a few. Many entrepreneurs do not yet have enough entrepreneurial skills and resources, thus discouraging entrepreneurship. With the passage of time, the public will become objective to entrepreneurship and be equipped with an entrepreneurial spirit and familiar with entrepreneurial laws and risks. Entrepreneurs can decide whether to start a business or not according to their own conditions that will improve the probability of success, and then influence entrepreneurial culture.

Protection of Entrepreneurs' Rights and Interests

2018 marks the 40th anniversary of China's reform and opening up. The growing group of entrepreneurs, especially private entrepreneurs, is playing an increasingly important role in promoting economic development and establishing a socialist market economic system in China. At present, China's economy is in a critical period of transformation and upgrading. It is urgent to vigorously stimulate and protect entrepreneurship, protect the legitimate rights and interests of entrepreneurs, and encourage more social subjects to engage in innovation and entrepreneurship.

Protection on Property Rights

In recent years, the legitimate rights and interests of entrepreneurs have been damaged due to property disputes, patent infringement, and improper government intervention. In order to reassure entrepreneurs, the Opinions of the CPC Central Committee and State Council on Creating an Environment for Healthy Growth of Entrepreneurs and Promoting Outstanding Entrepreneurship to Better Play the Role of Entrepreneurs (hereinafter referred to as the "Opinions") were released in September 2017, affirming the status of entrepreneurs and the value of entrepreneurship for the first time with special documents, and explicitly proposing to create a legal environment for protecting the legitimate rights and interests of entrepreneurs. In order to implement the opinions decision-making arrangements, the Division of Labor Plan for the Opinions was released, specifying 27 key tasks and 110 specific measures for implementing the opinions. At present, the key tasks are progressing in an orderly manner and various supporting measures are advancing steadily, which have played an important role in improving entrepreneurs' expectations and enhancing their confidence and have produced initial results in stimulating and protecting entrepreneurship.

Protect Entrepreneurs' Property Rights Under the Law

The property rights of entrepreneurs are protected under the law. The cooperation and consensus of the court, the people's procuratorate and the public security organ are needed to protect the property rights of entrepreneurs equally under the law, avoid using public power to infringe private property rights, illegally sealing up and freezing private enterprise property, and using criminal means to intervene in economic disputes. In December 2017, the Supreme People's Procuratorate issued a document demanding strict control of the definition between crime and non-crime. In December of the same year, the Supreme People's Procuratorate and the Ministry of Public Security jointly issued a document calling for the prudent seizure, detention, and freezing of enterprise property under the law. In January 2018, the Supreme People's Court issued a document calling for the resolute prevention of criminal interference in economic disputes.

Wrongful convictions relating to the property rights of entrepreneurs should be identified and corrected under the law so as to protect entrepreneurs' right to win lawsuits. The Supreme People's Court has set up an identification and correction working group to examine wrongful convictions relating to property rights in history. In December 2017, the Supreme People's Court announced to the public the retrial of the Zhang

Wenzhong case and the Gu Chujun case under the law. After a wrongful conviction is corrected, the people's court will initiate the state compensation procedure in accordance with the state compensation law to protect the legitimate rights and interests of entrepreneurs.

Protecting Entrepreneur's Innovation Rights and Interests Under the Law

Intellectual property is the foundation of innovative economic development. Measures to protect entrepreneurs' innovative rights and interests under the law include: (1) improving the legal system for the protection on intellectual property rights, (2) increasing the amount of compensation for infringement upon intellectual property rights, and (3) strengthening the protection of key core technologies and technological achievements in basic frontier areas.

In November 2016, the Opinions of the CPC Central Committee and the State Council on Improving the Property Protection System and Protecting Property Rights under the Law, which is the first top-level design for property rights protection in China in the name of the Central Committee.

In December 2017, the Supreme People's Court issued a document requesting people's courts at all levels to establish a judicial determination mechanism for infringement damage and to establish a punitive damage system for intellectual property rights in the trial of intellectual property rights.

In the area of judicial protection on intellectual property rights, China has set up three intellectual property courts. The State Intellectual Property Office has set up 19 intellectual property protection centers nationwide to promote one-stop services for intellectual property administrative protection.

Protect Entrepreneurs' Independent Management Rights under the Law.

Governments, authorities, and their officials may not interfere within independent operation activities carried out by entrepreneurs under the law.

The list of enterprise-related charges is under strict administration. Except for those specified in the list of charges of national government funds and administrative charges and the list of service charges priced by the government, no fees may be charged.

Efforts are made to explore and set up a unified enterprise rights protection service platform nationwide, and to establish a mechanism for joint rights protection by the government, industry associations, and other parties.

Fair Competition for SMEs

China released opinions and suggestions to strengthen the protection of entrepreneurs' fair competition rights and interests. The economic innovation-driven development requires competition policy to play its role. After the promulgation and implementation of the anti-monopoly law in 2018, the concept of "competition policy" was first introduced in the form of legislation. In 2015, the State Council issued the Several Opinions on Further Promoting the Reform of Pricing Mechanism and for the first time proposed gradually establishing the basic position of competition policy. In 2016, the State Council issued Opinions on Establishing a Fair Competition Review System in the Development of Market System and introduced a fair competition review system to prevent the government from suppressing competition by improper intervention, so that the government can truly seek its administration, perform its duties and perform its duties.

The market access negative list system is fully implemented.[2] The industries, sectors, and businesses outside the list may be subject to non-stop entry or non-stop entry, and all kinds of market players shall be guaranteed equal access to industries, sectors and businesses outside the negative list under the law.

Against monopoly and unfair competition. The amended Law of the People's Republic of China on Promotion of Small and Medium-sized Enterprises was officially promulgated in 2017, emphasizing equal rights. Property rights of SMEs and other civil subjects of different sizes

---

[2] In October 2015, the State Council issued Opinions on Implementing the Negative List System of Market Access and proposed to "create a market environment of fair trade and equal competition compatible with the negative list system of market access. The relevant departments should clean up and abolish all regulations and practices that restrict the market to play a decisive role in the allocation of resources and hinder the national unified market and fair competition, prohibit and punish all kinds of illegal preferential policies, oppose local protection, oppose monopoly and unfair competition, and prevent relevant policies from hindering the national unified market and fair competition."

and ownership are equally protected by law. In 2018, the newly established State Administration for Market Supervision is responsible for the enforcement of anti-monopoly law, ending the situation of multi-head[3] law enforcement. It is more conducive to the unification of law enforcement standards and the coordination of law enforcement actions, thus forming a regulatory force.

The fairness, standardization, and simplicity of supervision have been continuously improved. In terms of market regulation, China fully required "random inspection by random inspectors with results being made public on time",[4] to strengthen synchronized regulation of various departments across jurisdictions, eliminate multi-head law enforcement, improve the efficiency of comprehensive law enforcement, and reduce burdens on enterprises.

The market exit mechanism is improved to promote fair competition and survival of the fittest. In July 2016, the Supreme People's Court issued the Notice on Issues Related to the Filing and Acceptance of Bankruptcy Cases, focusing on clearing up obstacles to the commencement of bankruptcy cases from the litigation process. In August of the same year, the National Enterprise Bankruptcy Reorganization Case Information Network established by the Supreme People's Court officially put into operation, opening up a new situation of bankruptcy case adjudication with information technology.

---

[3] Previously, China's anti-monopoly law was enforced by the NDRC, the Ministry of Commerce and the State Administration for Industry and Commerce.

[4] "Random inspection by random inspectors with results being made public on time" means that the inspection subjects are determined at random, law enforcement officers are selected at random, and inspection and management results are made to the public on time.

Europe Union

The European Commission for Internal Market, Industry, Entrepreneurship, and SMEs is mainly responsible for creating a favorable environment for enterprise development, promoting innovation, and improving competitiveness. The EU's SME-Envoy Network is mainly responsible for providing advice on regulation and policy formulation, and timely understanding, coordinating, and promoting SME development in various countries.

In terms of fiscal and taxation support, the European Commission issued a law on value-added tax incentives for SMEs in early 2018 to reduce the tax burden. The Entrepreneurship 2020 Action Plan proposes to reduce the cost of tax compliance and improve the business environment for SMEs.

In terms of financing support, the SME-Envoy Network under the European SME-Action Program proposed to broaden financing channels for SMEs. The EU implements the programs and plans in the EU 2014–2020 COSME and Horizon 2020 for improving the financing difficulties faced by SMEs through the European Structural Funds and by developing progress microfinance and supporting SMEs to enter the capital market.

In terms of technical support, information support, market expansion, and business incubation services to support entrepreneurial innovation, the EU proposed in its 2017 Horizon 2020 2018–2020 Work Plan to launch the European Innovation Council (EIC) to support breakthrough innovations. The EU promotes the sharing of scientific research information among SMEs and the commercialization of research results by sharing public scientific research information and the incorporation of SMEs into the development of public pan-European information infrastructure. The COSME includes supporting SMEs to be international, creating a favorable environment conducive to competition, and providing market support and services for SMEs. The EU has also increased its service support by building EU Enterprise Europe Network (EEN) and European Cluster Collaboration Platform (ECCP). The "Data Pitch" program, a start-up accelerator funded by the European Commission, was officially launched in 2017. In 2020, the EU is using the impact of the Covid-19 on businesses as an opportunity to accelerate digital transformation. In March 2020, the EU SME Strategy for a Sustainable and Digital Europe came into force, supporting European SMEs and helping them benefit from digitalization to meet the challenges posed by the pandemic.

The Entrepreneurship 2020 Action Plan takes strengthening entrepreneurship education and training to support entrepreneurship and economic growth and reviving the European entrepreneurship culture to develop the next generation of entrepreneurs as its main tasks. The European Commission and EU member states have actively supported women and youth entrepreneurship. The Startup Europe Universities Network (SEUN) links up European universities, enterprises, and science park resources to provide better support for entrepreneurship.

The EU competition law prohibits large enterprises with market dominance from abusing their market dominance. For some special joint behaviors of SMEs, the EU competition law has exemption rules. The EU anti-trust penalty system also has provisions on the protection of SMEs, which determines the substantive criteria for judging the exemption of SMEs. In the long-term law enforcement practice, the EU has gradually formed a criterion for judging the restrictive condition of "not excluding effective competition in the market": market share.

Government Services

As the EU's basic framework of relevant policies on SMEs, the Small Business Act for Europe of 2008 (SBA) mainly includes promoting entrepreneurship, simplifying regulation on SMEs, easing policy environment, and removing development obstacles. Within this framework, the EU has formulated and promulgated a series of programs for entrepreneurship and SMEs:

The Entrepreneurship 2020 Action Plan (2013), which is the EU's blueprint of entrepreneurship promotion, calls on member states to jointly develop the potential of European entrepreneurs. It aims to remove barriers to entrepreneurship, change the European entrepreneurial culture, promote the development of SMEs, create a more suitable environment for entrepreneurs to grow, and thus enhance European economic strength.

The COSME, the promotion and implementation of the Action Plan, aims to facilitate SME financing, market access, support entrepreneurship, and provide a strong environment for enterprise incorporation and growth. The implementation period of the program is from 2014 to 2020.

The European SME-Action Program was issued in July 2017. It examines the existing SME policies and best practices from six aspects: regulatory system, market access, financing channels, entrepreneurship, skills training and SMEs digitalization. In addition, it determines the future direction and opportunities.

Horizon 2020 (2018–2020 Work Plan) was released by the EU in October 2017 and proposed an investment plan of 30 billion euros. Horizon 2020 is a scientific research plan proposal released by the EU in 2012, aiming to integrate scientific research resources of EU countries, improve scientific research efficiency, promote scientific and technological innovation as well as economic growth, and increase employment. It has a total investment of 77 billion euros. As of October 2017, it has provided 26.65 billion euros, of which nearly 3.79 billion euros have been spent on SMEs.

The European Commission for Internal Market, Industry, Entrepreneurship, and SMEs is mainly responsible for creating a favorable environment for enterprise development, promoting innovation, and improving competitiveness.

In 2011, the EU created the SME-Envoy Network, which each member state may nominate an envoy to join. The European Commission has also appointed a special envoy. Its incumbent envoy is Elżbieta Bieńkowska of the European Commission for Internal Market, Industry, Entrepreneurship, and SMEs. The main responsibility of the SME-Envoy Network is to provide advice relating to the formulation of regulations and policies on SMEs, and to understand, coordinate, and promote SME development in various countries in a timely manner. Any policy formulated by the European Commission calls for an assessment of the risks SMEs may encounter after the policy is introduced, to effectively reduce the bureaucratic style and regulatory burden.

Fiscal and Financial Support

The Entrepreneurship 2020 Action Plan proposes to reduce the cost of tax compliance and improve the business environment for SMEs. To make the current EU tax system better serve the development of start-ups, the European Commission is committed to removing tax barriers to start-up activities, including canceling registration fees for SMEs, reducing employment taxes, and implementing installment taxes.

In January 2018, the European Commission issued a law on value-added tax incentives for SMEs to reduce the tax burden on SMEs. The European Commission has proposed that all small businesses, whether they have been exempted from paying VAT, may be covered by a simplified measurement of VAT as long as their annual revenue does not exceed 2 million euros. In addition, small businesses registered in any member state may be covered by local VAT exemption, if they do business in another member state and their annual revenue does not exceed 85,000 euros.

Under the European SME-Action Program (2017), the SME-Envoy Network proposed to broaden the financing channels for SMEs, such as maintaining banking loan support for SMEs in the conventional financing, imposing less restrictions on the innovation forms of SME financing, and encouraging support for guarantee institutions, so as to make financing channels more convenient. As far as microfinance is concerned, the EU should improve and strengthen the activities of the European microfinance network and analyze the microfinance of specific target groups, while member states should design a regulatory framework for microfinance, improve the capacity of financial institutions through guidance, guidance and training, and support the digitalization of the microfinance industry. At the same time, the EU should also encourage the development of non-banking alternative financing, not limited to venture capital, reduce regulatory barriers, encourage cross-border non-banking financing, set up funds for non-banking equity and debt financing, and create expert groups that can provide inspiration and guidance for alternative financing. Member States should enhance SMEs' awareness of alternative financing through targeted measures and promote diversification of funding sources through banks and financial institutions in various countries.

The COSME also contains the content of helping SMEs finance. In order to provide more financing channels at different development stages, the EU will promote loans and equity investments for SMEs. The first channel is loan guarantee funds. This program will provide guarantee and counter-guarantee for financial institutions (such as guarantee associations, banks, and leasing companies) so as to provide more loans and lease financing. It is expected that the COSMEs will enable 220,000 to 330,000 SMEs to obtain financing, with a total value of 14 billion to 21 billion euros. The second channel is equity growth platforms. This program will provide venture capital for equity funds that mainly invest in the expansion and growth phase, helping 360–560 companies to obtain equity investment, with an estimated total investment of 2.6 billion to 4 billion euros.

The EU provides SMEs with access to financial support through the European Structure Funds, by developing Progress Microfinance, and supporting SMEs to enter the capital market:

European Structure Funds

With the support of this fund, the COSME and Horizon 2020 will be implemented in a bid to solve the financing problems faced by new SMEs.

The European Structure Fund is mainly composed of four funds: the European Social Fund (ESF), the European Regional Development Fund (ERDF), the European Agricultural Fund for Rural Development (EAFRD), and the European Maritime and Fisheries Fund (EMFF). The ESF mainly provides vocational training and employment assistance to solve the employment problems of young people and women. The ERDF is the largest of the four, accounting for about half of the total structure fund. Its main purpose is to support SME development in backward areas, promote investment, and improve infrastructure. Although the EU's regional coordination policy aims to strengthen the economic, social, and regional integration of the EU as a whole, its primary concern is job creation, instead of economic growth. Moreover, the eligibility, conditions, and the amount of support in the aided area are reviewed in a stringent way. The EARFD mainly provides financial support for rural areas to adopt new agricultural technologies, improve the agricultural industrial structure, and develop non-agricultural industries. The EMFF was set up to help fishermen in coastal areas affected by shrinking fishery production.

Progress Microfinance

The EU develops the microfinance market in Europe through the development of the Progress Microfinance and the Joint Action to Support Microfinance Institutions (JASMINE).

The European Progress Microfinance Facility is a microfinance tool jointly established in March 2010 by the European Commission and the European Investment Bank (EIB) with an investment of 200 million euros. It is mainly aimed at micro-businesses and self-employed persons and provides microfinance under 25,000 euros, including withdrawal, equity interest guarantee, direct guarantee, and counter-guarantee.

JASMINE is a joint program launched by the European Commission and the EIB in September 2008. It aims to provide technical services for small credit organizations and institutions in the European non-banking system and improve their ability to provide loans to micro-businesses.

European Investment Fund (EIF)

The EIF, which is affiliated with the EIB, mainly provides venture capital for SMEs. In 1992, the European Council proposed the establishment of the EIF to help European economic recovery. In 1994, the EIF was formally established. The shareholders of the EIF are composed of the EIB, the EU represented by the European Commission, and public or private banks and financial institutions. The EIF carries out projects with its own resources or funds from the European Commission, EU member states or other third parties. It provides financing channels for SMEs through intermediaries of the EIF, such as banks, guarantee companies, microfinance providers or private equity funds.

The goal of the EIF is to promote the EU's progress in entrepreneurship, growth, innovation, research and development, employment, and regional development by dispersing the risks of SMEs. Through the policy of commercial pricing and income based on the balance of cost and risk, it will create certain income for shareholders.

The EIF's support for start-ups and SMEs is mainly divided into the following three directions: (1) Equity products, which provide support in terms of venture capital and capital growth at different stages of enterprise development, including the earliest research and development of knowledge and technology, the transformation of technological achievements into products, and the more mature stage of enterprise development. Equity products are financed mainly by the EIB and the European Commission. (2) Debt Products, which, through securitization, provide guarantees and credit enhancement to improve the lending capacity of financial intermediaries to benefit more SMEs. The EIF cooperates with financial intermediaries, such as banks, leasing companies, guarantee funds, mutual insurance agencies, promotional banks, or other financial institutions that provide loans or loan guarantees for SMEs, in two ways. The first is credit enhancement and securitization. The EIF is the supplier of 3A credit enhancement in European SMEs securitization. Financial institutions should apply a 0% risk weight to assets guaranteed by the EIF. The second is the guarantee and counter-guarantee of the combination of micro-credit, SMEs loans, and lease. (3) Inclusive finance, including small loans (less than 25,000 euros) tailored to entrepreneurs and micro-enterprises (91% of the total number of European enterprises). In the EU as a whole, 99% of start-ups are micro or small businesses, one-third of which are initiated by the unemployed. As an important tool to overcome the impact of the financial crisis, the EIF has been involved in the European microfinance industry since 2000, providing financing (equity and loans), guarantees, and technical assistance for a wide range of financial intermediaries, including small non-bank financial institutions and microfinance banks.

Market in Financial Instruments Directive (MiFID)

Under this regulation, the EU has developed SMEs specialized in issuing stocks and bonds to promote their direct access to the capital market.

After the global financial crisis in 2008, the shortcomings of the regulation have gradually revealed. The MiFID II came into effect on January 3, 2018, which is the product of a successful response to the 2008 financial crisis. The goal is to enhance transparency and effective regulation of financial markets.

On October 20, 2011, the European Commission approved a proposal to amend the MiFID. After more than two years of discussion, the European Parliament and the Council of the European Union passed the MiFID II and the Market in Financial Instruments Regulation (MiFIR), which took effect on January 3, 2018.

The MiFID II strengthens the regulation on the securities market through the following measures. It ensures that organized transactions are conducted on a regulated platform. It introduces laws and regulations on high-frequency transactions. It improves transparency and supervision of financial markets, including derivatives markets. It strengthens investor protection and improves the enforcement of business rules, the competitive environment for trading financial instruments, and the liquidation of financial instruments. The revised MiFID II also restrains the organization and behavior of participants in the market.

The MiFID requires disclosure of trading data to the public and regulators, trading derivatives at designated trading places, removing barriers between exchanges and clearing service providers to ensure more competition, and launching special supervision on financial instruments and derivatives positions.

Entrepreneur Services

Information Services

The EU promotes the sharing of scientific research information among SMEs and the commercialization of research results by sharing public scientific research information and the incorporation of SMEs into the development of public pan-European information infrastructure.

Public Scientific Research Information Sharing
The Entrepreneurship 2020 Action Plan provides the sharing of information from the Framework Programs for Research and Development with SMEs and allows SMEs to commercialize their research results.

The European Commission requires that the EU's 7th R&D Framework Plan and all basic scientific research data of Horizon 2020 be made public in principle, and built up the E-infrastructure platform for scientific research information sharing to realize the interconnection between member states and between the EU and the outside world.

According to the 2016 European Commission evaluation report, the opening of scientific research data is conducive to EU innovation and scientific research cooperation. The European Commission will specifically apply for a budget for the opening of scientific research data, provide financial support, and launch a matching data management plan to attract more scientific researchers to participate in the opening of data.

Integration of SMEs into the Public Pan-European Information Infrastructure
In 2017, the European Commission issued Horizon 2020 (2018–2020 work plan), which focuses on promoting the long-term sustainable development of scientific research infrastructure and expanding the role and impact of facilities on the innovation chain. The work plan has a total budget of 1.2 billion euros over three years. The work plan proposes to stimulate the innovation potential of SMEs, establish an effective mechanism including financial support, and incorporate SMEs into the development of public pan-European information infrastructure.

Technical Services

In the Horizon 2020 (2018–2020 Work Plan) released in 2017, the EU stated that in the next three years, it will seek research funding to have a greater impact by focusing on smaller but key topics such as immigration, security, climate, clean energy, and the digital economy, and will devote more efforts to promoting breakthrough innovation.

The EU will launch the European Innovation Council (EIC) to support breakthrough innovation. The EIC will invest 2.7 billion euros in the next three years to support high-risk and high-return innovations in order to create a market for the future. In addition, it set up a crack challenge award to provide breakthrough technical solutions to pressing problems.

Market Support

The COSME includes supporting SMEs to be international and enter the market. It also creates a favorable environment conducive to competition, and provides market support and services for SMEs. The EU has also increased its service support for EU SMEs by building EU Enterprise Europe Network EEN and European Cluster Collaboration Platform (ECCP).

The COSME includes supporting SMEs to be international and enter the market:

1. providing support for European enterprises so that they can benefit from the single EU market and take full advantage of opportunities offered by markets outside the EU;
2. funding the EEN, which consists of more than 600 offices in more than 50 countries, helps SMEs find business and technical partners, understand EU legislations, and obtain EU financing;
3. funding network tools designed specifically for enterprise development, such as Your Europe Business Portal and SMEs Internationalization Portal. The former provides practical online information for entrepreneurs who want to be active in another member state, while the latter provides support measures for companies that develop business outside Europe; and
4. funding the SME intellectual property right (IPR) service desks in the Association of Southeast Asian Nations (ASEAN), China, and the South American Common Market (Mercado Común del Sur, MERCOSUR).[1] It provides advice and support for European SMEs facing problems relating to intellectual property rights, legal standards, or public procurement regulations in these areas. It also provides financial assistance for the EU-Japan Industrial Cooperation Center, promotes the exchange of experience and expertise between the EU and Japan by disseminating information on how to enter the Japanese market, and promotes various forms of industrial, trade, and investment cooperation.

---

[1] On March 26, 1991, the presidents of Argentina, Brazil, Paraguay and Uruguay signed the Treaty of Asunción in Paraguay's capital, announcing the establishment of the MERCOSUR.

The COSMEs is also committed to creating a favorable environment for entrepreneurship and SMEs to compete:

1. reducing unnecessary administrative and regulatory burdens, and improving the business environment of enterprises, especially SMEs. The goals include assessing the impact of relevant EU laws on SMEs, and strengthening the implementation of the principle of small business first in policy formulation at the national and regional levels;
2. supporting the emergence of competitive enterprises with market potential by helping SMEs adopt new business models and integrate into new value chains; and
3. promoting the development of the EU's world-class cluster, boosting its excellence and internationalization, with special emphasis on cross-sector cooperation and support for emerging industries, and accelerating the digitization of commercial communities.

The EEN was set up with the support of the COSME and the Horizon 2020, aiming to help SMEs innovate and go global. The organization provides three extensive services for SMEs:

1. International partnership. The EEN will help SMEs find suitable international partners. Typical examples are finding manufacturers of products, helping SMEs enter new markets abroad, developing technologies needed to promote business innovation, and cooperating in research projects. The EEN has more than 60 active state members, bringing together 3000 experts from more than 600 different organizations in the world, which can help SMEs find potential partners efficiently. After finding a partner, the EEN will send an expert to assist in supporting the whole cooperation process to ensure that SMEs can achieve the expected goal through this program and enhance their international competitiveness.
2. Suggestions on the direction of international development to SMEs. SMEs can get a series of consulting services free of charge, such as: how to export a product or service to a new market, how to get financial support for an enterprise's expansion plan, and how to protect intellectual property rights in another country. SMEs should

first go to the local EEN contact point, and then can get the help of an expert. The main services are: helping SMEs find suitable financing channels, upgrading management models according to the needs of enterprises, and learning EU regulations and standards.
3. Supporting business innovation. The aim is to help SMEs transform business innovation into commercial success in the international market. Firstly, the EEN will help SMEs understand innovation policies, laws, and regulations, financing channels. Secondly, it will designate experts to offer one-on-one consulting services to provide suggestions for the formulation of specific innovation strategies, financing, and intellectual property protection. Finally, experts will help enterprises manage their entrepreneurial activities and ensure that all aspects of business processes are consistent with the established innovation strategy.

The ECCP currently has nearly 1000 industrial clusters mainly of SMEs clusters registered on the platform and has signed cooperation agreements with 8 countries including Chile, Japan, and India to guide the SMEs of EU member states to gather and develop.

Enterprise Incubation

The "Data Pitch" program, a start-up accelerator funded by the European Commission, was officially launched in 2017.

According to the envision of the European Commission, the project will better link existing enterprises and organizations in the region with start-ups through a large amount of data, and experienced enterprises can use the accumulated data to help start-ups conduct information analysis. The project aims to build a data-driven innovation ecosystem across the EU.

The project will provide world-class business support for 50 European start-ups and SMEs, including interest-free funds of up to 100,000 euros, professional start-up guidance and investment opportunities, and data access services from mature enterprises and the public sector. Sectors supported by the Digital Pitch will include smart cities, food and agriculture, health and welfare, retail, data security, e-tourism, and financial telecommunications.

Digital Transformation Support

The EU launched "Digital Innovation Hubs (DIH)" in 2016, with the help of universities and research institutions, to provide a one-stop information platform for SMEs to understand relevant digital technologies, finance, market prospects, and resource docking. In June 2019, the "Digital Innovation and Scale-Up Initiative" (DISC) was launched to provide financial support for digital start-ups.[2]

In 2020, the EU is using the impact of the Covid-19 on businesses as an opportunity to accelerate digital transformation. In March 2020, the EU SME Strategy for a Sustainable and Digital Europe came into force, supporting European SMEs and helping them benefit from digitalization to meet the challenges posed by the pandemic. The measures are detailed as follows: the number of centers, whose function is to provide SMEs with the conditions to test new technologies and relevant market information and help them with networking, digital training, would be expanded from 166 to 240. And free digital transformation courses for SME employees are available as well.[3]

ENTREPRENEURSHIP EDUCATION

The Entrepreneurship 2020 Action Plan takes strengthening entrepreneurship education and training to support entrepreneurship and economic growth and reviving the European entrepreneurship culture to develop the next generation of entrepreneurs as its main tasks.

Women make up 52% of the total population in Europe and 30% of entrepreneurs. The Entrepreneurship 2020 Action Plan mainly takes the following measures to support women's entrepreneurship:

The first is to incorporate the women entrepreneurship policy into the national strategy. The second is to collect and filter entrepreneurship data by gender in order to clearly understand the situation of women's entrepreneurship every year. The third is to continue expanding the number of women entrepreneur ambassadors and mentors. The

---

[2] Assessment on the progress of G20 Entrepreneurship Action Plan, Entrepreneurship Research Center on G20 Economies, Oct 22, 2019.

[3] Evaluation and Prospect of G20 Members' Policies to Support Entrepreneurship in the Post-pandemic Era, Entrepreneurship Research Center on G20 Economies, Oct 22, 2020.

fourth is to take various measures to balance the business and life of female entrepreneurs, such as providing appropriate benefits for women entrepreneurs' families, especially children and the elderly, with the support of the ESF, the ERDF and the EAFRD.

The European Network to Promote Women's Entrepreneurship (WES), on behalf of member governments and institutions, is responsible for promoting women's entrepreneurship. It has the following goals: enhance the existing public image of women entrepreneurs; create an atmosphere suitable for women entrepreneurs to grow; expand the pool of women SMEs and increase the size of enterprises of women entrepreneurs through seminars; cooperate with existing networks and organizations; exchange information and experiences, and joint projects.

The European Commission has also set up the European Network of Mentors for Women Entrepreneurs, in which entrepreneurs from 17 European countries participate, to advise women-led enterprises at an early stage (the second to fourth year after their establishment) and help them grow.

The European Commission launched the WEGATE, a one-stop electronic platform, to help women start businesses in September 2016. Through this website, women entrepreneurs can obtain various information related to entrepreneurship, including entrepreneurship training, counseling, advice, and opportunities to expand their network. Entrepreneurship trainings include both online and offline offerings. For example, Rails Girls is an online community that helps women entrepreneurs better understand and master technology entrepreneurship and can teach entrepreneurs how to develop apps. It is a nonprofit organization, founded in Finland, and has now developed into a global organization with workshops in different European cities. Women PRO is an organization dedicated to helping young women become social entrepreneurs, providing them with entrepreneurial skills through entrepreneurial trainings so that they can start their own businesses. The organization has already launched relevant operations in Poland, Cyprus, Lithuania, and Bulgaria.

All EU member states have relevant institutions in place to improve women's entrepreneurial skills. The Ladies Enterprise Agency, set up by Finland's Ministry of Trade and Industry and 50% of private enterprises and associations in the capital Helsinki, is an organization dedicated to women entrepreneurs. Its goal is to stimulate and encourage women to start businesses and remove barriers to women's access to knowledge and technology.

The Entrepreneurship 2020 Action Plan has the following measures to promote youth entrepreneurship: (1) improving the learning mode of the youth who participate in the Youth Guarantee; (2) funding potential entrepreneurs to work with senior entrepreneurs through the Commission's Erasmus[4] for Young Entrepreneurs (YEY) for 6 months; and (3) providing technical assistance through the ESF.

As an important part of the Entrepreneurship 2020 Action Plan, the Erasmus for Young Entrepreneurs connects young entrepreneurs from different European countries with experienced SME entrepreneurs. Both sides can expand their interpersonal networks and lay the foundation for the development of international business. The project, which is partially funded by the European Commission and started in 2009, is planned to complete 10,000 pairs of entrepreneurs by 2020. The project has no restrictions on the age and industry of participants. According to the summary of the first five-year project in 2014, the project achieved 3000 pairs of combinations and good results. The survival rate of the enterprises established by new entrepreneurs participating in the project reached 87%, while the survival rate of ordinary European start-ups was 57% in three years. Since 99.8% of enterprises in Europe are SMEs. Therefore, this SME-oriented supporting program has a positive effect on promoting successful entrepreneurship in Europe.

The SEUN is an organization established under the support of the European Commission to connect European universities, enterprises, and science park resources to provide better support for entrepreneurship. Specific objectives and work carried out include: improving the quality of entrepreneurship education projects by understanding the operation of university entrepreneurship education projects; promoting the transformation of university scientific and technological achievements through online and offline activities; enhancing the interaction among entrepreneurs, investors, and enterprises. Through this network, entrepreneurs can expand their businesses and financing channels and find start-up incubators more easily within Europe, while large companies can find talents. At present, representatives from 20 EU countries have joined the organization.

---

[4] Desiderius Erasmus (1466?–1536, a Dutch scholar). The Erasmus Award of 1987, the first EU student exchange award was named after him.

The organization has been organizing the weeklong "Startup Europe Comes to Universes (Sec2U)", an annual offline event since October 2016. Its main goal is to promote the development of entrepreneurship and innovation culture in European universities. This effort brings together entrepreneurs, businessmen, local universities, and government personnel to exchange entrepreneurial experiences and lessons, share information, understand policies, and expand interpersonal networks. In 2016, there are 35 units from 18 countries joined the Sec2U, which held 38 events with 2800 participants.

FAIR COMPETITION FOR SMEs

The EU competition law prohibits large enterprises with market dominance from abusing their market dominance, and strictly controls these large enterprises to implement mergers that change the market structure.

For some special joint behaviors of SMEs, the EU competition law has exemption rules. The monopoly agreement that can be exempted needs to meet the conditions as follows: the monopoly agreement can promote technological progress, boost economic development, or improve the production or sales of commodities.

The EU anti-trust penalty system also has provisions on the protection of SMEs, which determines the substantive criteria for judging the exemption of SMEs. For example, the Treaty Establishing the European Community provides for that "the cooperation of SMEs can be exempted from the restriction of anti-trust law if it is conducive to the allocation of resources and products, technological upgrading, exploring the potential of enterprises, and improving social welfare, and does not exclude effective competition in the market".

In the long-term law enforcement practice, the EU has gradually formed a criterion for judging the restrictive condition of "not excluding effective competition in the market": market share. In other words, if the common market share of the enterprise that has reached a monopoly agreement in the relevant market is less than 30%, it can be considered that the agreement has not reached the level of excluding effective competition; if the common market share is greater than 50%, there is reason to suspect that the agreement will exclude effective competition; if the common market share exceeds 90%, it can be determined that the agreement seriously excludes effective competition.[5]

---

[5] Liu Jifeng, Zhang Ya; Perfection of China's Anti-Monopoly Fine System, Price Theory and Practice from the Perspective of SME Protection [J], No. 6, 2020.

France

The French Innovation and Research Law (1999) provides a legal basis for the commercialization of scientific research. In 2015, the French government released France-Europe 2020: National Research Strategy (2015). In 2017, the government invested 10 billion euros to implement the third Investment for the Future plan. Meanwhile, the Big Investment Plan 2018–2022 (GPI), with a total investment of 57 billion euros, was launched to bolster innovation.

Regarding the fiscal and financial support from the government, at the end of 2017, the 2018 Finance Bill was passed, with an announcement of new tax reduction plans. Moreover, in the same year, financial subsidies for SMEs were provided through the "Innovation Contest" program. Besides, the government provides various financing channels for SMEs and start-ups through banks such as Bpifrance and dedicated programs such as the Bourse French Tech program and Accélérateur de Start-up Fund.

Various plans and programs were launched to provide services for entrepreneurs and start-ups. In June 2016, the French government took actions to promote commercialization of scientific research, emphasizing the important role of higher education institutions in connecting public scientific research and businesses. At the end of 2017, the French government designed the Action Plan for Business Growth and Transformation (PACTE), aiming to facilitate business activities in France. French Tech, launched by the Ministry of Economy in 2013, was dedicated to linking French and overseas entrepreneurs, investors, engineers, large enterprises, and government agencies to form an ecosystem. This ecosystem promoted the growth of French start-ups and their international expansion. In October 2017, France launched the "French Fab" campaign to promote the brand of the French industry in the international market. In June 2017, Station F, the world's largest technology start-up incubator, began its operations in Paris. Apart from these plans and programs, the Concoursi-LAB is a national competition for technology companies and an important event for France to boost entrepreneurship. During the outbreak of Covid-19 in 2020, many SMEs found it difficult to adapt to teleworking, new sales tools, and other digital solutions that helped mitigate the impact of the epidemic. This epidemic is a challenge for telecommuting in France, but also an opportunity—to advance digital technology.

The Action Plan for Student Entrepreneurs launched by the French Ministry for Higher Education and Research integrates the course module of innovation and entrepreneurship into the entire university curriculum system. The entrepreneurship education in French higher education institutions also highlights international cooperation. To illustrate, in 2016, the Ecole Polytechnique, the ENSTA ParisTech, and the TélécomParisTech signed a double-degree partnership agreement with Zhejiang University in China. Progress has also been made in entrepreneurship education targeting women. For example, French BNP Paribas Wealth Management and Martine Liautaud's Women Initiative Foundation jointly launched the Women Entrepreneur Program for female entrepreneurs from fast-growing firms all over the world.

Closely related to the protection of SMEs in France is the regulation of corporate insolvency by bankruptcy law. One of the biggest characteristics of the Bankruptcy Law revised in 2005 is to shorten the liquidation time to one year. The government's intention to amend the bankruptcy law is to enable more enterprises to continue to survive.

Government Services

The French government has laws dedicated to innovation and scientific research. The Innovation and Research Law (1999) aims to solve the problems caused by the lack of collaboration between public research institutions and firms. It provides a legal basis for the commercialization of scientific research.

In 2015, the French government released the France-Europe 2020: National Research Strategy (2015), proposing five major action plans: applied big data research; earth observation for climate change; systematic biology research for medical and industrial applications; health research for serving patients; human behavior research for public policy making.

The French government invested 10 billion euros in 2017 to implement the third Investment for the Future plan. This plan was committed to the transformation of scientific and technological achievements into product innovation, connecting higher education institutions with business enterprises. The third Investment for the Future plan allocated 4.1 billion euros to promote innovation and SMEs.

GPI was launched by the French government in September 2017 with a total investment of 57 billion euros. The investment plan had a budget of 15 billion euros for improving the employment competitiveness of citizens, and planned to provide training opportunities for 2 million low-skilled people and help them find jobs. The investment plan also had a budget of 13 billion euros to encourage innovation, with an emphasis on the cooperation between public research institutions and firms in artificial intelligence, big data development, nanotechnology, and Internet security. In addition, the budget for digital development was 9 billion euros, dedicated to achieving 100% office automation for the government, reducing public expenditure, and improving the quality of public services.

FISCAL AND FINANCIAL SUPPORT

At the end of 2017, the French government passed the 2018 Finance Bill, announcing new tax reduction plans. In 2018, the corporate tax rate for firms with revenue lower than 500,000 euros was reduced to 28%. After 2018, the corporate tax for all firms will be gradually reduced to 25% by 2022. Small businesses continue to enjoy a preferential tax rate of 15%.

The "Innovation Contest" program was jointly launched by the French Ministry of Environment, Ministry of Economy, Ministry for Higher Education and Research, General Administration of Investment, Bpifrance, and Environment and Energy Control Agency at the end of 2017. The program was funded by GPI with 300 million euros, which would be offered to SMEs as government subsidies. The "Innovation Contest" program mainly supported digital technology, health technology, Internet security, French Fab, and so on.

Bpifrance provides financial support such as seed funds, innovation grants, and guarantees for micro-enterprises. For SMEs, Bpifrance offers innovation grants, guarantees, export financing, and growth funds. Bpifrance has 49 offices in France with a total of 2500 employees.

The French government has set up different projects to provide financing support for start-ups. For example, the Bourse French Tech program can provide 10,000–30,000 euros of financial support for the establishment of a start-up. Accélérateur de Start-up Fund also provides financing channels for start-ups.

Entrepreneur Services

Technical Services

In June 2016, the French government took actions to promote commercialization of scientific research, emphasizing the important role of higher education institutions in connecting public scientific research and businesses. For instance, research institutions were required to appoint a sole entrusted agent for intellectual property rights so as to accelerating the transfer of intellectual property rights. Another example was a study led by three universities to examine how to efficiently match researchers in public sectors and businesses in private sectors.

Market Support

At the end of 2017, the French government introduced PACTE, aiming to facilitate business activities in France. For example, it attempted to lower the entry barriers for SMEs, reduce obligations of SMEs, and advance a legal environment more conducive to the growth of SMEs.

The French Tech campaign was launched by the French Ministry of Economy in November 2013 and was dedicated to building an ecosystem that promoted the growth of French start-ups and their international expansion. So far, the "French Tech" has set up 9500 technology start-ups. Since 2015, the French Tech Ticket global entrepreneurship competition has been held to attract overseas entrepreneurs to France to establish technology start-ups. In June 2017, France announced the launch of French Tech Visa to provide four-year residence permits for entrepreneurial talents all over the world.

In October 2017, the French Minister of Economy announced the launch of French Fab. Through French Fab, French SMEs and large enterprises will form a network, in which firms will be uniformly certified by the government and will appear in the global market as a whole to represent France. This program aims to enhance the influence of the French industry in the global market.

Enterprise Incubation

On June 29, 2017, Station F, the world's largest technology start-up incubator, opened in Paris with an investment of 250 million euros and an area of 34,000 square meters. Entrepreneurs only need to pay 195 euros a month for each desk, and the incubator will not charge any service fees from projects.

In addition to Station F, there are themed incubators invested by world-renowned technology enterprises. For example, Start-up Garage of Facebook provides accelerator services for innovative data-driven companies. OuiCrea's China-Hexagon Accelerator (CHA) International Accelerator Program provides a cross-border incubation program to attract Chinese entrepreneurs to start businesses in France and encourage French start-ups to operate in China.

Communication Platform

The Concoursi-LAB is a national competition for technology companies and an important event for France to boost entrepreneurship. It is co-organized by the French Ministry for Higher Education and Research and Bpifance. Since its launch 19 years ago, Concoursi-LAB has invested a total of 418 million euros to support 1820 firms, of which 70% are still running.

Digital Transformation Support

At the national level, the "Actions to Promote the Digital Republic" 2015 and "La French Tech" (2013) are both in a bid to promote digital entrepreneurship and digital transformation of SMEs.[1]

During the outbreak of Covid-19 in 2020, many SMEs found it difficult to adapt to teleworking, new sales tools, and other digital solutions that helped mitigate the impact of the epidemic. This epidemic is a challenge for telecommuting in France, but also an opportunity—to advance digital technology. In response, France has introduced a number of measures to support the adoption of teleworking by SMEs. According to the latest amendments to the French Labor Code, during the epidemic, employers can make it mandatory for employees to telework if their jobs permit. This accelerated remote working during the epidemic and advanced the process of digital transformation. In the long run, this will also benefit technology innovation and development. In addition to this, a number of organizations also run programs to support SMEs. For example, the French digital technology company provided advice and technical support to SMEs during the crisis by distributing teleworking kits.[2]

Entrepreneurship Education

In 2013, the French Ministry for Higher Education and Research launched the Action Plan for Student Entrepreneurs (Plan d'actionenfaveur de l'entrepreneuriatétudiant). The program integrates the course module of innovation and entrepreneurship into the entire university curriculum system. Innovation and entrepreneurship courses run through undergraduate, master, and doctoral education. The program provides the "university student-entrepreneur" identity for university students or graduates under the age of 28 who are starting a business. This special identity helps students maintain their student identity and social welfare when they establish their companies.

---

[1] Assessment on the progress of G20 Entrepreneurship Action Plan, Entrepreneurship Research Center on G20 Economies, Oct 22, 2019.

[2] Evaluation and Prospect of G20 Members' Policies to Support Entrepreneurship in the Post-pandemic Era, Entrepreneurship Research Center on G20 Economies, Oct 22, 2020.

The entrepreneurship education in French higher education institutions also highlights international cooperation. In 2016, the Ecole Polytechnique, the ENSTA ParisTech, and the TélécomParisTech signed a double-degree partnership agreement with Zhejiang University in China. Its purpose was to cultivate top-notch Chinese scientists with international perspectives in innovation and entrepreneurship.

Progress has also been made in entrepreneurship education for women. In 2015, French BNP Paribas Wealth Management and Martine Liautaud's Women Initiative Foundation jointly initiated the Women Entrepreneur Program, a training program for female entrepreneurs from fast-growing firms all over the world. The training venue was at Stanford University in the US and the training generally lasted a week. In 2017, 40 women entrepreneurs from 12 countries joined the training. Besides, the programs of HEC Paris supporting women entrepreneurship mainly provide trainings for women from low-income regions. HEC plans to support 380 women entrepreneurs in 2018.

Fair Competition for SMEs

Closely related to the protection of SMEs in France is the regulation of corporate insolvency by bankruptcy law. The most basic text of the then-effect French bankruptcy law is the Judicial Reorganization and Liquidation Law of Distressed Enterprises in January 1985 (Law no. 85–98 of 25 January 1985).[3] According to the provisions of this law, this law applies to all businessmen, craftsmen, agricultural producers, and all private law juristic persons; natural and juristic persons with no more than 50 employees and less than the statutory turnover excluding tax shall apply the summary procedure stipulated in this Law.

One of the biggest characteristics of the Bankruptcy Law revised in 2005 is to shorten the liquidation time to one year. The main contents of the revision include: Firstly, the applicable subject of bankruptcy law has expanded from businessmen, handicrafts, and private law juristic persons to freelancers such as lawyers and doctors; secondly, more contents to listen to the opinions of bank creditors in bankruptcy proceedings are added; thirdly, the reorganization procedure is distinguished from internal reorganization and external reorganization (such as enterprise transfer and

---

[3] https://www.iiiglobal.org/sites/default/files/retentionoftitleclausesinfrenchlaw.pdf.

merger); fourthly, specific measures to prevent enterprise bankruptcy are added. The government's intention to amend the bankruptcy law is to enable more enterprises to continue to survive.[4,5]

---

[4] https://www.sohu.com/a/302623221_260616.
[5] http://bjgy.chinacourt.gov.cn/article/detail/2011/03/id/880999.shtml.

Germany

The specialized managing authority for SMEs in Germany is the German Federal Ministry for Economic Affairs and Energy (BMWi). An important initiative taken by the German government for serving start-ups and SMEs is to reduce administrative burdens on SMEs and improve government efficiency. In 2016, Germany released the Cutting Bureaucracy Act to reduce administrative burdens on enterprises. In addition, it launched the SME Test in 2017 to understand the administrative burdens on SMEs and their development demands.

The German government supports innovation, entrepreneurship, and SMEs through preferential financial and taxation policies, such as direct subsidy, the establishment of funds, and tax cuts. For example, the Cash Incentives Program (GRW) 2018 directly provides subsidy for SMEs, especially start-ups. The Central Innovation Program (Zentrales Innovations program Mittelstand, ZIM) is the largest program of the German government to support innovative SMEs. In 2017, the German government's financial budget plan set aside a budget of 548 million euros for the ZIM. In addition, the High-Tech Start-up Fund (HTGF) supports R&D-based start-ups by purchasing their shares. Moreover, the Innovation Assistant Program provides subsidies for SMEs that hire graduates. The German government exempted SMEs with a certain revenue from VAT to support their development.

Germany expands financing channels of start-ups and helps SMEs solve financing issues by providing bank guarantee and stimulating entrepreneurial investment sectors. To facilitate SMEs to get loans, Germany prescribed standardized guarantee conditions in 2017 to reduce procedural burdens on SMEs and simplify loan application procedures. In 2016, German guarantee banks supported 6200 financing projects and provided guarantee for loans of 1.7 billion euros. The German government announced to continue the INVEST—Grant for Venture Capital program from January 1, 2017, which helps start-ups find investments and encourages private investors to provide venture capital. In March 2016, the German BMWi, the ERP Special Fund, and the European Investment Fund (EIF) jointly set up the German Growth Joint Investment Fund (ERP/EIF-Wachstumsfazilität) with a total amount of 500 million euros to provide financial support for fast-growing enterprises in urgent need of capital growth. The EIF and the European Recovery Program (ERP) Special Fund jointly invested and established a parent fund of 2.7 billion euros in Germany to support venture investment funds invested in Germany.

The German government has been placing a priority on scientific research and innovation in promoting entrepreneurship and SMEs. In September 2017, the German government announced the five important action areas that encourage technology-based start-ups. German Digital Strategy 2025 (2015) proposed to invest 1 billion euros in launching the "Digital Investment Program for Small and Medium-Sized Enterprises" by 2018. In March 2017, the German government has begun to implement the Act on Implementing the EU's eIDAS Regulation to promote e-government.

To encourage and facilitate small enterprises to receive innovation and entrepreneurship consulting services, the German BMWi provides free consulting services for start-ups and SMEs through the Federal Funding Advisory Service on Research and Innovation, Start-up Portal information platform, and Start App. Taking standardization as an important means to promote innovation and entrepreneurship, the German government helps SMEs participate in standardization efforts and obtain the required standardization and normative information. In terms of business incubation services, Germany has nearly 40 years of business incubation experience, with more than 300 incubators providing various services for entrepreneurs as of 2017. The INSTI program set up by the German Federal Ministry of Education and Research (BMBF) provides an interface with potential investors for individuals and high-tech enterprises holding projects and patents. The program was originally set for a five-year period and has now been extended indefinitely.

The German entrepreneurship education runs through secondary, higher, and vocational education. While providing entrepreneurship courses, the entrepreneurship education of German universities places a priority on the development of entrepreneurship awareness, spirit, and skills, and sets up accelerators to facilitate the incorporation and growth of start-ups. Since 1998, the Exit-Business Start-Ups Program has played an active role in developing entrepreneurial culture and reinforcing cooperation and innovation between higher education institutions and research institutions. Also developed are German entrepreneurship education for specific groups such as refugees, young people, and women, including, for example, Start-up Your Future, Start-up Nights, and Guide programs. In addition, there are national entrepreneurship activities enriching the entrepreneurial culture in Germany, such as Founder Week 2018 and Women Enterprise led by the BMWi.

On January 19, 2021, the 10th Amendment to the German Competition Act officially took effect. The German Competition Act stipulates that market subjects may not abuse their market dominance to harm the interests of SMEs, and restricts large enterprises from easily entering the SME market. The German Competition Act also defines the cartel exemption system for SMEs to protect them. The purpose of exempting such cartels is to expand the cooperation of SMEs, enhance their competitiveness, and improve the competitive environment of the market.

Government Services

Germany has a series of laws and regulations supporting the development of SMEs and a relatively perfect legal environment for start-ups and SMEs.

Under the Constitution, all states released the SME Promotion Law in 1974. The national laws promulgated by the federal government include: (1) the Act against Restraints of Competition, which makes restraint regulations on the market monopoly, restraints of competition, and excessive concentration that cause market failure, and detailed provisions on promoting SMEs through government procurement such as principles and specific measures to support and promote SMEs through government procurement; (2) the Insolvency Law (1994), which adds reorganization procedures, protects not only creditors' rights and interests but also debtors' legitimate rights and interests, and establishes the reorganization system for salvaging debtors' businesses and liquidation funds for labor-related creditor's rights; and (3) the Reorganization Facilitation Act (2012), which introduces the interim self-management and special umbrella procedures, which allows debtors' to initiate insolvency proceedings and to formulate reorganization plans before the initiation.

Reducing administrative burdens on SMEs and improving government efficiency is an important effort of the German government to serve start-ups and SMEs.

In 2016, Germany started to implement the First Cutting Bureaucracy Act to reduce administrative burdens on enterprises, especially start-ups and fast-growing enterprises. According to the new regulations, increasing SMEs are exempted from the accounting and record-keeping obligations stipulated in the Commercial Code and the Financial Code. New companies are required to submit less official information and undergo simplifier tax payment procedures than before. By and large, administrative burdens on the private sector are reduced by 705 million euros.

In 2016, Germany decided to compulsorily enforce the SME Test. This plan is to work with universities and research institutions to understand the administrative burdens and development needs of SMEs, support the federal government to fully consider the needs of SMEs when formulating laws, and reduce the administrative burdens on SMEs as much as possible. According to a report released by the European Commission on SME Tests, 75% of the EU states responded believed that the SME Test had policy influences and benefited their SMEs in 2014.

In 2017, Germany introduced the Second Cutting Bureau Act to reduce administrative burdens on small companies further, especially those with only two or three employees. The legislation focus is to reduce the procedure and time in paying taxes and promote the implementation of e-government, such as providing unified information on supervision on the Internet-based platform, while simplifying relevant social security payment rules.

At present, Germany's specialized managing organization for SMEs is the German BMWi, which mainly works with the Federal Ministry of Education and Research (BMBF) to promote the development of SMEs, innovation, and entrepreneurship through the formulation and implementation of specific projects and programs.

Fiscal and Financial Support

Germany promotes the development of innovation, entrepreneurship, and SMEs by directly subsidizing investment projects in specific regions, implementing the Central Innovation Program (Zentrales Innovations program Mittelstand, ZIM), and setting up High-Tech Start-up Fund to support hi-tech research projects. In addition, tax preferential policies such as exemption from value-added tax are also implemented for eligible small enterprises.

In 2018, Germany Trade & Invest (GATI) launched the Cash Incentives Program (GRW) to directly subsidize investment projects in specific regions to promote the regional economy by creating jobs. By province and enterprise, the GATI made different subsidy standards for different provinces, under which SMEs may be subsidized for their eligible costs ranging from 10 to 40%, including capital expenditure and personnel costs upon their incorporation.

The 2017 Financial Budget of BMWi arranged a budget of 548 million euros for the ZIM. Founded by BMWi, the ZIM is the largest amount of monetary support provided by the German government for innovative SMEs. Every year, the BMWi allocates more than 500 million euros to the ZIM. SMEs may apply for the program's support at any time without submitting any proposal. Under the ZIM, there are three cooperation methods: (1) ZIM corporate program, which provides funds for the research effort jointly launched by companies and R&D institutions; (2) ZIM individual program, which provides funds for internal R&D of individual companies; and (3) ZIM cooperation network, which provides funds for the innovation network jointly developed by at least six SMEs. Enterprises cooperating with the ZIM may have access to financial assistance for any of their technical and application fields. The approval of their application for such financial assistance depends on the innovation degree of their R&D projects and the resulting feasibility.

The German government also subsidizes high-tech R&D projects. Germany's High-Tech Strategy Budget exceeds 6 billion euros and provides a subsidy for up to 50% of the eligible cost incurred during R&D. The High-Tech Start-up Fund (HTGF) was founded in 2005 to support innovative start-ups that require intensive capital support. It supports R&D-based start-ups by purchasing their shares. Under the HTGF, a start-up may receive a maximum financial support of 500,000 euros which may be used for R&D, production of sample machines, and market promotion. After 1–2 years, the HTGF withdrew its funds by transferring shares or extracting profits. The HTGF is funded by the German BMWi, policy banks such as KfW, Westarkade, and large-scale enterprises such as BASF Group, Deutsche Telekom, Siemens, Daimler, and Bosch.

The Innovation Assistant Program provides support for SMEs in hiring graduates and subsidizes up to 50% of their labor costs.

Financial Support

The German government helps SMEs solve their financing issues by providing loan guarantees, encouraging venture capital investment, and setting up venture capital funds.

In a bid to facilitate SMEs to get loans, Germany launched the standardized guarantee conditions (Allgemeine Bürgschaftsbestimmungen, or ABB), which applies to all of 16 German guarantee banks, in 2017 to reduce procedural burdens on SMEs and simplify loan application procedures. Banks are the main sources of loans for SMEs, but banks usually require collateral to meet their own standards. Since the establishment of Germany's first guarantee bank in 1950, the development of general guarantee clauses in various parts of Germany has been inconsistent. In the context of increasingly strengthened banking regulations and the gradual digitalization of SMEs and banking business, the German government proposed to modernize and harmonize the guarantee clauses. The simplified and modernized ABB can ensure faster, safer, and easier guarantee provision and loan disbursement for enterprises, banks, and partners. In addition, SMEs are easier to access finance by reducing administrative procedures of guarantee banks, promoting electronic guarantee procedures, and enabling automatic application procedures. In 2016, Germany's guarantee banks supported 6200 financing projects in total and guaranteed 1.7 billion euros of loans.

The German BMWi announced to continue the INVEST—Grant for Venture Capital program from January 1, 2017. Germany has implemented the INVEST—Grant for Venture Capital program since 2013, which helps start-ups find investments and encourages private investors to provide venture capital. The INVEST subsidy consists of two parts: (1) investment subsidy. Any private investor or angel investor who invests in eligible start-ups and holds them for at least three years may be entitled to the corresponding subsidy of up to 500,000 euros every year, and

(2) capital gain tax rebate subsidy. Any start-up that sells shares may be entitled to the lump-sum tax compensation for 25% of its profit from selling shares (of which the upper limit is 80% of the unit investment amount). The INVEST sets out certain requirements for the start-ups to be invested, including less than 7 years since its incorporation, less than 50 official employees, annual revenue or total assets and liability less than 10 million euros, headquartered in the EU and having at least one office in Germany, innovation-oriented sector according to the business registry, and continuous operation. Moreover, the INVEST has specific requirements for investors, including residing in the EU and without direct relationship with the invested and engaging in investment for no less than three years.

In March 2016, the German BMWi, the ERP Special Fund, and the EIF jointly set up the ERP/EIF-Wachstumsfazilität with a total amount of 500 million euros, of which 330 million euros came from the ERP Special Fund and the remaining 170 million euros from the EIF. The fund aims to provide financial support for fast-growing enterprises in urgent need to increase capital. Through cooperation with successful venture capital fund managers and their funds, the fund helps enterprises finance their expansion by acquiring their shares.

The EIF and the ERP Special Fund jointly invested and established a parent fund of 2.7 billion euros in Germany to support venture investment funds invested there. The parent fund with half of its fund invested by EIF and ERP is managed by EIF. In the capital venture market, the parent fund mainly invests in: (1) early funds eyeing the transfer of technology results, which can reach the public and private research centers and institutions and cooperate with them (such investments are usually initial investments); and (2) early technology-based companies in growth (expansion and development) as a subsequent investment.

Entrepreneur Services

Technical Services

The German government has been placing a priority on scientific research and innovation in promoting entrepreneurship and SMEs.

In September 2017, the German the German Federal Ministry of Education and Research (BMBF) announced the five important action areas that encourage technology-based start-ups, including: (1) encouraging scientific researchers to establish enterprises as an alternative way to utilize scientific research achievements, strengthening entrepreneurship programs for doctor candidates in German higher education institutions, and tapping the entrepreneurial potential of young scientific and technological talents; (2) incorporating financial support for entrepreneurship and start-ups in the scientific research programs, formulating proper funding measures for different disciplines, technologies, and application fields, and gradually eliminating obstacles of start-ups in applying for such support; (3) promoting regional innovation and development, strengthening the relation between start-ups and research institutions, and encouraging higher education institutions and research institutions to open to start-ups and provide them with infrastructure, instruments and equipment; (4) supporting scientific researchers in higher education institutions and research institutions for technology verification of their academic results for start-ups; and (5) creating a framework environment that facilitates entrepreneurship, including regulations on the license and patent use.

In Germany's Digital Strategy 2025 (2016), the German government proposes to invest 1 billion euros to launch the Digital Investment Program for Small and Medium-Sized Enterprises by 2018 to encourage SMEs to invest in digital transformation and strengthen the digital networking between Germany and Europe in the field of digital transformation. In addition, it implements tax incentives for digital technology and innovation, such as tax incentives for the R&D of SMEs and subsidies for losses of start-up enterprises. Moreover, it invests 10 billion euros in building gigabit networks in rural areas by 2025. Furthermore, it uses digital management to reduce the administrative burdens on start-ups.

In March 2017, the German government has begun to implement the Act on Implementing the EU's eIDAS Regulation to enable Germany to use the Electronic Trust Services, including electronic signatures, electronic seals, and electronic webpage certificates. Through the Electronic Trust Services, citizens can conduct online transactions more safely and promote the e-government.

Information Services

To encourage and facilitate small enterprises to receive innovation and entrepreneurship consulting services, the German BMWi provides free consulting services for start-ups and SMEs through the Federal Funding Advisory Service on Research and Innovation. The consulting services include but are not limited to an assessment of enterprises' potential to develop provision of development suggestions and business solutions, and introduction of technology partners.

The BMWi has a start-up portal information platform (http://www.existenzgruender.de) where start-ups may find detailed steps to incorporate. In addition, the start app can also provide entrepreneurs with the information they need to start a new business. The German government also sets up another website to provide women entrepreneurs with the information and assistance they need.

The German government also regards standardization as an important means to promote innovation and entrepreneurship. The BMWi manages and researches standardization through German Institute for Standardization (DIN) and promptly launches industry standards as required. Founded in 2008, the DIN's SME Commission (KOMMIT) is a platform where SMEs, freelances, public and private sectors, associations, and chambers of commerce may exchange information and share opinions. This platform helps SMEs participate in standardization efforts and obtain the required standardization and normative information.

Enterprise Incubation

Germany has nearly 40 years of business incubation experience and has developed three different incubation modules: (1) accelerators (fast service for technology industrialization), (2) enterprise workshops (modular customization for companies to promote commercial success), and (3) incubators (service for start-ups). By 2017, Germany had more than 300 incubators. The Federal German Association of Innovation, Technology and Business Incubation Centers (BVIZ) was founded in 1988, with a success rate of 90%. Factory Berlin provides timely technical and legal advice for graduates with entrepreneurial ideas and supports them in starting their own businesses. Some social service agencies in Germany also provide business incubation services for SMEs. For example, the founders club program of the German Federal Association of Young Entrepreneurs (BJU) provides free workshops to founders, supports exchanges between entrepreneurs and experienced businessmen, and helps start-ups run normally.

Communication Platform

The INSTI program provides a platform for individuals with projects and patents and high-tech enterprises to contact investors, allowing promising commercial projects to interface with potential investors. The program was established by the BMBF in 1995, which was originally set for a five-year period and has now been extended indefinitely. It is managed by the Institute for Economic Research (IW). The programs of INSTI related to SMEs are:

1. the INSTI SME Patent Action, which provides financial support for SMEs that apply for patenting their inventions (in such case, the application must be made for the first time or has not been made in last five years);
2. the INSTI innovation training, of which the long-term goal is to promote innovation activities by enhancing inventors' and enterprises' awareness of innovation, especially innovation management, innovation technology, industrial property, and system information management and consulting services provided by which include strategic management (strategic innovation management), finding new ideas about products, services, and processes (creativity and evaluation technique), legal protection on new products (industrial property and patent database information), and products and processes of developers (team cooperation and communication, successful internal structure, and individual work technology); and the INSTI-Innovation Market, which aims to help companies establish a global information network in terms of technology transfer and innovation and existed as an information provider for important European banks and joint ventures before being incorporated into the INSTI program.

Digital Transformation Support

Germany's Federal Ministry of Economic Affairs has founded the "Go-Digital" program in 2017 to help SMEs and start-ups on their way to the digital future. The program continued during the pandemic. With three modules "Digitalized Business Processes", "Digital Market Development", and "IT Security", the go-digital funding program not only supports optimizing processes and unlocking additional market shares through digitalization but also finances measures to protect SMEs from the loss of sensitive data. The Federal Ministry of Economic Affairs has authorized a number of competent consulting companies to help SMEs find individual solutions for online retail business, the digitalization of business day and the increasing security needs for digital networking.[1]

Entrepreneurship Education

The New Age for Entrepreneurship initiated by the BMWi contains a series of measures to encourage entrepreneurship, strengthening Germany's entrepreneurial spirit, and supporting more people to start businesses. Under this program, the BMWi launched the Entrepreneurship in Schools, on the basis of the Junior Expert Program 1994, to comprehensively promote entrepreneurship education for middle school students. The German Federal Government and German Trade Union founded the Alliance for Initial and Further Training for 2015–2018 in 2014, stressing that vocational education is important as college education, so that more young people in Germany and refugees entering Germany can enhance their employment and entrepreneurship by choosing to learn knowledge and skills from more than 300 professional technologies in the vocational education system.

While providing entrepreneurship courses, the entrepreneurship education of German universities places a priority on the development of entrepreneurship awareness, entrepreneurial spirit and skills, and sets up accelerators to facilitate the incorporation and growth of start-ups.

The Technical University of Munich (TUM) not only offers courses on basic knowledge of entrepreneurship for undergraduates, postgraduates, and researchers but also supports innovation with market-oriented concepts. As for entrepreneurship education courses, TUM offers undergraduate students, graduate students, and scientific researchers the basic knowledge of entrepreneurship, including finance, law, industrial design, innovation management, psychology, services and technology market, strategy and organization, etc. To better combine with practices, TUM founded the UnternehmerTUM, consisting of veteran businessmen,

---

[1] Assessment on the progress of G20 Entrepreneurship Action Plan, Entrepreneurship Research Center on G20 Economies, Oct. 22, 2019.

scientists, and professional managers, to comprehensively mentor startups and give them a hand from creativity to product development, establishment and improvement of business models, patent protection, investment introduction, and finally IPO. UnternehmerTUM also sponsored the AppliedAI, an artificial intelligence supporting platform, and partnered with many influential internet giants, including Google, NVIDIA, and PureStorage. While introducing industry experts, UnternehmerTUM has set up an international platform to help school start-ups develop overseas and also international companies enter the German market. TUM also organizes some entrepreneurial activities and competitions, such as the TUM Entrepreneurship Day, which sets up a principal entrepreneurship contest award to reward excellent entrepreneurial teams. In addition, The TUM has set up a social entrepreneurship college with other three universities to provide training and consulting services for entrepreneurs.

The University of Munich (Ludwig-Maximilians-Universität München, LMU) has set up an entrepreneurship center. Besides entrepreneurship research, its main work includes:

1. setting up entrepreneurship education courses for students;
2. helping start-ups establish and grow through accelerators; and
3. setting up an alumni entrepreneurship network. The LUM's accelerator provides free office space for students and selects 15 potential entrepreneurial teams for training each semester. At present, the accelerator has established more than 220 enterprises, of which 33% have been financed.

The accelerator links alumni entrepreneurial network for the entrepreneurial team, which now has 12,000 users, including alumni, investors, and other experts. The LUM also organizes entrepreneurship-related activities and competitions. For example, Hack@night is a two-day (weekend) entrepreneurship competition. Students who majored in different disciplines can form a 3–5-person entrepreneurship team, with special personnel on-site to guide them from creativity to a complete business plan. Enterprises, such as Siemens and BMW, are also be invited to participate in. entrepreneurship teams can cooperate with enterprises on developing products. The LUM's Entrepreneurship Center and German Accelerator cooperated to hold the CashWalk entrepreneurship competition, which was attended by 50 start-ups and more than 80 investors from all over the world, setting up a good platform for entrepreneurs to improve their entrepreneurial skills and expand their interpersonal networks.

Since 1998, the Exit-Business Start-Ups Program has played an active role in developing entrepreneurial culture and reinforcing cooperation and innovation between higher learning institutions and research institutions.

The program is a part of the High-Tech Strategy of the BMWi, including (1) developing the entrepreneurship culture of higher education institutions; (2) strengthening the transfer of high-tech research achievements of higher education institutions and research institutions; and (3) helping students and scientists establish and develop high-tech-based start-ups. Since 2015, the EXIST program has actively cooperated with Israeli universities and scientific research institutions. In addition to the support of the German government, the EXIST program also received funding from the European Social Fund (ESF).

Also developed are German entrepreneurship education for specific groups such as refugees, young people, and women.

In July 2017, the BMWi and the German Youth Chamber of Commerce jointly launched the Start-up Your Future program for refugees. The program was organized by veteran businessmen to train and mentor refugees in entrepreneurship and was piloted in Berlin-Brandenburg. Many refugees had some entrepreneurial experience before they came to Germany. Through this program, refugees can get an opportunity to intern in German enterprises and even take over enterprises and can be integrated into the Youth Chamber of Commerce, thus gaining more opportunities.

The BMWi organized the "Start-up Nights" event to connect young entrepreneurs with large companies, industry associations, and institutional investors in the same industry. Young entrepreneurs can get opportunities for cooperation by displaying their products, while large companies can also understand the new technology development trends of start-up companies. The event is divided into different themes, such as the medical industry, aerospace technology, social entrepreneurship, and digital energy.

The Guide program sponsored by non-profit organizations and supported by the Munich municipal government and the European Union provides women with advice and training on "how to start a business while taking care of their family". This program focuses on providing one-on-one consultation and regularly holds special seminars. The content of consultation and training covers business plans, market, sales, customer orientation, and policy subsidies. Veteran businesswomen, female entrepreneurs-to-be, and professional women who want to start a business share their experiences and expand their network at the party organized every month. The organization also holds entrepreneurial competitions. As of the beginning of 2018, there were about 5000 Munich women who had received consulting or training services, with an average of about 350 per year. Women entrepreneurs (both full-time and part-time) account for 40% of German start-ups established in 2016.

There are also some national entrepreneurial activities in Germany that enrich the entrepreneurial culture. For example, the Founder Week Germany 2018 led by the BMWi and jointly organized by several government agencies, industry associations, universities, and research institutions held a total of 1500 events, including themed seminars, entrepreneurship competitions, and forums each November. This event is part of the "Global Entrepreneurship Week", which was first held by the UK Enterprise and the US Kauffman Foundation in 2008. By 2017, the event has been attended by more than 9 million people from 167 countries. The BMWi has also launched the "Women Enterprise" program to encourage women to start businesses and encourage successful businesswomen or women entrepreneurs to participate in the "Women Entrepreneur Model" campaign as entrepreneurial models. At present, more than 100 women entrepreneurs or freelancers have become entrepreneurial models throughout the country. Some of them run large-scale enterprises and some are self-employed, but they are willing to contribute to the creation of women's entrepreneurial spirit.

Fair Competition for SMEs

On January 19, 2021, the 10th Amendment to the German Competition Act officially took effect.[2,3]

The German Competition Act stipulates that market subjects may not abuse their market dominance to harm the interests of SMEs. For example, the law stipulates that if an SME depends on supplying or demanding enterprises of a certain commodity or service so that the SME has no expectation possibility of turning to other enterprises, it will constitute unfair obstruction and discrimination against the SME. At the same time, it is stipulated that: compared with SMEs, enterprises with market dominance should not directly or indirectly hinder their competition in unreasonable ways. In addition, there are regulations on government procurement. For example, the interests of SMEs should be properly taken care of. The main method is to decompose public procurement according to certain standards and reserve a certain share for bidders of SMEs.[4]

The German Competition Act restricts large enterprises from easily entering the SME market. For example, when regulating vertical mergers and mixed mergers, it takes large enterprises' entry into the SME market as an inference to produce or strengthen significant markets. At the same time, the German Competition Act has "tolerance clauses" for mergers among SMEs. For example, enterprises with sales of less than 20 million Deutsch marks in the previous business year before the merger can merge with other enterprises without restrictions. If the merger takes place in a product market or service market with a life span of at least 5 years, and the total market sales in the previous business year are less than 30 million Deutsch marks, the merger is free from interference.[5]

The German Competition Act defines the cartel exemption system for SMEs to protect them. SME cartel is the cooperation among SMEs in

---

[2] https://www.bundeskartellamt.de/SharedDocs/Meldung/EN/Pressemitteilungen/2021/19_01_2021_GWB%20Novelle.html.

[3] In 1957, Germany promulgated the Competition Act, which created a fair market competition environment for SMEs by prohibiting cartel realization, prohibiting large enterprises from abusing their dominance, and controlling mergers.

[4] Shi Jianzhong, Competition Code of Thirty-One Countries [M], China University of Political Science and Law Press, 2009.

[5] http://www.iolaw.org.cn/showArticle.aspx?id=1036.

procurement, sales, or technical standardization to improve economic efficiency. The purpose of exempting such cartels is to expand the cooperation of SMEs, enhance their competitiveness, and improve the competitive environment of the market. In principle, price cartels among SMEs are not allowed, but price agreements can also be approved if prices are linked to certain measures of rationalization and are necessary for the success of these measures. However, they should not involve a market share exceeding 15%.[6]

---

[6] http://www.iolaw.org.cn/showArticle.aspx?id=1035.

India

The Indian government promotes innovation, entrepreneurship, and MSMEs by providing financial subsidies, introducing tax incentives, developing credit guarantees, and setting up venture capital parent funds. Qualified MSMEs may receive subsidies and services from the National Small Industries Corporation (NSIC) through the Raw Material Assistance Scheme and the Marketing Assistance Scheme. India's financial budget 2017 proposed preferential tax policies for SMEs, such as a reduction in the corporate tax and the capital gains tax. In addition, the Credit Guarantee Trust Fund for Micro and Small Enterprises (CGTMSE) has been increased by three times in recent years. Finally, the Indian government, together with the National Credit Guarantee Trust Company (NCGTC) and Small Industries Development Bank of India (SIDBI), set up a venture capital parent fund to promote venture capital in India.

In entrepreneurial service, the Indian government improves its efficiency and service quality by deploying online platforms. In 2016, The Mistry of MSME required all Indian MSMEs to fill in their registration information online, so that the government could monitor the execution of various official programs and schemes. Besides, the Ministry of MSME implements the Technology Center Systems Program (TCSP) through setting up Technology Centers (TCs). Moreover, the Indian government welcomes MSMEs to join government procurement. The Central

Government Public Procurement Policy for Micro and Small Enterprises Order 2012 stipulates a minimum amount of government procurement from MSMEs. The National Scheduled Caste/Scheduled Tribe Hub also helps MSMEs to win orders from the government and public sectors. The Marketing Assistant Scheme organizes international technology exhibitions, providing marketing support for MSMEs. In enterprise incubation, the Ministry of MSME has implemented A Scheme for Promoting Innovation, Rural Industry & Entrepreneurship (ASPIRE) which planned to establish 100 Livelihood Business Incubators (LBIs) in India. In 2017, ZDream Labs, the first China-India Internet incubator, was established in New Delhi.

The Indian government subsidizes entrepreneurship trainings, especially programs collaborating with multinational companies. The Scheme for Assistance to Training Institutions (ATI) 2016 and Samsung technical schools are representative examples. Moreover, Indian higher education institutions, such as the Entrepreneurship Development Institute of India (EDII) and Indian Institute of Technology (IIT), not only provide entrepreneurship education courses in their own curricula but also offer entrepreneurship trainings to specific demographic groups by working together with government agencies and businesses.

The Indian Competition Law prohibits acts that have or may have an appreciable adverse effect on competition (AAEC). It is also prohibited for any enterprise or group of enterprises to abuse a dominant position in the market. In addition, the anti-monopoly review system under the Competition Law and the Competition Commission of India Regulations 2011[1] sets thresholds for reporting assets and turnover in a transaction.

Government Services

The MSMED Act 2006 is Indian legislation dedicated to MSMEs. The Ministry of MSME was established under the MSMED Act 2006. The Office of Development Commissioner is a branch of the Ministry of MSME. It provides services such as entrepreneurship trainings, technical and management consulting, export assistance, and credit loans for MSMEs. The office also assists the central and local governments in designing policies for the development of MSMEs. In addition, through

---

[1] https://www.cci.gov.in/sites/default/files/regulation_pdf/Combination%20Regulations%202016%20-%20FINAL_0.pdf.

CPGRAMS, the Ministry of MSME deals with complaints and suggestions from SMEs. Till March 2018, the CPGRAMS accepted a total of 8400 complaints/suggestions, of which 8345 were resolved or adopted.

In addition, the Indian government initiated the "Start Up India", an innovation and entrepreneurship program, in 2016, which aimed to shore up the sustainable development of the Indian economy by championing innovation and entrepreneurship. This program consisted of three themes: first, simplification and operability, such as reducing administrative burden and simplifying procedures; second, financial support and incentives, such as providing parent funds and start-up business loans; third, incubation and cooperation between businesses and higher education institutions, such as organizing start-up exhibitions and creating incubation networks.

Fiscal and Financial Support

The Raw Material Assistance Scheme of NSIC is designed to provide financial support for SMEs to purchase raw materials, drawing SMEs attention to quality improvement. NSIC's Marketing Assistance Scheme helps SMEs assess the market environment and analyze customer demand. SMEs can also find partners with the assistance of this scheme and get access to a platform for technology transfer.

India's financial budget 2017 proposed preferential tax policies for SMEs. The corporate tax rate of domestic SMEs with revenue below 500 million rupees (equivalent to 7.8 million US dollars) in the fiscal year 2015–2016 has been reduced to 25% from 30%. Companies listed on India's SME Exchange are entitled to a 100% reduction in long-term capital gains tax and an 85% reduction in short-term one. The time limit for carrying forward Minimum Alternative Tax (MAT) has been raised from 10 to 15 years. For SMEs with revenue of less than 20 million rupees (equivalent to 310,000 US dollars), the presumptive tax is reduced by 2%.

With the support of the Indian government, the CGT-MSE was increased to 75 billion rupees (equivalent to 1.17 billion US dollars) from 25 billion rupees (equivalent to 390 million US dollars) by the end of 2016. In 2014–2018, the CGT-MSE supported loans totaling 51.65 billion rupees (equivalent to 800 million US dollars).

According to Start Up India, the Indian government, together with NCGTC and SIDBI, set up a venture capital parent fund with an initial principal of 25 billion rupees (equivalent to 390 million US dollars). The fund was expected to provide 5 billion rupees (equivalent to 78 million US dollars) a year for SMEs to boost India's innovation and start-ups. This parent fund was managed by a board of directors composed of representatives from industry, academia, and start-up companies.

Entrepreneur Services

Information Services

In July 2016, The Ministry of MSME released the MSME Development (Furnishing of Information) Rules 2016, which required all Indian MSMEs to register their firm information online. This move not only helped the Indian government supervise the execution of its programs and schemes but also enabled MSMEs to update their information in real time to get government procurement orders. So far, the system has 132,000 registered users.

Technical Services

The Ministry of MSME implements TCSP and will set up 15 TCs nationwide. In addition, it will upgrade TCs in Bhubaneswar, Mumbai, and Aurangabad, of which the cost budget is about 22 billion rupees (equivalent to 34.33 million US dollars).

Market Support

The Central Government Public Procurement Policy for Micro and Small Enterprises Order 2012 stipulates a minimum of 20% of the total annual government procurement from MSMEs. In October 2016, the government launched the National Scheduled Caste/Scheduled Tribe Hub, which was operated by the NSIC. By the end of the first quarter of 2018, the program had implemented 98 supplier development projects to support MSMEs to become government and public sector suppliers.

The Marketing Assistant Scheme organizes international technology exhibitions and supports SMEs to participate in international and domestic trade exhibitions. The "Business Fair" included in this scheme gathers bulk buyers/government agencies and MSMEs on one platform.

Enterprise Incubation

Since March 2015, the Ministry of MSME has implemented ASPIRE which planned to establish 100 LBIs and 20 Technology Business Incubators (TBIs). By March 2018, 62 LBIs had been built, of which 33 began to incubate. Of the 17,000 enterprises that have been incubated, 30% have set up their own businesses or started formal operations.

In September 2017, ZDream Labs, the first China-India Internet incubator, was established in New Delhi. Based on China's experience in the rapidly- growing Internet-based industries, ZDream Labs will explore the Indian market which is highly similar to the Chinese market, incubating and accelerating premium Indian start-up programs and searching for the next Indian unicorn.

Digital Transformation Support

Digital India Programme was launched by the Government of India in July 2015. It is centered around three key areas: Digital Infrastructure as a Utility to Every Citizen, Governance and Services on Demand and Digital Empowerment of Citizens. MSMEs offering IT and IT-enabled services (ITeS) are expected to develop significantly as the program aims to ensure digital empowerment of citizens by strengthening public IT infrastructure, improving governance and providing services on demand.[2]

On July 20, 2020, India's MSME sector urged e-commerce major Amazon to list products from small businesses separately on its platform and help micro-entrepreneurs market their goods globally. Besides, during the pandemic, government, industry leaders, and other key stakeholders have made efforts to support vulnerable MSMEs and given them a fighting chance by creating a technology-empowered entrepreneurial ecosystem. Initiatives like conducting video KYC, as approved by the Reserve bank of India (RBI), have vastly helped lenders offer quick and easy remote onboarding services to small business owners. A groundbreaking government initiative revolutionizing the Indian digital lending infrastructure is the India Stack. As a part of the Digital India initiative, it can help lenders provide credit to borrowers, especially small businesses, through quick, hassle-free Aadhar-based authentications. India Stack has

---

[2] Assessment on the progress of G20 Entrepreneurship Action Plan, Entrepreneurship Research Center on G20 Economies, Oct 22, 2019.

brought rapid growth of the digital payment ecosystem in India, with more and more businesses adopting digital payment solutions, and is helping lending channels to either invest in the digital transformation of small businesses or partner with the right fintech platforms to help MSMEs stay competitive.[3]

ENTREPRENEURSHIP EDUCATION

The Ministry of MSME launched the Scheme for ATI 2016 to subsidize training institutions registered with official organizations such as the Ministry of MSME and facilitate them to provide training programs of entrepreneurial skills for entrepreneurs. Under this scheme, eligible training institutions may be subsidized up to 25 million rupees ($390,000).

The Ministry of MSME and Samsung Electronics signed a memorandum and jointly set up 10 Samsung technical schools to provide training courses for Indian young people. Till March 2018, 2175 people received training, among whom 1538 had already been employed. The Indian government plans to set up two more technical schools in Jamshedpur and Bengaluru in the future. In 2017, India's Ministry of MSME also signed a memorandum with SAP India to implement SAP B1, an employment training program, in five TCs.

Indian higher education institutions, represented by EDII and IIT, not only provide entrepreneurship education courses and programs by themselves, but also offer entrepreneurship trainings to specific groups such as young people, college students, and women by collaborating with government agencies and businesses.

The Indian government's Rural Entrepreneurship Program (January 2016–March 2020) aims to help young people in rural areas start sustainable, self-employed businesses while connecting rural entrepreneurs with banks and financial institutions. In 2018, the Ministry of Science and Technology partnered with EDII to provide entrepreneurship trainings for 7000 young people from 40 regions in India.

The Society for Innovation and Entrepreneurship (SINE), an innovation and entrepreneurship platform of IIT, provides training programs for

---

[3] Evaluation and Prospect of G20 Members' Policies to Support Entrepreneurship in the Post-pandemic Era, Entrepreneurship Research Center on G20 Economies, Oct 22, 2020.

a variety of start-ups. Take the Plugin Program as an example. It is a one-year program supported by the Ministry of Science and Technology, Intel Corporation, and SINE to support hardware design and development firms. It attempts to help hardware start-ups in product development and commercialization. In addition, it provides firms with opportunities to access international resources. It mainly focuses on technologies such as artificial intelligence, machine learning, blockchain, and the Internet of Things.

FAIR COMPETITION FOR SMEs

The Indian Competition Law[4,5] prohibits acts that have or may have an appreciable adverse effect on competition (AAEC). These include restriction of competition agreements, abuse of market dominance, and concentration of enterprises. The Indian Competition Law mainly protects SMEs by regulating the above three types of monopolistic behaviors.

The Indian Competition Law clearly stipulates that no enterprise, individual, or association of individuals may enter into an agreement on the production, supply, distribution, storage, acquisition of control of goods, or the provision of services, which has or may have AAEC; otherwise, the agreement is invalid. It is also prohibited for any enterprise or group of enterprises to abuse a dominant position in the market, and the Competition Commission of India can order an enterprise to cease the abuse and at the same time impose a fine of up to 10% of the average turnover of the previous three fiscal years, can order an enterprise with a dominant position in the market to split up to ensure that the enterprise cannot abuse the dominant position, and can also impose penalties on the individuals responsible for the company in the event that the company engages in conduct that violates the Competition Act.

In addition, the anti-monopoly review system under the Competition Law and the Competition Commission of India Regulations 2011[6] sets thresholds for reporting assets and turnover in a transaction, and if either

---

[4] The current anti-trust law in India is the Competition Act 2002 adopted by the Indian Parliament in December 2002, which came into effect in January 2003.

[5] https://www.cci.gov.in/sites/default/files/regulation_pdf/Combination%20Regulations%202016%20-%20FINAL_0.pdf.

[6] https://www.cci.gov.in/sites/default/files/regulation_pdf/Combination%20Regulations%202016%20-%20FINAL_0.pdf.

threshold is exceeded, both parties will be required to obtain approval from the Competition Commission of India before the transaction can be implemented. In case of failure to comply with the requirements, the Competition Commission may impose a fine of up to 1% of the concentrated turnover or assets, whichever is higher.

Indonesia

The Indonesian government attaches importance to the role of SMEs in boosting the economy and has arranged supportive measures in its economic stimulus plan. The Indonesian government has launched a national entrepreneurship campaign, promulgated a micro-credit agency law and a national financing strategy to promote SME and start-up developments, and committed itself to simplify the registration and business license processes. The Ministry of Cooperatives and SMEs are mainly responsible for these affairs in Indonesia.

The Indonesian government has taken a series of measures to reduce the fiscal and taxation burdens for SMEs. In early 2018, the preferential income tax rate for SMEs was lowered and a tax cut was granted to foreign investment projects. In 2017, the import of raw materials for SMEs will be exempted from customs duties. In 2016, the amount of taxes paid by SMEs was reduced. In order to encourage venture capital companies to support emerging SMEs, the government also introduced a preferential income tax policy for venture capital in early 2018.

Indonesia provides financing support for SMEs through commercial banks that mainly serve SMEs, in which Bank Rakyat Indonesia (BRI) and PT Bank Danamon Indonesia TBK (BDI) play an important role. PT. Askrindo (Persero) mainly provides a guarantee for banks of SME lending. In recent years, Indonesia's venture capital also developed rapidly.

Indonesia's digital economy has considerable growth potential. Therefore, the government has implemented the Indonesia Broadband Plan, given priority to network infrastructure development, and encouraged the country to start businesses and develop SMEs in the field of digital economy. The ongoing Palapa Ring program will provide faster broadband services, and Internet platforms such as Indonesia MALL's website and Tokopedia platform of the People's Bank of Indonesia (PBI) will also facilitate SMEs to use the Internet to expand their market. In Indonesia, there are various incubators, mainly active in the fields of digital start-ups, digital financial enterprises, and digital media. In addition, Indonesian government departments have also initiated the development of an entrepreneur community and provided an information, technology and resource exchange platform for entrepreneurial activities. In 2020, the Government of Indonesia launched a national initiative called "BanggaBuatanIndonesia" to encourage start-ups to make greater use of online platforms to grow their businesses. With this measure, the government hopes to mitigate the impact of Covid-19 on the economy and that more start-ups will benefit from it.

In Indonesia, international organizations and multinational companies have actively promoted local entrepreneurship education and training, and have set up different programs to provide entrepreneurship training for special groups such as youth and women and high-growth enterprises. Such initiatives include the Indonesia Green Entrepreneurship Program of the International Labor Organization (ILO) and the "Womenwill" program sponsored by Google, a campaign launched by US-based non-profit organizations in 2016. In addition, increasing higher learning institutions are carrying out entrepreneurship education, and they have also started projects aimed at providing entrepreneurship education for middle school teachers.

The contents of the Indonesian Competition Law relating to SMEs are mainly of the regulations on the vertical agreement and abuse of market dominance. The Indonesian competition law prohibits vertically restrictive agreements that are themselves illegal because they can lead to unfair business competition and adversely affect consumer welfare. And, abuse of market dominance by all Indonesian enterprises is illegal per se.

GOVERNMENT SERVICES

Indonesia Company Law (2007) and Small and Medium Enterprises Law (2008) (SMEs Law 20/2008) have prescribed the definition and legal status of SMEs in Indonesia, as well as the basic policies and management measures of Indonesian governments at all levels for SMEs, which are the basic laws of the Indonesian government to support SME development.

In recent years, the Indonesian government has arranged supportive measures of start-ups and SMEs in its economic stimulus plan, reducing the amount of required capital, improving the business environments, improving the financing opportunities for new ventures and SMEs, and simplifying the registration and licensing processes.

The Indonesian government issued a new regulation in 2016 to reduce the required capital for the establishment of a limited company to 200,000 rupiahs (equivalent to 15 US dollars), with the previous minimum capital requirement of 3800 US dollars, to reduce the cost of starting a business. According to the new regulations, the parties to a limited company can provide proof that they have the same amount of net assets and can be exempted from the minimum capital requirement of 3800 US dollars, but the asset certificate must be submitted to the Ministry of Law and Human Rights (MOLHR) within 60 days after signing the registration of the company.

The 16th Economic Stimulation Plan[1] in 2017 is mainly aimed at improving and speeding up the processing of various investment licenses so as to improve the entrepreneurial environment and facilitate the administrative licensing of enterprises and businesses. The plan implements a new service system, using high technology to process comprehensive license applications and services. License application procedures are submitted online to improve and speed up the efficiency of various investment license processing. In order to improve Indonesia's ranking in the Ease of Doing Business (EODB) index, the Indonesian government has abolished the requirement to extend the business license for enterprises (Surat Izin Usaha Perdagangan, SIUP) and enterprises are no longer required to extend their trade license.[2]

---

[1] In 2015, the Indonesian government introduced the 4th Economic Stimulus Plan and increased small loan support for SMEs. Its main goal is to maximize and promote employment through stimulating enterprise vitality and expanding investment.

[2] According to the EODB index, Indonesia ranked 72 in 2018 and 91 in 2017.

The Indonesian government announced in early 2018 that it would do its best to improve its EODB index and business regulations in the coming years. Indonesia's Coordinating Ministry of Economic Affairs will give priority to improving the EODB index, including start-ups, tax payment, and cross-border trade. In April 2018, the Gubernatorial Regulation No. 30/2018 allowed first-time entrepreneurs to use their homes as office spaces. In the same month, the "Ayo UMKM Jualan Online" (Let SMEs Sell Online) was launched, and government agencies and trading markets landed on the online platform to help start-ups and SMEs operate online and increase profits. The plan aims to have 8 million SMEs operating online by 2020.

The National Entrepreneurship Movement (Gerakan Kewirausahaan Nasional, GKN) was launched by Indonesia's Ministry of Cooperatives and SMEs in 2011. The Indonesian government provides entrepreneurship training, cooperation, and Environmental Partnership Program (Program Kemitraan Bina Lingkungan, PKBL), corporate social response financing, and small business loan support, etc. The Indonesian government promulgated the MFI Law 1/2013 and the national financing strategy in 2012 to coordinate various government agencies to improve SMEs' financing opportunities.

The Indonesian government has been simplifying the registration and licensing processes since 2010 and promoting the One-Stop-Shops system throughout the country to make it easier for entrepreneurs to get the needed registration information. In 2014, Indonesia promulgated President Regulation No. 98, which allows SMEs to register new legal entities through a one-page application, a more simplified process at a lower cost.

The Ministry of Cooperatives and SMEs is responsible for domestic SME affairs, with 49 service centers in 24 provinces with 293 experts providing consulting, guidance, and other services. The BKPM is a one-stop processing center for all business licenses and permits. The MOLHR and the Ministry of Trade provide name approval, permanent business license, and company registration certificate approval services.

FISCAL AND FINANCIAL SUPPORT

The Indonesian government supports start-ups and SMEs development by reducing corporate income tax, reducing taxes payable, and exempting related duties, and implementing preferential incentive measures to exempt venture investment from income tax.

In early 2018, the government lowered the preferential income tax rate for SMEs from 1 to 0.5%, and stipulated that SMEs with annual revenue not exceeding 4.8 billion rupiahs (equivalent to 350,000 US dollars) may be entitled to the preferential tax rate. At the beginning of 2016, the 12th Economic Policy Package promulgated by the Indonesian government reduced the number of taxes to be paid by SMEs from 54 to 10, all of which can be paid online.

At the same time, the government also announced a 50% reduction in corporate income tax for a five-year period for newly established foreign direct investment projects in Indonesia, if the investment is between 100 billion rupiahs (equivalent to 7.4 million US dollars) and 500 billion rupiahs (equivalent to 37 million US dollars). Before that, Indonesia has implemented legislation to provide 100% exemption from enterprise income tax for foreign direct investment projects with an investment of 500 billion rupiahs (equivalent to 37 million US dollars) or more.

In early 2017, the government announced the exemption of tariffs on raw materials and other materials imported by export-oriented SMEs. According to the newly passed Exemption of Imported Materials from Customs Duties on Exported Goods, eligible companies must export at least 75% of their products. This will reduce the production costs of such enterprises by 25% and eventually promote exports. Eligible SMEs can also apply for low-interest loans from the Indonesian Export–Import Bank—Indonesia's export financing institution.

In order to promote e-commerce investment, the Indonesian government granted exemption from income tax in early 2018 to venture investment companies that provide financing for start-ups. Ministry of Finance said that the government will not take the continued lending of venture capital companies to innovative enterprises as the target of income taxation. This is the first set of incentives adopted by the Indonesian government to promote the development of venture capital to increase the incentive to invest in innovative enterprises, especially the development of new online enterprises.

Indonesia provides financing support for start-ups and SMEs through commercial banks that mainly serve SMEs, increases the loan guarantee number of SMEs, and expands the financing of start-ups and SMEs. Among them, BRI, BDI, and Persero played important roles. In addition, the development of venture capital also provides diversified financing channels for Indonesia's venture development.

BRI's key loan customers include SMEs. As of December 2017, the BRI issued 739.3 trillion rupiahs (equivalent to 54.6 billion US dollars) in 2017, and increased by 11.4% year on year, of which 73.5% was SME loans (72.5% in 2016) and made a profit of 29.04 trillion rupiahs (equivalent to 1.5 billion US dollars) for the whole year, becoming the bank that kept making profits for 13 consecutive years in Indonesia, with SMEs as the main contributor to its profits. The BRI was founded in 1895. It officially launched the microfinance business in 1969 to provide policy financial services in rural areas. After restructuring in 1985, it positioned its business as microfinance and went public in Jakarta in 2003.

The BDI was established in 1976 and was taken over by the Indonesian government during the Asian financial crisis in 1998, positioning its business mainly on SME credit. In the fiscal year of 2017, the BDI's SME banking business realized SME loans of 29.2 trillion rupiahs (equivalent to 2.16 billion US dollars), up to 10% year on year. The BDI also launched the "Danamon Connect" in 2017 to provide a comprehensive financial transaction service model for enterprises, especially start-ups, SMEs, and financial institutions.

The Persero was established in 1971 to provide bank loans to SMEs (People's Enterprise Credit, KUR) to expand financing for SMEs and promote SME development in Indonesia. Such guarantees can be used for working capital and investment loans up to 500 million rupiahs (equivalent to 370 US dollars). In 2017, Indonesia's Ministry of Cooperatives and SMEs increased the loan guarantee for SMEs (KUR) to 110 trillion rupiahs (equivalent to 8.11 billion US dollars), up 10% year on year, and the applicable interest rate was 7% (down from 9 to 7% in January 2016).

In recent years, Indonesia's venture capital industry has developed rapidly. The total VC investment in 2012 was 44 million US dollars, in 2016 it was 1.4 billion US dollars, and in the first eight months of 2017, it reached 3 billion US dollars. From 2012 to August 2017, 58% of the capital flow went to e-commerce start-ups, 38% to transportation start-ups, and 5% to others.

Entrepreneur Services

Indonesia has a population of 260 million, of which 93.4 million are Internet users, and its digital economy has considerable room for growth. The government gives priority to developing network infrastructures and encourages the country's entrepreneurship and development of SMEs in the field of digital economy. In Indonesia, there are various incubators mainly active in the fields of digital start-ups, digital financial enterprises, and digital media. In addition, the government departments have also initiated an entrepreneur community and provided an information, technology, and resource exchange platform for entrepreneurs by organizing activities.

Technical Services

The Indonesia Broadband Plan launched by the Indonesian government in 2014 is expected to provide mobile Internet access to 52% of Indonesia's population. The total budget of the plan is 278 trillion rupiahs (equivalent to 20.5 billion US dollars), of which 10% comes from government funding. The plan will also extensively improve the nation's e-government network, data center, passive infrastructure, and wireless connection facilities.

The Palapa Ring project being implemented by the Indonesian Ministry of Communication and Information consists of three parts (western, central, and eastern) and is one of the Indonesian government's priority infrastructure projects. It includes a huge undersea fiber optic cable network, which will provide a backbone of fiber optic networks to Indonesia's entire archipelagos and provide faster broadband services.

In 2017, the BRI built a website called Indonesia Mall to encourage SMEs to use the Internet platform to expand their product markets. Tokopedia platform, with a total of 2 million users in Indonesia, directly sold 60 million items to customers through the platform, bypassing middlemen and overcoming the logistics problems faced by conventional businesses. The Indonesian government believes that the emergence of this business model is conducive to entrepreneurship and the development of SMEs.

Enterprise Incubation

Indigo Incubator is a start-up incubator project of Telkom, which supports the development of digital start-ups. Start-ups can get six months of incubation support and services, such as market access, business and technical consulting, and a start-up fund of 250 million rupiahs (equivalent to 18,000 US dollars), and have the opportunity to get advanced financing of 2 billion rupiahs (equivalent to 147,000

US dollars) from Telkom. Telkom, Indonesia's largest telecommunications company, has 150 million customers, multi-country operations, and subsidiaries of more than 100 companies.

Mandiri Digital Incubator was set up by Indonesia's Mandiri Bank to provide one-on-one professional guidance for entrepreneurs in cooperation with Indigo Incubator and get support funds after six months of incubation. The purpose of the incubator is to create world-class financial digital products and promote Indonesia's economic development.

SkyStar Ventures is an incubator project that started in late 2013. This incubator supports start-ups of products and services related to digital media, including distribution, publishing, social media, and e-commerce. SkyStar Ventures provided an initial investment of 60 million rupiahs (equivalent to 4400 US dollars) to 960 million rupiahs (equivalent to 70,000 US dollars).

The Jakarta Founder Institute (JFI) currently has nearly 40 mentors, and each trainee has an average of 2 mentors. Participants are required to attend seminars every week, report to their mentors and receive training on specific topics, and complete business plans on schedule. The agency has now raised 70 million US dollars.

Communication Platform

Indonesia Entrepreneur Center (IDEC) is a government initiative, which hopes to create an entrepreneurial ecosystem by establishing an entrepreneurial community so that anyone can access entrepreneurial knowledge anywhere, accelerate the growth of Indonesian entrepreneurs and improve Indonesia's socioeconomic developments through entrepreneurship.

The BRI has implemented some measures to support innovation and entrepreneurship. For example, the BRI held the Coworking Festival 2017 and set up Coworking Space in Indonesia to provide entrepreneurship training and space for entrepreneurs and SMEs, creating a platform to exchange experiences and share potential business opportunities.

PLUS (Platform Usaha Sosial) is an online network that helps Indonesian entrepreneurs get the resources they need. It helps them establish contact with mentors, experts, and capital that can support their growth, and provide free learning materials on the website. PLUS has established an open enterprise search directory in Indonesia. PLUS's mission is to build development communities for Indonesian entrepreneurs, provide them with learning resources and financial and other support opportunities through online platform training.

Digital Transformation Support

In 2017, Indonesia's Ministry of Industry launched the Smart IKM Program, which has established cooperative relations with several e-commerce platforms in Indonesia to encourage SMEs to integrate into the Internet economy and expand sales channels. By September 2019, the total value of e-commerce transactions of SMEs is 2.3 billion rupiah ($162,800). The Government of Indonesia launched a national initiative called "BanggaBuatanIndonesia" in 2020 to encourage start-ups to make greater use of online platforms to grow their businesses. With this measure, the government hopes to mitigate the impact of Covid-19 on the economy and that more start-ups will benefit from it.[3]

BanggaBuatanIndonesia encourages sales through online platforms, provides specialized training, and provides a total of Rp 34.1 trillion in funding to help start-ups grow their online businesses, with the hope that entrepreneurs can help improve Indonesia by building stronger digital businesses. The competitiveness of the brand in the global market.[4]

ENTREPRENEURSHIP EDUCATION

In Indonesia, international organizations and multinational companies have actively promoted local entrepreneurship education and training, and have set up different programs to provide entrepreneurship training for special groups such as youth and women and high-growth enterprises. In addition, increasing higher learning institutions in Indonesia are carrying out entrepreneurship education, and they have also started projects aimed at providing entrepreneurship education for middle school teachers.

Youth unemployment and environmental pollution are problems Indonesia faces at the same time. In order to solve these problems,

---

[3] Assessment on the progress ofG20 Entrepreneurship Action Plan, Entrepreneurship Research Center on G20 Economies, Oct 22, 2019.

[4] Evaluation and Prospect of G20 Members' Policies to Support Entrepreneurship in the Post-pandemic Era, Entrepreneurship Research Center on G20 Economies, Oct 22, 2020.

the ILO launched the Indonesian Green Entrepreneurship Program in Indonesia in 2016, with the main goal of encouraging and developing entrepreneurs in the field of environmental protection, especially young people. It covers men and women, urban and rural areas. It mainly focuses on six specific industries: food and agriculture, renewable energy, tourism, garbage disposal, transportation, and creative industries. The training content of the whole project is divided into several modules, including one general module, five industry-related modules, one teacher module, and 50 case studies.

The women entrepreneurship training program "Womenwill" is a global project initiated by Google to help women start their own businesses. It mainly uses Google's Internet technology advantages to help women learn better online or improve economic benefits through online tools. The Womenwill project in Indonesia provides both online and offline training opportunities for women entrepreneurs to learn digital marketing skills. In 2017, more than 8000 Indonesian women participated in the offline conference in six cities. Through the conference, women entrepreneurs can not only learn knowledge and skills but also expand contacts and inspire each other. In addition, women entrepreneurs in 10 cities in Indonesia can participate in the "Gapura Digital" training program online, learn about business operations weekly, and share their views and experiences in online forums.

Endeavor is a US-based non-profit organization dedicated to assisting start-ups with high-growth potential. Endeavor has more than 1400 entrepreneurs from 880 companies worldwide (in 2017), creating 600,000 jobs. In Indonesia, Endeavor assessed more than 2000 start-ups and selected 35 of them for training. The organization's main way to help entrepreneurs is through its organizational resources to help entrepreneurs expand their global resource network and provide guidance in marketing, e-commerce, sales, talent management, and financing so that enterprises can develop more rapidly.

Indonesia has more than 2900 higher education institutions, with more than 1 million graduates each year. Indonesia's Ministry of Education has included entrepreneurship education for university students in its strategic development plan and provided certain financial supports. In order to promote employment, increasing higher education institutions are launching entrepreneurship education and related activities.

The Center for Entrepreneurship Development and Studies (CEDS) of the University of Indonesia (UI) provides students with entrepreneurship training programs, which can be divided into four categories. The first category is IGNITE Business Class, which aims to develop entrepreneurs' skills and provide them with the opportunity to contact investors after the project ends. The second category is Business Case Competition Mentoring, with the goal of enabling students to learn relevant entrepreneurial skills by preparing for the competition and having someone to provide mentoring to win the competition. The third category is entrepreneur networking (UI Entrepreneur Networking) which aims to expand the entrepreneur's interpersonal network and share knowledge and experience. The fourth category is company visits, by which participants have the opportunity to visit local companies or foreign-funded enterprises and learn about entrepreneurship and management through close contact with enterprises.

The Business School of Bandung Institute of Technology has launched undergraduate programs in the entrepreneurship track and will also provide students with opportunities for practical exercises. Its main goal is to develop students' ability to identify opportunities and start businesses, pay attention to innovation and practice, and contribute to Indonesia's economic development. In order to develop students' entrepreneurial spirit, the institute organized students majoring in entrepreneurship to visit and inspect enterprises. For example, in July 2017, the institute organized students to visit resorts, handbag factories, and milk processing factories set up by alumni in Bogor, Indonesia. Students can understand the original intention of the founders to set up enterprises and the problems and experiences in setting up and managing enterprises. Students can absorb these contents and apply them to the process of setting up their own enterprises.

There are also youth entrepreneurship training programs in Indonesia, such as Manulife Indonesia and PuteraSampoerna Foundation School Development Outreach (PSF SDO) jointly launched the youth entrepreneurship development program for young entrepreneurs, which mainly provides training in entrepreneurship education for middle school teachers. In addition to teachers offering entrepreneurship education courses to students, Manulife Indonesia's employees will give school teachers and parents a wide range of economic knowledge. These measures are conducive to fostering Indonesia's entrepreneurial culture and atmosphere.

Fair Competition for SMEs

The contents of the Indonesian Competition Law[5] relating to SMEs are mainly of the regulations on the vertical agreement and abuse of market dominance.

Vertical agreement refers to the agreement concluded between enterprises in different economic stages. The characteristic of a vertical competition restriction agreement is that the payment of both parties is complementary.[6] The Indonesian competition law prohibits vertically restrictive agreements that are themselves illegal because they can lead to unfair business competition and adversely affect consumer welfare.

With respect to abuse of market dominance, an enterprise is in possession of a dominant position if it is one of the following: An enterprise or a group of enterprises controls 50% or more of the market share of a commodity or service; or two or three companies control 75% or more of the market share of a particular commodity or service. Abuse of market dominance by all Indonesian enterprises is illegal per se.

---

[5] Law No. 5 of 1999 regarding Prohibition of Monopolistic Practice and Unfair Business Competition (Competition Law).

[6] By Wang Xiaoye. Research on Competition Law. Beijing: China Legal Publishing House 1999.

Italy

The Italian government supported the internationalization of innovative start-ups and SMEs through financial subsidies to enhance their international competitiveness and influence. "Trademarks + 3" was open for application in March 2018. The "Industria 4.0" plan provides tax relief and preferential policies to innovative start-ups and SMEs. Since 2017, for example, the Italian government has reduced 30% of personal income tax or enterprise income tax for capital investors of innovative enterprises, start-ups, and SMEs. It has also implemented the super- and hyper-depreciation taxation system, and added the nominal purchase cost in calculating depreciation of new machines and equipment. In addition, the taxable amount of enterprises has been reduced and R&D credits has been given to enterprises The Innovative Startups Policy/Innovative SMEs Policy exempts innovative start-ups and SMEs from stamp duty, business registration fees, and annual chamber fees, as well as a certain amount of value-added tax. The policy also provides discounts of service fees for expanding the international market and expands financing channels for innovative start-ups and SMEs by allowing online equity crowdfunding and setting up SME Guarantee Fund.

The Italian government has been attaching great importance to the technological R&D and innovation of SMEs. The 2015 Stability Law implements tax credits for enterprises' R&D incremental investment and reduces regional taxes. The Patent Box 2015 strengthens the protection of intellectual property rights. In order to support the knowledge innovation and achievement transformation of SMEs, the government has set up a Technology Innovation Fund (FIT) and a Research and Development Fund (FAR) to encourage national scientific research institutions and enterprises for scientific R&D. To promote the development of e-commerce of SMEs, the Italian government began to implement the voucher system for SMEs in 2014. In 2017, the government announced the continuation of the Italia Startup Visa program and the Italia Startup Hub program. On March 12, 2020, the Italian Minister for Technological Innovation and Digitization launched the Digital Solidarity program, in response to the outbreak of Covid-19.

The Italian government put forward various policies and actions to create a culture of youth entrepreneurship. For example, the Italian government designed and implemented the National Youth Plans, set up the Department for Youth and the National Youth Agency, and cooperated with non-governmental agencies such as Confindustria. The European Social Fund, the Youth Employment Initiative, and the Youth Guarantee also increased efforts to support youth entrepreneurship in Italy. The support for youth entrepreneurship is mainly tilted to innovative high-tech projects. Italian universities launched entrepreneurship-related courses to promote the development of entrepreneurship among students and scientific researchers, such as Bologna University's technical entrepreneurship education course and Padova University's newly established postgraduate training program in entrepreneurship and innovation. There is a national-level development path in technical and vocational education.

Italian anti-trust law prohibits one operator or several operators as a whole from abusing their market dominance in the domestic market or a substantial part of the domestic market. In addition, when the concentration of operators reaches a certain limit, it should be reported to the competent authority for approval. Through the declaration system of concentration of operators, Italian anti-trust law eliminates the high concentration of operators which is not conducive to the development of SMEs.

Government Services

Italy has launched special laws on SMEs, for instance, the Law on Supporting Innovation and Development of Small and Medium-sized Enterprises (1991), which encourages SMEs to adopt advanced technology and carry out technological innovation to promote structural adjustment. In 2012, the Innovation and Entrepreneurship Law was promulgated to stimulate the innovation and entrepreneurship of innovative SMEs.

In 2016, Italy launched the "Industria 4.0", a national plan, to digitalize new industries and enhance the competitiveness of Italian industries. In addition, Italy formulated a series of measures to encourage venture capital development, such as financial incentives for equity investment only for innovative start-ups and SMEs, asset depreciation and tax incentives for their R&D activities. The government believes that, compared with other European countries such as France, Germany, and Spain, its venture capital scale is far behind and the gap is increasing. The Refinancing of Smart & Start Italia, which provides financing for start-ups, was launched in the 2017 Budget Law, and a new two-year visa is granted to non-EU citizens who have made major investments in Italy's strategic areas.[1] Such investments include capital investments of no less than 500,000 euros to innovative start-ups and no less than 1 million euros to other types of enterprises.

Decree-Law No. 3 of January 24, 2015, reformed the company registration process. It reduced registration fees and improved registration efficiency and online registration. The new process is free of charge except for registration documents and stamp duty. In addition, the new process has fewer registration steps and does not require third-party identity verification. It can be registered by electronic signature and has adopted the standard articles of association and regulations, which is conducive to rapid drafting of company registration documents. The new process also allows online company registration.

The Italian Ministry of Economic Development, Ministry of International Trade and Ministry of Economy and Finance are mainly responsible

---

[1] According to the European Venture Capital Report (EVCR) 2016, the size of Italian venture capital increased from 98 million euros in 2015 to 162 million euros in 2016 (vs. 2.7 billion euros in France, 2 billion euros in Germany, and 611 million euros in Spain in 2016).

for SMEs, innovation, and entrepreneurship. For instance, the ministries carry out research on SME development, formulate relevant policies, give feedback on the situation and opinions of SMEs, and simplify administrative application procedures.

Fiscal and Financial Support

The Italian government supported the internationalization of innovative start-ups and SMEs through financial subsidies to enhance their international competitiveness and influence. The "Trademarks + 3" was open for application in March 2018.

The program provides subsidies totaling 3,825,000 euros for SMEs applying for registration in the European Union Intellectual Property Office (EUIPO) and the World Intellectual Property Organization (WIPO). In order to promote the internationalization of SMEs' brands, improve their innovation capacity and competitiveness, and enhance their international competitiveness and influence, the Italian government began to implement the "Trademarks + 2" plan in 2015. To encourage SMEs to register trademarks in the EUIPO and the WIPO, SMEs are grant subsidies of up to 20,000 euros under the plan. The "Industria 4.0" plan provides tax relief and preferential policies to innovative start-ups and SMEs. Starting from 2017, capital investors of innovative start-ups and SMEs may receive a 30% (vs. maximum deduction up to 25% and 27% over the past years) deduction of personal income tax or enterprise income tax. These incentive measures are applicable to venture capital, Collective Investment Undertakings (CIUs), asset management companies, and investment companies mainly investing in start-ups, innovative enterprises, and SMEs.

The new super-and hyper-depreciation taxation system has increased the nominal purchase cost of depreciation calculation of new machinery and equipment by 40 and 150%, respectively, resulting in a substantial and long-term decrease in the taxable income of enterprises. The application of super-depreciation or hyper-depreciation depends on the type of new machinery and equipment. Tangible assets such as the Internet of Things, big data, cloud computing and augmented reality technologies, and connectivity devices will adopt hyper-depreciation (150%), while the rest will adopt super-depreciation (40%).

The R&D credit is given to R&D projects. From 2017 to 2020, companies that increase R&D costs will receive a tax credit of 50% of the incremental costs (deducted from the tax payable), with a maximum credit of 20 million euros per year, up from the previous maximum of 25% or 5 million euros.

The Italian government's Innovative Startups Policy/Innovative SMEs Policy provides tax exemptions and financing supports for innovative enterprises, start-ups, and innovative SMEs.

Innovative start-up companies and accredited incubators can be exempted from stamp duty and business registration fees, without paying the annual chamber fees, and are entitled to a maximum exemption of 50,000 euros of value-added tax. In this way, innovative start-up companies avoid liquidity risk in the fragile stage of venture investment. Unlike innovative enterprises and start-ups, SMEs are imposed no limits on duration in that they are exempted from stamp duty when registered with a specific department of the Business Registration Department.

For companies or individuals investing in innovative enterprises or start-ups/innovative SMEs, 30% of the company/individual investment will be exempted from the corporate income tax or personal income tax, with the maximum exemption limit of 1.8 million euros for companies and 1 million euros for individuals. Innovative enterprises or start-ups/innovative SMEs are able to conduct equity crowdfunding on authorized websites. The Italian government has simplified the procedures to enable crowdfunding to be conducted online throughout the process and has added two types of investors, i.e., professional investors on request and investors in support of innovation, including angel investors.

The Italian Trade Agency provides business assistance in the international market for innovative enterprises or start-ups/innovative SMEs, while start-ups may be entitled to a 30% discount on the charges for this service.

The Italian Guarantee Fund for Small and Medium Enterprises (FGPMI) provides a financing guarantee for SMEs with a maximum guarantee ratio of 80% and a maximum guarantee amount of 2.5 million euros. In 2013, the Italian government standardized and simplified the operation of the FGPMI and optimized the financing guarantee for innovative start-ups and certified incubators, which not only exempted the cost of credit but also provided guarantee priority channels for such enterprises. For example, if an enterprise has a bank credit rating, its application will be submitted to the fund management committee for approval with priority and may increase its credit line by applying for a personal guarantee. From the issuance of the first guarantee in 2013 to June 30, 2017,

3062 guarantees were issued, benefiting 1748 innovative start-ups with a guarantee amount of about 740 million euros. Among them, the total amount of guaranteed credit in the past four years was about 323 million euros, while in the past calendar year, innovative enterprises and start-ups received 200 million euros of new bank loans under guarantee.[2]

Entrepreneur Services

The Italian government has been placing a high priority on technology R&D and innovation of SMEs. It encourages SMEs to carry out R&D and innovation activities. Tax credits, Technology Innovation Fund (FIT) and the Research and Development Fund (FAR), and way of vouchers are put in place to support SMEs.

The Stability Law L190/2014 in 2015 introduced a 25% tax credit for the incremental investment of enterprises in R&D in 2015–2019. If new investment is related to the employment of highly qualified personnel, the tax credit will be increased to 50%. As part of the Stability Law, the government has provided a total of 4.7 billion US dollars (equivalent to 3.5 billion euros) in financial incentives to private employers who permanently employ new employees. The law also reduced regional taxes on production activities. The Paten Box 2015 provides incentives for the use of intellectual property rights, industrial patents, trademarks, designs, and processes in the legal protection fields of industry, commerce, and science.

The Italian FIT supports the knowledge innovation and achievement transformation of SMEs and encourages the establishment of industry research centers. The fund is supervised by Italy's former Ministry of Production Activities (now the Ministry of Economic Development) and mainly supports the industrialization and commercialization of research results for the purpose of developing new technologies, processes, and products. The fund's support for research activities that meet the standards is mainly in the following forms: (1) subsidized financing, which provides research projects costing less than 3 million euros with a 50% subsidy loan for research costs at 20% of the benchmark interest rate; and (2) interest rate subsidy, which covers 50% of the research costs for research projects costing more than 3 million euros and payments are

---

[2] Evaluation and Prospect of G20 Members' Policies to Support Entrepreneurship in the Post-pandemic Era, Entrepreneurship Research Center on G20 Economies, Oct 22, 2020.

made in advance, discounted at the current benchmark interest rate on the bank loan payment date. In addition, the direct subsidy for research expenses is 20%, which can also be a subsidy that increases the nominal cost of small enterprises by 20% or medium-sized enterprises by 10%.

The Italian FAR encourages national scientific research institutions and enterprises to jointly carry out scientific R&D and provides technical support for the improvement of production technology. The fund is managed by the Italian Ministry of Education, Universities, and Research and mainly supports applied research projects, national research programs, international cooperation projects in applied research projects conducted by some authorized laboratories. Only scientific research consortia composed of enterprises and universities or scientific research institutions can apply for this funding, and no single party has the right to apply for it. In general, the funding form is low-interest loans, which in principle do not exceed 55% of the total research funds, but the proportion of loans to SMEs can be up to 65%. Enterprises may apply for part of the grant, but the amount cannot exceed 50% of the loan amount. If an enterprise applies for a full grant, the grant generally does not exceed 35% of the total research funds and 40% for SMEs. 10% of the fund is available for technical training.

In order to promote e-commerce, the Italian government passed a regulation in 2014 to implement e-vouchers for SMEs, who can use it to develop e-commerce solutions, provide broadband Internet connection, and provide qualified training for employees among others. Each enterprise may have a voucher of no more than 10,000 euros, with a maximum deduction of 50% of the total eligible expenses.

In 2017, the Italian government announced the continuation of the two projects: Italia Startup Visa (ISV) and Italia Startup Hub. The ISV program was launched in 2014. All foreigners holding an ISV can enter Italy to start a business independently or jointly with others. The ISV may be applied for in English online for free, which also allows business teams to submit joint applications. As of June 30, 2017, 252 applications for Italia Startup Visa had been received and 151 (59.9%) of which had been approved. The main reason for the rejection was the lack of project innovation. In the first six months of 2017, 91 applications were received, a significant increase over the 99 applications for the whole year in 2016. There were 44 in 2015 and 18 in 2014.

The Italian Startup Hub Program, launched at the end of the same year, allows non-EU nationals holding Italian residence permits to change residence permits into Permit for Startup Self-Employment after the permit expires so that they could stay in Italy and start innovative enterprises. As of June 30, 2017, six applications had been received, two from South Korea, two from Iran, one from the United States, and one from Malaysia. All applications were approved and eventually, two start-up companies were set up, Recyclinnovas.r.l.s. and Armnets.r.l.

As to the digitalization, Digital Promotion Plan encourages (larger) SMEs to actively communicate to establish contacts, build transnational digital manufacturing projects, share successful cases and digital solutions online, and exchange management experiences of digital centers. And on March 12, 2020, the Italian Minister for Technological Innovation and Digitization launched the Digital Solidarity program, in response to the outbreak of Covid-19. Digital Solidarity is an online platform created by the Italian Government that allows companies to set up their services and users to register. As the government encourages all businesses to provide free services, most of the use of the platform is currently free of charge, especially for services related to online office and business, with free access to teleconferencing, cloud data, and other services for both businesses and employees.

Entrepreneurship Education

There was a culture of encouraging entrepreneurship in Italian history. The current Italian government has also recognized the importance of youth entrepreneurship and committed itself to various policies and actions to create a culture of youth entrepreneurship.

In the past decade or so, the Italian government has put forward the National Youth Plans and set up the Department for Youth and the National Youth Agency. Among them, the National Youth Agency plays an important role, such as "encouraging young people's initiative, creativity and entrepreneurship". The Italian government also cooperates with non-governmental organizations, for example, the Confindustria, a public NGO, and young entrepreneurs jointly launched the National Business Plan Competition. Policies and measures to support youth entrepreneurship at the EU level, such as the European Social Fund, the Youth Employment Initiative and the Youth Guard. Italy's support for youth entrepreneurship is mainly tilted to innovative high-tech projects founded by university graduates, for instance, large-scale training programs such as Smart Startup, and programs initiated by non-governmental organizations (public: Unioncamere and the Chambers of Commerce, Confindustria's Young Entrepreneurs' Network; private: ItaliaCamp, Confcommercio).

Italian universities have set up entrepreneurship-related courses to promote the development of entrepreneurship among students and researchers. The School of Engineering and Architecture of Bologna University has offered an entrepreneurship education course called "Technology Entrepreneurship", which aims to develop students' awareness of entrepreneurship and the ability to identify opportunities for technology entrepreneurship. The University of Padova launched a graduate student training program for entrepreneurship and innovation in 2018, with its main goal to train future entrepreneurs and managers. The course includes both theoretical knowledge learning and learning-by-doing.

Entrepreneurship education is still at an early stage in Italy's secondary schools. Italy has a development path in technical and vocational education at the national level. Although there is no specific guidance for entrepreneurship education, the government has made sound progress. For example, the Jobs Act (Decree 15 June 2015, n.81) requires an increase in entrepreneurship-related training programs for high school teachers. Some secondary schools have also launched pilot programs. Under the sponsorship of the Ministry of Labor and Social Policies, Italia Lavoro provides technical support for secondary schools and universities to improve students' ability to shift from school to work by strengthening vocational guidance and links between schools and local industries. The "School, Creativity and Innovation" award set up by the Italian Unioncamere is an annual competition award for entrepreneurship education in primary and secondary schools to promote creativity and innovation among the youth and their schools.

FAIR COMPETITION FOR SMEs

Italian anti-trust law prohibits one operator or several operators as a whole from abusing their market dominance in the domestic market or a substantial part of the domestic market. Such acts include directly or indirectly imposing unfair purchase and sale prices or other unfair contract terms; restricting the production of goods, channels of distribution, market entry, investment, development of technology or improvement of technology; treating counterparties differently with significantly different terms that put certain counterparties at a competitive disadvantage in the market; and attaching other obligations that are not necessarily linked to the contract in any way.

In addition, when the concentration of operators reaches a certain limit, it should be reported to the competent authority for approval. Through the declaration system of concentration of operators, Italian anti-trust law eliminates the high concentration of operators which is not conducive to the development of SMEs. In 2013, the Amendments to the Competition and Fair Trading Act changed the pre-merger filing threshold as follows: firstly, the total turnover of mergers and acquisitions in Italy (including the acquirer and the acquired party) exceeded 468 million euros; secondly, the total turnover of the acquired party in Italy exceeded 47 million euros. This threshold will be adjusted according to the annual GDP price deflator.

Japan

The Japanese government provides subsidies for SMEs, especially those using local industrial resources. The Japanese government allocated 46 billion yen (equivalent to 407 million US dollars) to subsidize economic entities such as SMEs in the fiscal year 2017. Tax cuts and preferential policies have also been provided for SMEs. The 2016 Tax Reform Outline stipulated policies such as reducing tax rates, providing tax credits for employees' wages, and tax preferential policy for the depreciation of fixed assets. The Japanese government also provides loans and guarantees for SMEs and micro-businesses through JFC. For SMEs affected by natural disasters, the Japanese government has set up special loan projects as well as a credit guarantee system. Venture capital, together with the Angel Tax System and the Japan Association of Securities Dealers Automated Quotation (JASDAQ), also provides financing channels for SMEs.

The Japanese government highlights the importance of transferring R&D achievements from public research institutions to private sectors. Following the Small Business Innovation Research (SBIR) model in the US, Japan's SBIR has been formulated to promote the innovation of SMEs. In addition, the Japanese government supports the market development of start-ups and SMEs through government procurement, with an emphasis on promoting fair trade between subcontracting enterprises and subcontractors. The Basic Policies for Future-Oriented Trade Practices were issued in September 2016. Based on these policies, the execution standard of the Act against Delay in Payment of Subcontracting Proceed was revised in December 2016 and the Subcontract G-men Door-to-Door Investigation began in January 2017. The Japanese government also promoted this work by other means, such as inter-ministerial liaison meetings and investigation interviews. In May 2016, the Strategy to Boost Export Power of Agriculture, Forestry and Fisheries was formulated, which would bring huge overseas market opportunities for SMEs. After the epidemic, the Japanese government provided support for the digital transformation of MSMEs by establishing a special framework for the government's original productive development support, relaxing the application requirements, and increasing the subsidy rate and ceiling.

SMRJ provides entrepreneur services and support for entrepreneurs through incubators nationwide. It also provides online services including J-GoodTech and CEO Network Enhancing Project to help SMEs expand domestic and overseas markets and establish business networks.

The Startup School Accreditation Scheme began in the fiscal year 2017 to provide services for start-up schools that meet the Japanese government's accreditation standards. Since 2017, Japan has launched a number of entrepreneurship training campaigns for young people and women, such as the Global Tech EDGE NEXT program and the Tokyo Women's Entrepreneurship Acceleration Program. JFC organizes the High School Student Business Plan Grand Prix every year to improve high school students' entrepreneurial ability. International cooperation is a key feature of Japanese entrepreneurship education. The Consortium for Next-Generation Entrepreneurship Education led by Waseda University was established in 2017.

Japan's anti-trust law restricts the abuse of market dominance by large enterprises. At the same time, Japan's anti-trust law also has provisions on the exemption of SMEs, provided that the merger cannot restrict the competition of other enterprises. In terms of enterprise merger regulation, Japan attaches importance to the use of industrial policies to guide SMEs to implement horizontal and vertical mergers. In addition, the Law on Prohibiting Private Monopoly and Ensuring Fair Trade clearly expresses special protection for SMEs in the design of fine system.

GOVERNMENT SERVICES

The Act on Strengthening the Management of SMEs came into effect on July 1, 2016. This law provides the policy framework to improve SMEs' productivity. According to this law, firms can get tax and financial supports. The law also supports the development of SMEs through organizations such as chambers of commerce and local financial institutions.

The Industrial Competitiveness Enhancement Act promulgated by the Japanese government in December 2013 was formulated in accordance with the Japan Revitalization Strategy (approved by the Japanese Cabinet on June 14, 2013) with the aim of revitalizing the Japanese economy, promoting industrial development, and enhancing the competitiveness of start-ups in Japan. According to this act, local governments and private sectors should work together to provide support for start-ups. Specifically, local governments formulate the Start-up Support Business Plans according to the central government's Business Start-up Support Implementation Guidelines and submit them to the central government for approval. Besides, according to this act, qualified start-ups can get subsidies from local governments, with a maximum of 2 million yen (equivalent to 18,000 US dollars).

METI has set up the Small and Medium Enterprise Agency to guide and support the development of SMEs. SMRJ is responsible for formulating national SME policies, helping SMEs obtain more financial support, and providing management advice. Policies are implemented and services are provided through organizations such as Japan External Trade Organization (JETRO), National Federation of Small Business Associations, JFC, Shoko Chukin Bank, Japan Chamber of Commerce and Industry (JCCI), and Credit Guarantee Corporation.

FISCAL AND FINANCIAL SUPPORT

The Japanese government provides subsidies for SMEs. Specifically, the government encourages SMEs to use local industrial resources. Local industrial resources refer to local production technologies, agricultural products, and tourism resources, which are identified by county-level administrative authorities. Approved business plans involving these resources may apply for subsidies up to 5 million yen (equivalent to 44,200 US dollars). This subsidy policy is part of the government's SBIR program. In the fiscal year 2017, the Japanese government allocated 46 billion yen (equivalent to 407 million US dollars) to subsidize economic entities such as SMEs.

Tax cuts and preferential policies were also provided for SMEs. The 2016 Tax Reform Outline adjusted the income tax of SMEs. From April 2016, the corporate income tax rate for SMEs with revenue lower than 8 million yen (equivalent to 70,000 US dollars) fell from 19 to 15%. This policy lasted until March 2018. For SMEs with revenue higher than 8 million yen (equivalent to 70,000 US dollars), the corporate income tax rate was dropped from 23.9 to 23.4% from April 2016 and further dropped to 23.2% from March 2018. Besides, the 2016 Tax Reform Outline also gave tax credits up to 22% to SMEs that increased the wages of their employees. Finally, the outline also stipulated that SMEs using certain production equipment (e.g., machinery, tools, and software) could benefit from a one-time depreciation or be entitled to a 7% tax credit.

The Japanese government also provides loans and guarantees for SMEs through JFC. JFC is a state-owned enterprise established in 2008. In 2016, the Japanese government authorized JFC to provide 7 loans and guarantee projects. For example, the Safety Net Loans Program provided loans up to 768 million yen (equivalent to 6.8 million US dollars) to SMEs whose revenue or profit was affected by short-term economic fluctuations. The Managerial Improvement Loans for Micro Business provided low-interest loans for micro-enterprises without guarantee. It granted 36,863 loans in the fiscal year of 2016, totaling 218.7 billion yen (equivalent to 1.937 billion US dollars). The SME and Micro-Business Management Enhancement Loan/Guarantee Program was committed to the diversification and business transformation of SMEs and micro-businesses. Women, young people, and advanced start-up companies can get loans at a rate 0.4% below the benchmark interest rate. The Safety Net Guarantees provided guarantees for SMEs affected by the bankruptcy of their business partners, natural disasters, etc.

For SMEs affected by natural disasters, the Japanese government has set up special loan projects for the East Japan Earthquake and Kumamoto Earthquake. From its establishment in 2011 to December 2016, the East Japan Earthquake Special Loan Project granted 297,000 loans with a total amount of 6.357 trillion yen (equivalent to 56.313 billion US dollars). As of the end of 2016, the Kumamoto Earthquake Special Loan Project granted a total of 12,000 loans with a total amount of 165 billion yen (equivalent to 1.461 billion US dollars). The Japanese government has also launched the Disaster-Related Guarantees and Safety Net Guarantees, which aim to reduce the interest burden on SMEs caused by disasters.

The total amount of venture capital in Japan in 2016 was 104.8 billion yen (equivalent to 928 million US dollars), with 1025 transactions. Capital flowed to seed enterprises (23.9%), early enterprises (42.9%), expansion enterprises (23.8%), and mature enterprises (9.5%). Japan's Angel Tax System was established in 1997, and the current Angel Tax System was revised in 2008 to provide tax incentives for investors investing in start-ups and selling shares of unlisted start-ups. Besides, in 1991, the Japanese government introduced the JASDAQ following the practices of the United States. JASDAQ encourages SMEs with high potential, especially high-tech enterprises, to enter the capital market.

Entrepreneur Services

Technical Services

The Japanese government highlights the importance of transferring R&D achievements from public research institutions to private sectors. Following the SBIR model in the US, Japan's SBIR has been formulated to promote the innovation of SMEs and enhance SMEs' participation in national research programs.

Every fiscal year, SBIR has a budget to subsidize SMEs. Qualified research projects are entitled to loan benefits. For example, low-interest loans up to a maximum of 600 million yen (equivalent to 5.315 million) are provided by the New Business Development Fund, with special interest rates in the first five years. Women, Young People/Senior Entrepreneurs Support Funds provide loans of up to 720 million yen (equivalent to 6.378 million US dollars) to women, young people, or experienced entrepreneurs. SBIR's website has set up a page for each SME qualified for the SBIR subsidy, with information on their R&D and commercialization. SBIR is also actively involved in connecting SMEs with financial institutions and facilitating the establishment of business partnerships.

Market Support

The Japanese government supports the market development of start-ups and SMEs through government procurement, with an emphasis on promoting fair trade between subcontracting enterprises and subcontractors. According to the Act on Ensuring the Receipt of Orders from the Government and Other Public Agencies by Small and Medium-Sized Enterprise, government agencies should take actions in government procurement to enhance SMEs' possibility of winning the bid. Actions that can be taken include setting up supplier qualification, separately extending contracts, and splitting out contracts to reduce purchase quantities. In addition, the Japanese government issued the "Basic Policies for Future-Oriented Trade Practices" in September 2016 to promote fair trade between major subcontracting enterprises and subcontractors. In particular, these policies stress the need to strictly prevent major subcontracting enterprises from forcing their subcontractors to pay the costs that should be borne by major subcontracting enterprises. At the same time, they require major subcontracting enterprises to improve the payment conditions for subcontracting costs, taking cash payment as the basic rule. Based on these policies, the Japanese government revised the execution standard of the Act Against Delay in Payment of Subcontracting Proceed in December 2016.

In January 2017, the Japanese government began the Subcontract G-men Door-to-Door Investigation. The Small and Medium Enterprise Agency planned to appoint Subcontract G-Men to interview 2000 or more SME subcontractors every year. The information obtained from the interviews would be shared with firms and industry organizations when necessary, under the premise of confidentiality, in order to urge the promotion of fair trade. The Japanese government also promoted this work by other means, such as inter-ministerial liaison meetings and investigation interviews. In December 2015, the Japanese Prime Minister's Office held its first liaison meeting to assess the actual trading environment of SME subcontractors and review the necessary improvements. Till March 2017, 11 liaison meetings were held. From December 2015 to March 2016, more than 15,000 large enterprises were surveyed in writing, while 10,000 SMEs were surveyed online and 200 subcontractors were interviewed.

The Japanese government formulated the Strategy to Boost Export Power of Agriculture, Forestry and Fisheries in May 2016, promoting cooperation between the public and private sectors, and setting a target of exporting 1 trillion yen (equivalent to 8.86 billion US dollars) by 2020. One of the actions called for in the strategy is to take advantage of the popularity of Japanese food and expand the overseas market of Japanese food and food culture.

Enterprise Incubation

SMRJ has 32 incubators nationwide and 2 new Business Creation Hubs in Tokyo to provide workspace leasing services, organize consulting and training activities for entrepreneurs, and establish links among potential business partners.

Communication Platform

J-GoodTech online service provided by SMRJ helps Japanese SMEs establish ties with overseas enterprises. At present, the platform has more than 7000 active registered users at home and abroad. "Rin crossing", another online service, links small conventional handicraft enterprises with buyers. The CEO Network Enhancing Project of SMRJ helps Japanese SMEs establish business partnerships with overseas companies through on-site visits, business meetings, lectures, and network activities. From 2012 to 2016, a total of 10,285 business talks were held. 775 CEOs from overseas and 3288 Japanese SMEs participated in the project.

Digital Transformation Support

Japanese government provided support for the digital transformation of MSMEs by establishing a special framework for the government's original productive development support after the epidemic, relaxing the application requirements, and increasing the subsidy rate and ceiling. Priority approval may be given to businesses that are actively engaged in life and business to overcome the impact of the epidemic.[1]

On April 8, 2020, the Japanese government announced an additional package of 86.4 trillion yen (16.4% of GDP) in economic measures, including 10.2 trillion yen to support telecommuting for businesses. Small

---

[1] Assessment on the progress of G20 Entrepreneurship Action Plan, Entrepreneurship Research Center on G20 Economies, Oct 22, 2019.

and medium-sized businesses and small-scale operators that introduce IT equipment that enables them to work remotely from home and improve their work efficiency during the epidemic period, and set up teleworking systems, receives a subsidy of 300,000 to 4.5 million yen (about $30–40 thousand) at a rate of 50%, with the rate increased to a special framework or specific purposes (e.g., responding to supply chain damage). MSMEs that have been certified for telecommuting receive a special tax discount (up to 20% of taxable corporate income tax). The government supports office equipment manufacturers in providing digital services to MSMEs by providing funding.[2]

Entrepreneurship Education

The Start-up School Accreditation Scheme began in the fiscal year 2017 to provide services for start-up schools that meet the Japanese government's accreditation standards. These certified schools are run by school management companies and provide basic entrepreneurship courses including finance, taxation, and business planning.

Since 2017, Japan has launched a number of entrepreneurship training campaigns for young people and women. The Global Tech EDGE NEXT Program is an ongoing project funded by the Japanese government to train global entrepreneurial talents and establish an ecosystem for entrepreneurship. The education program is provided by four universities, namely, Tokyo University, Tsukuba University, Ochanomizu University, and Shizuoka University.

The Acceleration Program in Tokyo for Women launched by the Tokyo municipal government provides short-term intensive training courses for Tokyo women aspiring to expand their business scale. It aims at improving their management skills and setting up a platform for them to expand their interpersonal network. This program plans to develop several role models of female entrepreneurs, stimulating women's entrepreneurial enthusiasm.

Since the fiscal year of 2013, JFC has organized the High School Student Business Plan Grand Prix every year to improve high school

---

[2] Evaluation and Prospect of G20 Members' Policies to Support Entrepreneurship in the Post-pandemic Era, Entrepreneurship Research Center on G20 Economies, Oct 22, 2020.

students' entrepreneurial ability. JFC also sends professionals with experience in helping start-up projects to give lectures in high schools. By using the knowledge gained from 26,000 start-ups funded by JFC, the company is able to solve problems encountered by high school students who are developing their business plans. The content of these plans has become increasingly diversified. For example, senior high school students in various regions wanted to address the problem of population reduction. They developed business plans to revitalize the regions, such as using local resources to cooperate with local industries and enterprises. Another example is the SGH Program initiated by the Ministry of Education, Culture, Sports, Science and Technology (MEXT), which supports students' business plans with international perspectives.

International cooperation is a key feature of Japanese entrepreneurship education. The Consortium for Next-Generation Entrepreneurship Education led by Waseda University was established in July 2017. The consortium consists of four universities and 31 institutions (including scientific research institutes, enterprises, and government agencies) from Asia, Europe, and North America. The project was selected under the EDGE NEXT program of the MEXT. The EDGE NEXT program aims to connect universities at home and abroad to promote commercialization of scientific research and cultivate entrepreneurial talents. Currently, five research projects led by five universities (Tohoku University, Tokyo University, Nagoya University, Kyushu University, and Waseda University) have been selected. The Waseda University-led consortium will run for five years from 2017 to 2022, with a total enrollment of 5200 students.

Fair Competition for SMEs

Japan's anti-trust law restricts the abuse of market dominance by large enterprises, which plays a good role in regulating the possible behaviors of restricting competition and hindering the sound development of the market. At the same time, Japan's anti-trust law also has provisions on the exemption of SMEs, provided that the merger cannot restrict the competition of other enterprises. For example, in the Law on Prohibiting Private Monopoly and Ensuring Fair Transaction, it is stipulated that the merger behavior that may cause substantial restriction on competition in a certain field is illegal, but the joint behavior between SMEs, which has a positive impact on consumers, is not prohibited.[3]

In terms of enterprise merger regulation, Japan attaches importance to the use of industrial policies to guide SMEs to implement horizontal and vertical mergers. Horizontal union is to unite many SMEs together, so that capital is relatively concentrated and the production scale of SMEs is expanded; the vertical union is to add SMEs to the large enterprise system vertically, form "enterprise series", and realize professional cooperation. These are to improve the competitiveness of SMEs through the indirect expansion of enterprise scale. In addition, Japan also restricts the expansion of large enterprises to the production and operation fields exclusive to SMEs, and has enacted laws such as the Department Adjustment Law and the Large-Scale Retail Store Law.

In addition, the Law on Prohibiting Private Monopoly and Ensuring Fair Trade clearly expresses special protection for SMEs in the design of fine system. (1) Clarifying the definition standard of SMEs in anti-trust law. (2) Applying anti-trust penalty exemption to SMEs. (3) Setting a lower penalty rate for SMEs.

[3] Wang Xiaohua. Research on Competition Law [M]. China Legal Publishing House 1999.

Korea

In terms of fiscal and financial support, the South Korean government has implemented tax cut incentives for innovation, entrepreneurship, and provided policy loan support for SMEs. The corporate tax of SMEs in South Korea can be reduced by 5–30%. In addition, investment in the commercialization of core technologies and investment in facilities or equipment to improve productivity can be deducted from the corporate income tax. In July 2017, the South Korean government provided loans of 800 billion won (equivalent to 750 million US dollars) for SMEs in the form of "SME Policy Grants" through the supplementary budget. A financing system composed of SBC and banks provides financing support for South Korean start-ups and SMEs. Among them, the Bank of Korea, the central bank of South Korea, increased the credit limit for SMEs in 2015 and 2017, respectively, bringing the total size of the Bank Intermediated Lending Support Facility to 25 trillion won (equivalent to 23.37 billion US dollars). Angel investment has become the main sector of South Korean venture capital, expanding financing channels for South Korean start-ups and SMEs. By the end of 2016, total angel investment in South Korea posted 212.6 billion won (equivalent to 198 million US dollars), a record high. In addition, the legalization of crowdfunding in South Korea and the Korean Securities Dealers Automated Quotations (KOSDAQ) market provide diversified financing channels for start-ups.

© The Author(s), under exclusive license to Springer Nature Singapore Pte Ltd. 2022
J. Gao et al., *G20 Entrepreneurship Services Report*,
https://doi.org/10.1007/978-981-16-6787-9_14

The globalization of SMEs is one of the most important policy objectives of the Ministry of SMEs and Startups (MSS) in South Korea, and also an important service measure for start-ups and entrepreneurs. To this end, South Korea has implemented an export promotion program that includes a series of projects, such as the establishment of an export support center and the implementation of the "Global Highway Program". In 2016, the Online Reverse-Direct Purchase Store Project for Best SME Products will be implemented, combining SMEs with large enterprises to expand overseas markets using the online platform of large enterprises. In addition, South Korea signed several free trade agreements and MOUs with many countries. The South Korean government has also set up a platform for the exchange of information and experience among entrepreneurs. For example, more than 10 own hall-type meetings were held in all parts of South Korea in 2017 to help South Korean exporters share best practices of major exporters. The slogan is "Startup 101, Pick Me Up". In March, 2021, South Korea government has proposed a goal of raising the services sector's share of GDP, it will support the construction of a smart digital system of 100,000 mom-and-pop shops and 1350 SMEs and start-ups to implement automation such as digital payment solutions. The industry-wide digital transformation helps adding new jobs for young workers in the information and communication technology sector.

At the government level, South Korea has a number of entrepreneurship training programs for the population, including youth and college students, in such fields as software. Relevant indicators of entrepreneurship education in South Korean higher learning institutions are the indicators for universities to obtain financial support. South Korean higher learning institutions attach importance to cooperation in entrepreneurship education among themselves, jointly launching various campaigns and creating platforms for entrepreneurship. In addition, South Korea's "Work-Study Dual System" has special training programs for students from high schools and higher vocational colleges. The efforts made by the South Korean government and universities in the field of entrepreneurship education have promoted the development of entrepreneurship and entrepreneurship culture in South Korea.

On December 9, 2020, the Korean National Assembly formally deliberated and adopted the Fair Trade Law[1] (Draft), which would be officially implemented one year after the date of promulgation.

South Korea's anti-trust law only prohibits the combination of enterprises that essentially restrict competition in a certain trading field. For mergers with enterprises, Korean anti-trust law has special exemption clauses for mergers of innovative SMEs.

GOVERNMENT SERVICES

Before the establishment of the MSS in 2017, the Department of SMEs was the driving force of the South Korean entrepreneurship support system. In 2017, Moon Jae-in was elected as the 19th President of South Korea, who launched a new round of restructuring of government agencies, upgraded the Department of SMEs office to the MSS, merged relevant managing authorities of small merchants, self-employed, and SMEs into a single authority, and formulated unified policies and measures to improve policy effectiveness.

The MSS aims to promote the shift of the economic structure to SMEs and venture capital enterprises, and is responsible for creating a social environment that encourages innovation and entrepreneurship, creating a good growth environment for SMEs, and promoting cooperation Ministry of SMEs and Startups. Moon Jae-in's government plans to release 2.5 trillion won (equivalent to 2.3 billion US dollars) every year, accounting for about 7% of the total budget, to support start-ups and SMEs.

The South Korean government has also formulated relevant laws and regulations on venture capital development. The South Korean government revised the Law on Special Measures for Developing High-Tech Enterprises in 1998 and 2002 respectively, encouraging venture investment in SMEs, introducing a stock exchange system, simplifying the merger and acquisition process of enterprises, and improving the specific

---

[1] The Exclusive Regulation and Fair Trading Law, also known as the Exclusive Regulation Law or the Fair Trading Law, namely the Korean Anti-Trust Law, which was promulgated and implemented by the Korean National Assembly on December 31, 1980. It mainly regulates the abuse of market dominance, the concentration of enterprises and economic power, improper joint behavior, and unfair trading behavior.

system for venture capital enterprises. In 1999, the Special Law on Scientific and Technological Innovation was enacted, which clearly defined the policy of supporting the development of SMEs and defined the national responsibility for the development of SMEs.

Fiscal and Financial Support

The South Korean government has implemented tax cut and policy loan incentives for innovation and entrepreneurship and SMEs.

The corporate tax of SMEs in South Korea can be reduced by 5–30%, depending on the company's geographical location, size, and type of business. The maximum amount of reduction is 100 million won (equivalent to 93,000 US dollars). This tax incentive applies to tax years up to December 31, 2020.

By the end of 2018, 10% (SMEs), 7% (medium-sized enterprises), and 5% (large enterprises) of the investment for the commercialization of core technologies will be deducted from the corporate income tax. Before the end of 2019, the investment quota of 3% (medium-sized enterprises) and 7% (SMEs) will be deducted from the corporate income tax to increase productivity, investment in facilities and equipment, and safety investment for industrial purposes. Unused tax credits can be carried forward to the next five years.

In July 2017, the South Korean government provided loans of 800 billion won (equivalent to 750 million US dollars) for SMEs in the form of "SME Policy Grants" through the supplementary budget. Of this amount, 200 billion won (equivalent to 187 million US dollars) will be loaned to SMEs for equipment investment; 200 billion won (equivalent to 187 million US dollars) to SMEs with financial difficulties; and 400 billion won (equivalent to 373 million US dollars) to start-ups.

The SME Policy Grants is a government low-interest loan to innovative start-ups and high-tech SMEs to help them solve their bank financing difficulties. It is jointly implemented by the MSS and SBC. In screening loan applicants, the MSS and SBC will give priority to start-ups and SMEs with employee recruitment plans. In the assessment, the "quality" of the job is also assessed in conjunction with wages and employee benefits. In addition, if start-ups and SMEs get loans and hire new employees within three months, the MSS and SBC will refund the interest paid by the company. For each employee hired, 0.1% of the amount, up to 2.0%, can be returned, but only if the company continues to hire new employees within six months after obtaining the loan can it get the interest refund.

The financing system composed of SBC and commercial banks, and the development of venture capital in South Korea provide diversified financing support for South Korean start-ups and SMEs.

The SBC provides financial support according to the different stages of development of SMEs (start-up—growth—restart), including providing start-up funds for start-ups, providing financial support during the growth stage, restart stage of SMEs and commercialization of research results of high-tech enterprises, and also helping enterprises to survive the unstable stage caused by natural disasters or difficulties. SBC's global cooperation plan and other consulting projects support start-ups and SMEs to enhance their global competitiveness.

The Bank of Korea is the central bank of South Korea and the main institution providing low-interest loans to small businesses. In 2017, the Bank of Korea said in its report to the parliament that it would improve the credit policy of the Bank's Intermediate Lending Support Facility, include enterprises with difficulty in corporate restructuring in the scope of loan support, and increase the total loan limit for SMEs by 5 trillion won (equivalent to 4.67 billion US dollars), bringing the total size of the Bank's Intermediate Lending Support Facility to 25 trillion won (equivalent to 23.37 billion US dollars). In 2015, the Bank of Korea raised the loan limit for SMEs by 5 trillion won (equivalent to 4.67 billion US dollars) and the Bank's Intermediate Lending Support Facility reached 20 trillion won (equivalent to 18.7 billion US dollars).

Angel investment has become the main sector of South Korean venture capital, expanding financing channels for South Korean start-ups and SMEs.

By the end of 2016, total angel investment in South Korea posted 212.6 billion won (equivalent to 198 million US dollars). Of these, 174.7 billion won (equivalent to 163 million US dollars) was invested by private investors, with a total of 3984 private investors investing 37.9 billion won (equivalent to 35.43 million US dollars) through private investment associations, a new record since 2004.

The MSS believes that the private investment associations in South Korea continue to grow and are superior to private investors in terms of expertise, economies of scale, investment risk control, and portfolio development. As of June 2017, there were 273 private investment associations with a capital of 137.8 billion won (equivalent to 129 million

US dollars). Since the end of 2015, the number of private investment associations has increased by 206.7% and the size of funds by 209.0%. In 2016, private investment associations' investment reached a record high. By August 2017, the investment had totaled 86.7 billion won (equivalent to 81.06 million US dollars).

In July 2015, the Korea's National Assembly passed a bill to legalize crowdfunding and crowdfunding websites in South Korea. Before the bill was introduced, entrepreneurs in South Korea could only use their own funds, small venture capital pools, or foreign crowdfunding platforms to raise funds.

KOSDAQ, South Korea's technology stocks market, was set up on July 1, 1996 by the Korean Securities Dealers Association after the US NASDAQ market and officially opened for trading. The South Korean Government's Plan to Revitalize the KOSDAQ includes a series of measures to promote its development, such as increasing the capital of KOSDAQ listed companies, expanding the tax exemption scope for the transfer income of KOSDAQ's listed corporations, relaxing the conditions for listing on KOSDAQ, and giving more preferential tax treatment to listed SMEs.

Entrepreneur Services

Market Support

The globalization of SMEs is one of the most important policy objectives of the Ministry of SMEs and Startups (MSS) in South Korea, and also an important service measure for start-ups and entrepreneurs. Therefore, the MSS has formulated the Export Promotion Plan, and its SMBA is responsible for its specific implementation.

The MSS has set up 14 export support centers in regional offices across the country to provide one-stop support and solve the difficulties faced by export SMEs. SMEs can not only get policy support from these export support centers, but also get policy support on exports from SBC, Korea Trade Promotion Corporation (KOTRA), and other government organizations. For example, SMEs are helped solve difficulties in certification of origin so that they could make full use of the Free Trade Agreement (FTA).

The Export Promotion Program of the MSS also includes participating in global exhibitions, sending trade delegations, and helping SMEs join international supply chains. In addition, the MSS also provides export promotion programs in policy areas such as R&D and financing, such as the "Global Highway Program".

Unlike previous programs focusing on marketing support, the "Global Highway Program" provides guidance and policy support for enterprises to enhance their global capabilities and help them grow into "strong global SMEs".

The technological development leading the market, the rapid localization, and the management system responding to the changes in the global market environment are the key factors that determine the fate of enterprises in the global market. After a period of growth, many companies have stagnated in the domestic and foreign markets due to conceptual and technical reasons. Therefore, the "Global Highway Program" helps start-ups and SMEs overcome growth stagnation, take opportunities to expand the global market, and quickly grow into strong global SMEs.

The "Global Highway Program" provides systematic and highlighted support in three steps: diagnosis of globalization capabilities, designing of globalization strategies, and provision of marketing, R&D, and financial support. In the first two steps, global consulting companies with global networks and rich consulting experience will provide consulting service and take measures to improve the enterprises' capability to go global. In the third step, enterprises, MSS, SMBA, and other government departments jointly implement these measures, so that enterprises could have customized supports.

The focus of the "Global Highway Program" is on enterprises that are currently exporting on a small scale but need to establish a global management system to expand their exports, or are in urgent need of finding a breakthrough in export stagnation.

The SMBA started to implement the Online Reverse-Direct Purchase Store Project for Best SME Products in 2016, combining SMEs with large enterprises to expand overseas markets using the online platform of large enterprises.

Since 2014, the SMBA has been implementing the Global Online Store Project for SME Products. As of the launch of the program mentioned above, 2571 SMEs have sold about 54 billion won (equivalent to 54.08 million US dollars) of products through the global online stores.

The program entrusts specialized agencies to maintain the overall sales process running on the five global online stores (Amazon, eBay, Taobao, Lotte, and Qo10), such as from product website development (translation) to promotion and final shipment. It will involve the operation platforms of three large enterprises (SK Planet, Lotte.com, Hyundai Home Shopping) and the products of about 1000 SMEs. The platform opens "Best Products Store" to promote SME products and provides the following services:

- Web page creation. Create a product web page with detailed product description and translate it into the language of the target country.
- Training and consultation. Global export training, consultation based on sales record analysis and warehousing and logistics services dedicated to global transportation of products.
- Promotion. Provide a wide range of promotional campaigns, including Korean brand sales day, purchase mileage, and free delivery vouchers.

In addition, SMEs participating in the program can also benefit from the preferential loan interest rate provided by the Shared Growth Loan Program of the Industrial Bank of Korea (IBK).

In October 2016, the SMBA signed the MOU for the Promotion of SME Exports through Online Channels with Alibaba, which is also the follow-up action of the "Online Reverse-Direct Purchase Store Project for Best SME Products" mentioned above. The MOU will allow South Korean SMEs to benefit from Alibaba's B2B platform and help SMEs with potential to expand their overseas business through a joint e-commerce training program.

The SMBA works in tandem with Alibaba to allow SMEs recommended by the South Korean government to access Alibaba's TA (Trade Assurance)[2] service. This service is expected to improve the reliability of South Korean SMEs to overseas buyers and promote online B2B transactions.

The main features of the MOU are as follows:

---

[2] TA is a service provided by Alibaba (Alibaba.com), which provides buyers with guarantees of payment, product quality, and punctual delivery. This service is currently available only to Chinese suppliers.

- Through the use of tools such as Global Gold Supplier Membership (GGS), the SMBA will cooperate to improve the user experience on the platform provided by Alibaba for SMEs in South Korea.
- Alibaba B2B platform (Alibaba.com) offers its quality members a wide range of benefits, including exposure of search results lists, mini-sites for individual suppliers, and unlimited product registration.
- The SMBA selects quality South Korean SMEs and helps them apply for and take advantage of the GGS benefits, such as subsidizing up to 70% of membership fees and helping create foreign language product pages.
- Alibaba B2B Platform (Alibaba.com) provides support such as discounts on member fees and exposure of search results lists to SMEs recommended by the SMBA.

Within the framework of the MOU, the SMBA and SBC jointly announced the establishment of an "Industrial Hub" for South Korean SMEs on Alibaba B2B platform (Alibaba.com) in March 2017 to provide diversified and quality services, including preferential recommendations in search results pages and provision of strategic convenience for them to enter the global online B2B market.

South Korea's first free trade agreement was signed with Chile in 2004. By the end of 2015, South Korea had signed free trade agreements with 51 countries. In order to promote the overseas entry and exit of South Korean SMEs and cope with changes in overseas markets, the South Korean government has also signed the MOU on SMEs with new developing countries other than FTA countries. In 2015, South Korea signed the MOU on SMEs with Kuwait, Brazil, Chile, Denmark, and Hungary. In 2018, South Korea signed the MOU on SMEs with Ecuador, which includes expanding trade and investment between the two sides, exchanging experiences and information on SME policies, formulating training and education plans, and sending experts to inspect progress. The MSS will identify and promote cooperation projects that can help South Korean SMEs enter the Ecuadorian market.

Communication Platform

The SMBA regards "expanding the global export of South Korean SMEs" as one of its primary goals in 2017. To this end, the South Korean government has also set up a platform for the exchange of information and experience among entrepreneurs.

In 2017, more than ten "town hall-type meetings" were held across South Korea to help South Korean exporters share best practices of major exporters and discuss solutions to various problems faced by exporters, such as obtaining market information and ensuring the safety of potential buyers and distribution networks. The first Exporter's Town Hall-Type Meeting was held in Seoul in April 2017, attended by about 200 representatives of exporters, SMEs, and export agencies. Unlike previous meetings attended by only a few companies, the Seoul meeting was held in the form of "town hall-type meetings", in which the groups and the audiences held two-way free discussions. At the meeting, the SMBA's director-general, chief executive officers of major exporters, senior executives of export agencies, and audiences discussed the method of "promoting exports through market/product diversification". For those entrepreneurs who could not attend the meeting, the SMBA broadcasts the meeting live on YouTube and Facebook, and entrepreneurs could take part in real time through the chat window.[3]

In May 2017, the South Korean Start-Up Youth Job Festival[4] was held at Yonsei University. This job festival was organized by the Youth Committee, SMBA, Seoul Business Agency, and seven universities, including Yonsei University. The slogan of this youth job festival is "Startup 101, Pick Me Up".

As a job fair for start-ups, the job festival selected 101 promising start-ups, such as Mimi Box, Flitto, and Wadiz, through recommendation by venture capital companies, in a bid to enhance the public opinion toward start-ups. The start-ups could get 500,000 won per month as Startup-Youth Employment Talent Grant for six months from the Youth Hope Foundation. The job festival also takes the form of literature and art programs to raise social awareness of start-ups and help the public understand their positive contribution to society. In addition, the job festival

---

[3] http://www.youtube.com/bizinfo1357, http://www.facebook.com/bizinfo1357.
[4] Official website: www.startup.kban.or.kr.

can also receive brain competence tests (200 first-time tourists), career counseling, cover letter counseling, and entrepreneurship counseling.

Digital Transformation Support

In March, 2021, South Korean government has proposed a goal of raising the services sector's share of GDP from 60 to 65% and create 300,000 new jobs by 2025. To this end, it will support the construction of a smart digital system of 100,000 mom-and-pop shops and 1350 SMEs and start-ups to implement automation such as digital payment solutions. The industry-wide digital transformation helps adding new jobs for young workers in the information and communication technology sector. The government promised to guarantee about 2 trillion won ($1.78 billion) in funding to be provided to service companies that embrace digital transformations through use of big data and artificial intelligence. Eight sectors including tourism, health care, logistics, and finance receives intensive support to improve their high-value-added services.[5]

ENTREPRENEURSHIP EDUCATION

At the government level, South Korea has a number of entrepreneurship training programs for the population, including youth and college students, in such fields as software.

The program "Leaders in Industry-University Cooperation (LINC+)", launched by the South Korean Ministry of Education and the National Research Foundation of Korea, is a large-scale financial support program with a total amount of about 300 million US dollars. The plan hopes to combine university courses with the actual needs of society, mitigate the crisis of youth employment, and solve the demand for talents in enterprises. The Korea Business Incubation Association provides short-term training for college students or assists in the start-up competition.

TWO Smart Ventures Institute, a subsidiary of the SMBA, provides a 28-week support for software-related start-ups, including education and training, consulting services, and up to 94,000 US dollars in financial support, as well as interfacing with venture capital. After the training, it

---

[5] Evaluation and Prospect of G20 Members' Policies to Support Entrepreneurship in the Post-pandemic Era, Entrepreneurship Research Center on G20 Economies, Oct 22, 2020.

will continue to help enterprises for 5 years and help start-ups achieve a 90% survival rate.

The South Korean government attaches great importance to promoting entrepreneurship education in higher learning institutions, and regards the relevant indicators of entrepreneurship education as a consideration factor for universities to obtain financial support. South Korean higher learning institutions attach importance to cooperation in entrepreneurship education among themselves, jointly launching various campaigns and creating platforms for entrepreneurship. In addition, South Korea's "Work-Study Dual System" has special training programs for students from high schools and higher vocational colleges.

The "Leading Universities for Start-up Business" program of the KISED aims to help a number of South Korean universities set up platforms for youth entrepreneurship. This program includes student entrepreneurship training, counseling, and financial support. These universities and KISED jointly organized the "Youth Entrepreneur Travel Festival" and regional start-ups exhibitions, which provided a good opportunity for entrepreneurial students to show themselves and created an entrepreneurial culture among them.

The KAIST officially launched the Startup KAIST Campaign in April 2014 with the slogan of "Stop Thinking, Start Doing". In promoting entrepreneurship culture, the KAIST organizes some activities, such as "Startup Network Program" and "Again Let's Meet Then x Doryong Venture Forum", and invites guests to speak, so that entrepreneurs can exchange information about entrepreneurship with one other. In terms of helping enterprises grow, there will be different programs to provide corresponding assistance for entrepreneurs at different stages, from stimulating students' entrepreneurial enthusiasm to establishing the basic knowledge and skills of the company, helping obtain financial support, and accelerating the development of enterprises.

The Business School of Korea University has set up a special start-up institute, which consists of two parts. The first part is an incubator, which mainly holds start-up contests and provides start-up counseling (including law, taxation, technology, and market), networking opportunities (entrepreneurs, investors), and office space. The second part is entrepreneurship education courses, which mainly include systematic courses on entrepreneurship, lectures by teachers or guests inside and outside the university, special seminars led by entrepreneurs, and related courses offered by teachers in other departments. Korea University was included in the LINC+ program of the Korean Ministry of Education and the Korea National Research Fund in 2017 and will receive about 4.6 million US dollars every year from 2017 to 2021.

Korea University has signed a cooperation agreement with Korea Institute of Science and Technology to build Anam-Hongreung Valley, a platform similar to the US Silicon Valley.

The MSIT and the MOE launched the policy of "Fostering Creative Individuals" in 2013, which includes promoting the development of vocational education, establishing a work-study dual system, and developing entrepreneurship-friendly education. The "work-study dual system" released later is a way to combine practical work with theoretical study, drawing on the German apprenticeship system. The Ministry of Labor and the MOE are responsible for the joint promotion of such system. The Uni-Tech program, which was piloted in 9 high schools since March 2015 and officially implemented in 2015, is a two-system program and is aimed at students from high schools and higher vocational colleges.

FAIR COMPETITION FOR SMES

On December 9, 2020, the Korean National Assembly formally deliberated and adopted the Fair Trade Law[6] (Draft), which would be officially implemented one year after the date of promulgation.[7]

South Korea's anti-trust law only prohibits the combination of enterprises that essentially restrict competition in a certain trading field. According to the current law, if an enterprise meets one of the following conditions, it can be presumed that there is "substantial restriction of competition" in a certain transaction field. (I) The combination of enterprises with dominant market position; (II) the combination of enterprises led by large-scale enterprises: A combination of companies with a market share of more than two-thirds of the SMEs referred to in the Basic Law

---

[6] The Exclusive Regulation and Fair Trading Law, also known as the Exclusive Regulation Law or the Fair Trading Law, namely the Korean Anti-Trust Law, which was promulgated and implemented by the Korean National Assembly on December 31, 1980. It mainly regulates the abuse of market dominance, the concentration of enterprises and economic power, improper joint behavior, and unfair trading behavior.

[7] https://www.yna.co.kr/view/akr20201209141151002; official account: Review of anti-monopoly practice; Dentons antitrust team.

for Small and Medium-Sized Enterprises; a combination of such companies can achieve a market share of more than 5%. The purpose of this system is to prevent large-scale enterprises from entering the market of SMEs, and to combine enterprises that disturb the competition order.

For mergers with enterprises, Korean anti-trust law has special exemption clauses for mergers of innovative SMEs: "Business combination between an SME venture capital firm or SME venture capital partnership and an entrepreneur or venture capital firm as defined in the SME Venture Promotion Law" is eligible for exemption. In addition, South Korea's anti-trust law allows small-scale joint behavior under certain conditions, and the behavior of small-scale entrepreneurs or consumers to set up certain joint organizations for the purpose of mutual support is not restricted. For example, (1) for the purpose of helping each other by small-scale operators or consumers; (2) setting up an organization at will, and joining or quitting the organization at will; and (3) all members have equal right to make decisions, etc..[8]

---

[8] Ding Yuanqiang, Research on Korean Anti-Trust Law—From the Perspective of Historical Evolution, Jinan University, 2010.

Mexico

The Mexican government has helped start-ups and SMEs solve their financing problems through tax reform, guarantee system development, and special financing programs and projects, but these measures were mostly formulated before 2016. In Mexico fiscal and taxation reform, the Regime of Fiscal Incorporation (El Régimen de Incorporación Fiscal, RIF) is conducive to promoting the regularized operation of small businesses.

The National Economic Prosecutor (Fiscalía Nacional Económica, FNE) is the main financial tool of the Mexican government to support Mexican entrepreneurs and MSMEs. Through the guarantee system, it promotes loans from the commercial banking system to support entrepreneurs and small enterprises. In 2016, the total amount of the FNE was 7.2 billion pesos (equivalent to 365 million US dollars). By May 2016, the Financing Program for Entrepreneurs had supported 626 projects with 178 million pesos (equivalent to 9 million US dollars).

The High Impact Entrepreneurship Program (HIEP) provides financial subsidies for start-ups with innovative products, business models that with high-growth potential and high impact, and enterprises in the expansion period. In 2016, the program provided subsidies for 150–200 enterprises and in 2017 it is expected to subsidize 200–250 enterprises.

The Mexican government has also implemented some programs to finance start-ups and MSMEs, such as the Youth Credit Program, the

© The Author(s), under exclusive license to Springer Nature Singapore Pte Ltd. 2022
J. Gao et al., *G20 Entrepreneurship Services Report*,
https://doi.org/10.1007/978-981-16-6787-9_15

SME Productive Projects, the National Programs of Franchises, and the National Microenterprise Financing Program, and provided loans at preferential interest rates for specific groups, regions, and purposes. The Mexican government encourages the creation of venture capital funds, expands financing channels, and promotes the development of innovation and entrepreneurship by implementing the Program to Foster the Venture Capital Industry.

In terms of serving entrepreneurs, the Mexican government pays attention to the function of government procurement policy to help innovative enterprises and SMEs expand the market. The Law on Public Sector Procurement, Leasing and Services and the new government procurement network system support more MSMEs to participate in government procurement. The chapter of "government procurement" in the TPP also has favorable provisions for Mexican MSMEs, including allowing Mexican MSMEs to participate in government procurement projects in other contracting countries.

The Mexican government set up the Entrepreneurship Network (La Red de Apoyo al Emprendedor, RAE) to optimize the registration process and improve the entrepreneurial environment of start-ups. Incubators such as Endeavor, StartupMexico, 500 StartupMexico provide incubation services for entrepreneurs and start-ups. As to the digitalization, the Monterrey Digital Center was established in July 2018 to provide space for the creation of a digital transformation community. During the outbreak of Covid-19, electronic platforms were used to promote sustainable business development.

The Mexican government attaches great importance to international exchanges on innovation and entrepreneurship. For example, Mexico and France established the "Entrepreneurship and Innovation Commission Mechanism" in 2015. Mexico hosted the Startup Nations Summit 2015 as the first country in Latin America and the Caribbean.

The Mexican government has set up entrepreneurship training programs and courses and attaches great importance to promoting entrepreneurship and innovation culture in universities. The "Entrepreneur University" run by the INADEM provides entrepreneurs with a platform for online learning of entrepreneurial knowledge, as well as training programs and courses specifically for young entrepreneurs. National contests such as "National Entrepreneur Week" are conducive to fostering a culture of entrepreneurship.

The I-Corps and NoBI-U projects in cooperation with the United States focus on helping entrepreneurs understand the real market demand and commercialize technology. In Mexico, there are also special institutions to support women's entrepreneurship. For example, the Crea Communities of Social Entrepreneurs, AC (Crea) is dedicated to helping female entrepreneurs or businesswomen improve their business ability.

In 2015, the INADEM signed a cooperation agreement with the National Association of Universities and Higher Education Institutions (Asociación Nacional de Universidades e Instituciones de Educación Superior, ANUIES) to strengthen coordination and promote a culture of entrepreneurship and innovation in higher learning institutions. Represented by the Monterey Institute of Technology (Instituto Tecnológico y de EstudiosSuperiores de Monterrey), Mexican higher learning institutions have incorporated entrepreneurship education into the curriculum system and set up the Network of Centers for Entrepreneurial Families in connection with family business issues. The university has also set up incubators and accelerators to help entrepreneurs start and develop businesses.

Government Services

Mexico made strategic plans to promote entrepreneurship and strengthen the development of MSMEs in its National Development Plan 2013–2018, and proposed measures to promote innovation and entrepreneurship in its Special Plan for Science, Technology and Innovation 2014–2018. For example, the Mexican government increased national R&D investment and will increase the ratio of R&D investment to GDP from 0.43% (2013) to 1% (2018) year by year. In addition, it established a stable cooperation mechanism among universities, scientific research institutions, and enterprises, promoted knowledge transfer and transformation, and encouraged the creation of scientific and technological enterprises. Moreover, it established a national information network system for scientific and technological infrastructure, formulated open access policy, and invested in building scientific research information knowledge base.

Compared with other member states of G20 economies, the Mexican government has earlier started to create a more efficient market environment for innovation and entrepreneurship by promoting the Rapid

Business Opening System (SARE) to improve the efficiency of enterprise registration, providing one-stop service for enterprise registration, and abolishing the minimum capital requirements for the establishment of companies. In 2002, Mexico began to gradually promote the SARE system in different cities, and then launched a new business registration website www.tuempresa.gob.mx to provide one-stop shop for business registration. Entrepreneurs can register through a simplified registration process using the network. In 2013, the Mexican Corporate Law removed the minimum capital requirement for the creation of a limited liability company (SRL) and a stock company.

The Federal Law on Competitiveness Development of Micro, Small, and Medium Enterprises (2006) stipulates that the Mexican Ministry of Economy is responsible for the issuance of rules, initiation, and implementation of plans, and revision of relevant regulations. In 2013, the Mexican Ministry of Economy set up the INADEM, which is specifically responsible for innovation and entrepreneurship-related work. The INADEM, as a subsidiary of the Mexican Ministry of Economy, is responsible for the implementation and coordination and ensures the proper and effective implementation of various support policies and measures through the RAE.

Fiscal and Financial Support

The Regime of Fiscal Incorporation (El Régimen de Incorporación Fiscal, RIF) is conductive to promote regular operation of small businesses and increase tax revenue. In the 2013 Mexican fiscal and tax reform, important adjustments were made to the tax regulations for small businesses, such as introduction of the RIF to encourage unformal enterprises to be formal ones and creation of "My Account" on the website of the Mexico's Tax Administration Service to provide tax preferential policies for small businesses: Taxpayers earning less than 100,000 pesos (equivalent to 5000 US dollars) a year are exempted from VAT and special taxes on production services (IEPs) for 10 years. Enterprises with an annual income of 100,000 to 2 million pesos (equivalent to 100,000 US dollars) are entitled to a 10-year step-by-step reduction of IEPs. Through this network platform, taxpayers can register their income and expenditure, file tax returns, complete tax payment procedures and issue invoices. This measure promotes the regulated operation of small enterprises and is conducive to increasing the national tax revenue.

The fund of the FNE under the auspices of the INADEM comes mainly from the federal budget. The Mexican Ministry of Economy formulates specific regulations for its use every year, and the INADEM is responsible for its specific implementation. The FNE was established in 2014, formerly known as the Fund for the Support of the Small and Medium Enterprise (SME Fund), and is the main financial tool for the Mexican government to support Mexican entrepreneurs and MSMEs.[1] The INADEM allocates one-third of the budget of the FNE to the National Guarantee System (Sistema NacionaldeGarantías) every year to support loans to entrepreneurs and small businesses through the commercial banking system. In 2016, the FNE totaled 7.2 billion pesos (equivalent to 365 million US dollars), focusing on supporting entrepreneurs and SME financing and the use of advanced technology.

The "Financing Program for Entrepreneurs" launched by Mexico's Ministry of Economy in 2011 is a guarantee fund financed by the INADEM to encourage commercial banks to broaden their channels to help entrepreneurs raise funds. In the first two years of credit, the fund assumed 100% risk and adjusted to 75% in the third and fourth years. According to the technical complexity of entrepreneurs' projects, conventional entrepreneurs can get credit ranging from 50,000 (equivalent to 2500 US dollars) to 500,000 pesos (equivalent to 250,000 US dollars), while high-tech start-ups can get credit ranging from 350,000 (equivalent to 170,800 US dollars) to 1.5 million pesos (equivalent to 76,000 US dollars). The term of the loan was extended from 36 to 48 months and a grace period of 3–9 months was available, with interest calculated at a fixed interest rate of 13.0%. As of May 2016, the project has supported 626 projects with a total amount of 178 million pesos (equivalent to 9 million US dollars).

The INADEM launched the HIEP in 2014 to provide financial subsidies for start-ups in their expansion period with innovative products or business models, high-growth potential, and high impact. Start-ups that have passed the application review process can receive up to 170,000 US dollars, while those in the expansion stage can receive up to 280,000 US dollars in subsidies. The applications submitted by enterprises will be evaluated and examined by two groups, namely, a group composed of

---

[1] In 2004, the Mexican government set up the SME Fund, which was directly included in the national budget and was the most tightly managed and largest SME support fund project in Mexico at that time.

government staff and a group composed of industry experts with rich experience. Only those enterprises whose scores exceed the prescribed standards will be eligible for subsidies. In 2016, the project provided subsidies for 150–200 enterprises out of 1000 applications. It is expected to subsidize 200–250 enterprises in 2017. Along with the HEIP program, a study on the impact of governmental subsidies on start-ups and SMEs is also in the pipeline that 400 enterprises will be considered qualified in 1000 applications and half of which will be randomly subsidized by the government and the other half will be considered as the comparison group. The preliminary results of the study are to be produced in 2019.

The Mexican government has also implemented some programs to finance start-ups and MSMEs, such as the Youth Credit Program, the SME Productive Projects, the National Programs of Franchises, and the National Microenterprise Financing Program, and provided loans at preferential interest rates for specific groups, regions, and purposes.

The Youth Credit Program, launched in early 2015, aims to provide guaranteed commercial loans to young people aged 18–35. The plan is based on bank financing and is usually backed by loans from the INADEM. The loan can be up to 100% of the project cost with a fixed annual interest rate of 13.0%. From the beginning of the program until September 2017, 4248 loans worth 1545.5 million pesos (equivalent to 78.86 million US dollars) have been granted to young entrepreneurs.

The SME Productive Projects mainly provide loans for enterprises in rural areas, which can be used to purchase production equipment, infrastructure and up to 50% of working capital, with a maximum loan of 2 million pesos (equivalent to 100,000 US dollars) per project. The four-year loan interest rate is 12%, and a monthly repayment interest rate is as low as 6%, if monthly repayment can be ensured. The requirement for obtaining a project loan is that the enterprise needs to be registered for at least one year and contribute at least 30% of its capital to the investment of new projects.

Under Mexico's National Program of Franchises, business owners can get zero-interest loans from cooperative financial institutions to cover up to 50% of franchise expenses, but they must pay off the loans within the next 36 months. If Mexican enterprises have been operating in at least two places for more than two years, they can also be entitled to the benefits of this loan if they want to expand their business.

The National Microenterprise Financing Program, initiated by Ministry of Economy of Mexico, was the second largest project after SME

Fund at that time, with the main goal of helping low-income and poorer entrepreneurs through microfinance, loans, consulting, and training. It operates through two trust funds: the Trust of the National Program for Microenterprise Financing (FINAFIM) and the Trust of the Fund for Microfinance for Rural Women (FOMMUR).

In 2013, the INADEM formulated and began to implement the "Program to Foster the Venture Capital Industry", which aims at encouraging the creation of venture capital funds, expanding financing channels, and promoting the development of innovation and entrepreneurship. From 2013 to 2017, 142 companies from 17 different sectors had received investments with the support of more than 40 funds, totaling 28.29 million US dollars. In addition to obtaining investment, these companies or projects received guidance and consulting services on entrepreneurship and business development.

Entrepreneur Services

The Mexican government pays attention to the function of government procurement in order to regulate the advance payment and encourage more MSMEs to participate in government procurement, and uses the new government procurement network system to promote the development of MSMEs. In 2010, new rules under the Law on Public Sector Procurement, Leasing, and Services were promulgated to regulate advance payments and encourage more SMEs to participate in government procurement. According to the new rules, if the production process of the products exceeds 60 days, the winning SMEs can get 10–50% of the total contract amount in advance, and the preferential margin for international bidding will also be increased to 10–15%. The Mexican government began using the new government procurement network system in 2010. The new system established a new supplier database, added more qualified SMEs, and made public the evaluation documents for each supplier's contract performance, including the termination of the contract and the corresponding fines. Suppliers and enterprises can register on the government procurement website (compranet.gob.mx) and then receive bids and related bidding information from the website in electronic form. After Mexico joined the TPP, the government procurement section of the TPP also has favorable provisions for Mexican MSMEs: (1) Mexican MSMEs are allowed to participate in government procurement projects in other contracting member states; (2) Mexican MSMEs are facilitated to participate in government procurement projects in other contracting member states to the TPP; and (3) a special protection ratio is set for Mexican MSMEs to participate in government procurement projects in their own country.

The RAE is a digital platform for entrepreneurship support built by the INADEM to provide services for MSMEs, with the goal of receiving, processing, and tracking support requests from MSMEs and entrepreneurs in a simple, effective, and transparent manner. The RAE is a joint effort of Mexican government agencies and reputable non-governmental organizations and enterprises to provide support projects, products, services, and solutions for entrepreneurs. 695,000 registered entrepreneurs, 284 partners, 417 related organizations, and 270,000 participating enterprises had been established as of 2016.

In terms of business incubation, Mexico provides services for entrepreneurs and start-ups through, for example, Endeavor, StartupMexico, and 500 StartupMexico incubators. Endeavor was an incubator founded in 2002 and has set up nine regional centers in Mexico. Up to now, it has provided more than 20,000 hours of guidance for entrepreneurs, indirectly creating more than 8600 high-value jobs, and 50% of entrepreneurs in its incubators have patents or are applying for them. In addition, Endeavor has launched an innovative franchise strategy to attract promising entrepreneurs from all over Mexico and has set up regional offices in cooperation with top universities and local businessmen in seven states. StartupMexico Incubator, where participants can attend incubation meetings by phone to obtain products or services, or join a shared space to participate in activities and courses, has hatched 150 enterprises. The 500 StartupMexico Incubator, part of the 500 Startup Global Incubator, was established in 2011 and has invested more than 100 enterprises so far, mainly in financial technology, transportation, tourism, education, e-commerce, civic technology, and healthcare, providing incubators in Mexico City with a 16-week seed program, 47,500 US dollars in cash and service worth of 12,500 US dollars, as well as open investment courses for free.

The Mexican government attaches great importance to international exchanges on innovation and entrepreneurship. There are new mechanisms for innovation and entrepreneurship in Mexico and France, as well as global innovation and entrepreneurship competitions. In 2015, the governments of Mexico and France established the "Entrepreneurship and Innovation Commission Mechanism" with INADEM as the leading agency. The mechanism consists of three committees: The Entrepreneurship Commission, the Innovation Commission, and the Strategic Sector Commission. Under the Innovation Commission also set up Mexico-France Innovation Research Center to expand cooperation and exchanges between the two countries in the fields of intellectual property and patent protection. In 2015, the INADEM hosted the Startup Nations Summit 2015, becoming the first country in Latin America and the Caribbean to host the event, attended by 104 representatives from 60 countries and 30 innovative companies from 31 countries participating and 15,000 young entrepreneurs.

As to the digitalization, the Monterrey Digital Center was established in July 2018 to provide space for the creation of a digital transformation community, realize a fast and dynamic learning system through digital technology, and enhance the interaction among entrepreneurs, investment funds, digital talents, universities, organizations, accelerators, and other participants.[2]

During the outbreak of Covid-19, electronic platforms were used to promote sustainable business development. The Mexican Secretariat of Economy made MYPYMES MX, its e-platform, available to all MSMEs since June 2020. This e-platform provides guidance for the start-up, sales, expansion, and export of MSMEs, helping them to obtain timely information on government support measures and financing policies, and helping entrepreneurs to improve their managerial skills and enhancing the competitiveness of their businesses. In June 2020, the Mexican government launched the Solidarity Market, an online platform, in hope of helping MSMEs survive the difficulties with the solidarity of Mexican citizens. Through this platform, consumers can purchase nearby goods and services online in multiple formats, and MSMEs can discover and transact with local markets and consumers, thereby promoting the consumption of their own products and services and helping artisans, producers, and providers of certain non-essential services that may have been shut down

---

[2] Assessment on the progress of G20 Entrepreneurship Action Plan, Entrepreneurship Research Center on G20 Economies, Oct 22, 2019.

during the epidemic, with 14,989 registered transactions currently on the platform.[3]

Entrepreneurship Education

The "University of Entrepreneurs" set up by the INADEM not only contains rich entrepreneurship programs and courses, but also training programs and courses for young entrepreneurs. The INADEM has opened a platform for entrepreneurs to learn about entrepreneurship online—University of Entrepreneurs. The University of Entrepreneurs contains many training programs and courses related to entrepreneurship, such as online incubation programs, entrepreneurship leadership courses, courses on innovation, e-commerce marketing, and talent recruitment. Some courses are offered independently by the INADEM, while others are offered in cooperation with experienced enterprises in various industries, enabling entrepreneurs to acquire knowledge and skills that are closely integrated with practice. The National Entrepreneurship Week was also launched by the INADEM to promote entrepreneurship and entrepreneurship culture for a period of six days, during which several entrepreneurship training programs and forums will be organized and entrepreneurs can choose to participate according to their own conditions. National events such as the "National Entrepreneur Week" are conducive to fostering a culture of entrepreneurship.

The I-Corps and NoBI-U projects in cooperation with the United States focus on helping entrepreneurs understand the real market demand and commercialize technology. The Mexico-US I-Corps and NoBI-U projects are pilot projects of I-Corps in Mexico launched in 2015 by the National Council of Science and Technology (CONACYT) and the US-Mexican Science Foundation (FUMEC) with the support of the US National Science Foundation (NSF). In 2017, the CONACYT began to promote the project and will set up 5 NoBI-Us among universities in Mexico, each of which will be jointly built by different universities or scientific research institutions. One of the experimental sites was set up in cooperation between the Universidad Nacional Autónoma de Mexico

---

[3] Evaluation and Prospect of G20 Members' Policies to Support Entrepreneurship in the Post-pandemic Era, Entrepreneurship Research Center on G20 Economies, Oct 22, 2020.

(UNAM) and the Universidad Anahuac. The training content of the I-Corps project is based on Steven Blank's Lean Startup Theory. 23 teams selected from two universities will be instructed on commercializing the technology during the 7–8 week training period. One of the important contents is that each team will conduct no less than 100 interviews with potential customers to understand the real market demand. Of the 23 teams participating in the project in 2017, the project involves technologies in biodiesel, wastewater treatment, 3D printing, education, and medical care. Under Mexico's I-Corps pilot project in 2015, a TOCO project was relatively successful. They developed a portable instrument for cornea detection, which was recognized by the market for its high cost performance, and established a start-up to develop the new products.

In Mexico, 22% of Youth (aged 15–29) are neither in employment, education, or training (NEET). The University of Entrepreneurs of the INADEM provides learning opportunities for the youth interested in entrepreneurship. In order to improve young people's innovative entrepreneurship and international vision, the Mexican Youth Bureau (Instituto Mexicano de Juventud, Imjuve) and youth entrepreneurship related organizations (StartupMexico, PlugBridge, etc.) jointly launched the Young Course (RUMBO JUVEN) Program, an international youth entrepreneurship exchange program, for outstanding young Mexican entrepreneurs aged 18–29. The program requires entrepreneurs to have innovative products in their entrepreneurial projects, preferably at the industry leading level. Through international exchanges, they can share experiences and learn from each other and find opportunities for expanding the international market. In 2018, the program is mainly aimed at young entrepreneurs in the field of life sciences. The selected participants will travel to Boston, USA, to attend seminars and visit enterprises for a week. In 2016, the program's young entrepreneurs went to Paris, France, to visit and experience the fashion and clothing industries in Paris, and attended seminars and exchange studies with industry experts.

The Crea was established in 2008 and helps women entrepreneurs or businesswomen improve their business ability and avoid marginalization of their social and economic status. The organization and its partners have developed training programs that are closely integrated with practice. The Crea means to create opportunities and start businesses. The Crea has face-to-face training and online training. The Crea and the INADEM jointly launched the Women Moving Mexico (Mujeres-Moviendo Mexico), a face-to-face training program, which trains women entrepreneurs who want to start a business or develop their own business. The program has six training centers nationwide, providing business training, technical support, seminars, etc. This activity has set up a national network of entrepreneurs for women entrepreneurs and can provide online diagnosis and support nationwide. During the National Entrepreneurship Week organized by the INADEM, there was also a special female entrepreneur forum. Participants discussed and shared their views on the problems existing in the process of women entrepreneurship.

In October 2015, the INADEM and the ANUIES signed a cooperation agreement, aimed at strengthening coordination, promoting entrepreneurship and innovation culture in institutions of higher education, and promoting youth development and close ties with the production field. Educational institutions are invited to participate in entrepreneurial support projects and support entrepreneurs and MSMEs.

Represented by the Monterey Institute of Technology, Mexican higher learning institutions have incorporated entrepreneurship education into the curriculum system. The institute has been conducting entrepreneurship education programs since 1978. It is one of Mexico's first universities to carry out entrepreneurship education and currently has cooperation with Stanford University. The curriculum covers three parts: senior middle school, undergraduate students, and graduate students (master and doctor candidates). In Mexico, 90% of companies are family businesses. 55% of family businesses fail within two years of establishment and 85% of family businesses fail because of family problems, not business problems. In order to deal with this problem, the institute has set up a network of family business start-up centers (network of centers for entrepreneurs) to help solve the problems of small and medium-sized family businesses, pay attention to practice, improve the skills of entrepreneurs so that family businesses can achieve sustainable development and promote regional economic prosperity through the development of family businesses.

The institute set up an incubator in 2001 to help entrepreneurs transform ideas into enterprises and grow. According to the technological level of start-ups, incubators are divided into incubators of technological base, intermediate technology incubators, and social incubators. Incubators of technological base are mainly for enterprises in agricultural engineering, biotechnology, information technology, pharmaceutical engineering, aerospace, automobile, and other fields. Intermediate technology incubators are mainly for enterprises in consulting, chain, software, and other fields. Social incubators are mainly for small and microenterprises and help them solve employment problems through education and training. At present, the institute has 101 incubators all over the country, including 8 incubators of technological base, 25 intermediate technology incubators, and 67 social incubators. The institute's incubators are open to not only students, faculty, staff, and relatives, but also people who are interested in starting businesses.

The accelerator system was established in 2006, mainly for enterprises with potential to achieve high growth. Specifically, it mainly assists entrepreneurs from three aspects: market, innovation, and capital. The market side provides suggestions on international trade, market plan, value chain, and public relations. Innovation includes business model, production process improvement, and new product development. Funds include financial management, tax planning, and financing. Currently, the institute has 17 accelerators. Alumni of Monterey Institute of Technology also organized an E+E link network to bring together experienced entrepreneurs from various industries to provide more support and help for start-ups.

Russia

Russia's economy has been sluggish since 2014. Though recovered slowly from 2017, it still causes negative impact on Russian SMEs. In a bid to provide SMEs and start-ups with good legal environment, the Russian government has released a swathe of laws and regulations, including the Federal Law on State Support for Small Business in the Russian Federation and the Federal Law on the Protection of Competition. In addition, the Russian government supports and promotes the development of start-ups and SMEs by adjusting industry structure of SMEs and improving business environment. To this end, it released the SMB Development Strategy until 2030 in 2016 and launched the Scheme of "Simplifying the Registration Procedure for Entities and Individual Entrepreneurs". Russian SMEs are managed by the Department for the Development of Small and Medium-Sized Businesses and Competition, Ministry of Economic Development of Russia.

Russian government has initiated a series of financial policies to support the development of SMEs. On the one hand, it simplified the tax procedure for SMEs and reduced the tax burden through tax reform, such as expanding the scope of enterprises using the "simplified tax system" in 2016; on the other hand, the Russian central bank has eased bank regulation for SMEs in 2017. During 2017–2018, Russian central bank launched SME loan subsidies to implement the loan program with interest rate at 6.5%. Besides, Russian Federal SME Corporation has expanded the financial channels for SMEs. The growth of Russian venture investment also ameliorated the financing environment for start-ups and SMEs.

The Russian government devised strategies and plans in 2017, highlighting the importance of digital economy and supporting SMEs (digital service and R&D). In addition, it encourages universities and research institutions to cooperate with enterprises by providing continuous fiscal subsidies. Russia helps SMEs explore market by lifting procurement limits of governments and state-owned enterprises on SMEs, improving relevant measures, and providing subsidies. The Russian Network Innovation and Development Fund and the Skolkovo Fund provide incubation services for software tech start-ups. In June 2019, the Russian Ministry of Economic Development cooperated with Inline Technology Co., Ltd. to establish a national digital ecosystem to support SMEs. On 22 September, 2020, Russian First Deputy Prime Minister held a meeting on updating the national project "Small and Medium-Sized Businesses and Support for Individual Entrepreneurship".

Russian universities are governed by the state; and the entrepreneurship education has been implemented by these universities and academic institutions. A prominent feature of entrepreneurship education in Russian academic institutions is the cross-disciplinary cooperation, university-industry cooperation, and international cooperation. Moreover, it promotes the transfer of technology results and development of start-ups through various entrepreneurship platforms and incubators. Russia provides entrepreneurship training programs not only for young people and women, but also for high-growth enterprises.

Russian anti-trust law achieves general protection for SMEs by regulating four types of monopoly: monopoly agreement, abuse of market dominance, administrative monopoly, and concentration of operators. Article 11 of the Law clearly stipulates that agreements, resolutions, or concerted actions of operators to restrict competition are prohibited. For the determination of market dominance, Russian law sets different criteria for different industries, and the criteria for determining market dominance in individual industries.

Government Services

The Russian government places a high priority on the services rendered to start-ups and SMEs. In recent years, it has continuously introduced a series of policies and measures to support and promote entrepreneurship and the development of SMEs by adjusting the industrial structure of SMEs and improving the business environment to reduce their operating costs.

Russia has a special small and medium-sized enterprise law—the Federal Law on State Support for Small Business in the Russian Federation (2007). In June 2016, the Russian government adopted the SMB Development Strategy until 2030 to determine the important position of SMEs in Russia's long-term stable economic growth as a national strategy. The strategy is designed to increase the percentage of SMEs in processing sector from 11.8 to 20% by 2030, which requires the financial system to provide more financial support, especially long-term financial support for innovative and high-tech SMEs. Additionally, the strategy proposes to promote the mass production of new and high-tech products of small enterprises, enable them to develop to medium enterprises in an accelerated pace, and improve the technology of SMEs by encouraging small high-tech enterprises to develop product lines for large companies.

Russian tax authorities started the registration of SMEs in 2016, which was carried out in accordance with the Federal Law No. 408 Concerning the Amendment to the Law on Supporting SMEs (2015). In 2013, Russia implemented a series of measures to promote innovation and entrepreneurship. For example, the Scheme of "Simplifying the Registration Procedure for Entities and Individual Entrepreneurs" proposes to shorten the registration duration from 30 working days to 5 working days by 2018 and promote the Russian ranking of Global Business Environment to the 20th. In addition, Russian Federation released the Federal Law on Public–Private Partnership which improves the investment environment and serves as the legal basis for private and foreign investment in monopolized sectors, entering in public service, and regulating government procurement.[1]

The Department for the Development of Small and Medium-Sized Businesses and Competition under the auspice of the Ministry of Economic Development of Russia is responsible for SMEs affairs, including formulating development policies relating to SMEs and, together with other institutions and organizations such as financial institutions including the SME Corporation, providing financial, consulting, and market expansion support for Russian start-ups and SMEs.

---

[1] According to the World Bank's Doing Business 2017: Equal Opportunity for All, Russia ranks the 40th in terms of global business environment, and China 78th.

Fiscal and Financial Support

In October 2016, Russian President Putin ordered the government to further simplify the tax payment for SMEs, requiring enterprises earning less than 150 million rubles (equivalent to 2.6 million US dollars) per year to have the right to use "simplified tax system".[2] This is another increase after the Russian government raised the annual income standard of enterprises using the "simplified tax system". Russia approved an amendment to the tax law in June 2016, stipulating that starting from 2017, the annual revenue of enterprises eligible to use the "simplified tax system" will be increased from 80 million rubles (equivalent to 1.39 million US dollars) to 120 million rubles (equivalent to 2.08 million US dollars). In 2007, the Russian government laid down the Basic Principles of Tax Policy of the Russian Federation for 2008–2010 to cut the enterprise income tax to 20% by 2009, while implementing the "simplified tax system" to assist the development of micro and small enterprises.

The Russian government supports banks in lending to SMEs by continuing to provide loans subsidies to SMEs, sets up a unified guarantee system, and promotes the development of venture capital to improve the financing situation of start-ups and SMEs.

After the Russian Ministry of Finance and Ministry of Economic Development added 50 billion rubles (equivalent to 868 million US dollars) in 2017 to provide SMEs with a "loan program with interest rate at 6.5%", the Russian government announced in 2018 that it will continue to subsidize banks that make loans to SMEs launching projects in prioritized areas. The Russian government has an annual interest rate discount of 3.5% for bank loans to small enterprises and 3.1% for bank loans to medium-sized enterprises, and the discount period for the above-mentioned enterprise investment projects does not exceed 10 years, and the discount period for loans to obtain working capital does not exceed 3 years. The purpose of the Russian government's subsidy to banks is to ensure that the annual interest rate of SMEs' loans from banks is not higher than 6.5%. The program originated in 2016 when the Central Bank of the Russian Federation (Bank of Russia) coordinated to invest 30

---

[2] From 2002 to 2012, Russia carried out the second round of tax reform, implementing a simple single tax system for micro, small, and medium enterprises, which is also known as "simplified tax system" to replace the value-added tax and enterprise income tax and simplify tax declaration procedures.

billion rubles (equivalent to 521 million US dollars) with annual interest rate of 6.5% to support 12 large banks, including VTB Bank, that provide preferential loans to SMEs.

In April 2017, the Bank of Russia allowed banks to increase the ratio of foreign loans to bank capital from 0.2 to 0.5%, relaxed the regulation on banks serving SMEs, and allowed banks to raise the ceiling of loans to SMEs from 50 to 60 million rubles (equivalent to 860,000 US dollars to 1.04 million US dollars).

According to statistics, the SME Corporation guaranteed loans totaling 192 billion rubles (equivalent to 3.33 billion US dollars) in 2016. The SME Corporation was established by the Russian government in 2015 within the framework of Russia's National Guarantee System Development Strategy for SMEs by 2020. The SME Corporation provides financing assistance to SMEs through some regional commercial banks and non-bank financial institutions such as leasing companies, microfinance institutions, regional SME support funds, and other organizations. Small businesses receive loans at an annual interest rate of 11% and medium-sized businesses receive loans at an annual interest rate of 10% under the guarantee of the SME Corporation.

In 2015, the Ministry of Economic Development of Russia released the Basic Terms on Approving the Russia's National Guarantee System Development Strategy for SMEs by 2020. The main purpose of this strategy is to establish a unified guarantee system to improve the financing situation of SMEs. It is stipulated in the document that the state guarantee system will provide effective support for SME infrastructure projects backed by banks and other institutions at the federal and regional levels in mutual cooperation. At the same time, the document also defines the development goals and methods of promoting regional guarantee agencies, loan guarantee agencies, and other institutions within the national guarantee systems. Credit Guarantee Corporation is the authority center of the national guarantee system. Its main objective is to expand the scale and scope of the guarantee support for SMEs within the framework of strategic alliance with financial institutions and regional guarantee agencies. In the development of the national guarantee system, SMEs can be given priority to development by means of guarantee support and current market demand.

The development of Russian venture capital has also expanded financing channels for innovation entrepreneurship for SMEs. Russia's total number of venture capital investments in 2016 was 217, with a total value of 816 million US dollars, which is at a moderate level among G20 members, although it is higher than the size of G7 members Britain and Italy in the same year, China, which is also a member of the BRICS countries, is 22 times as large.

Entrepreneur Services

Technical Services

In terms of technical services, Russia aims to focus on developing the digital economy and supporting SMEs in digital services and R&D. The Russian government encourages universities and other research institutions to cooperate with enterprises by fiscal subsidies.

In May 2017, Russian President Putin signed Presidential Decree No. 203 Russian Federation Information Society Development Strategy 2017–2030. Within this strategic framework, the Russian government announced the Russian Federation's Digital Economy Plan in July 2017, planning to improve the availability and quality of public services and products through modern digital technology so as to create opportunities for building an informational society. According to the plan, Russia will focus on supporting 500 SMEs that provide digital services.

Russia's Resolution No. 218 (2010) concerning Measures of State Support for Cooperation between Russian Academic Institutions and Industrial Enterprises stipulates the procedures and conditions for the State to provide financial support for organizations and institutions implementing comprehensive high-tech projects. For those high-tech projects completed jointly by industrial enterprises and universities, subsidies will be provided for a period of 1–3 years, with an annual subsidy of 100 million rubles (equivalent to 1.73 million US dollars). In addition, the State will also provide subsidies for enterprises to purchase foreign patents, give preferential depreciation period to enterprises' assets, and support universities, scientific research institutions, and large companies to establish the "innovation belts" through development banks and venture capital companies.

Market Support

In terms of market services, Russia has increased the procurement quota of government and state-owned companies for SMEs, hoping that SMEs will modernize their equipment through government procurement and that they will further expand their production capacity. In addition, the Russian government has helped SMEs expand overseas markets through subsidies and other sound measures.

The Russian Federation's SMB Development Strategy until 2030 proposes to increase the share of SMEs in government procurement from 18% in 2016 to 25% in 2018. In 2016, the Russian government determined the list of enterprises and instructed them to purchase innovative and high-tech products developed by SMEs in order to improve their technology and production capacity. Previously, the Russian government announced in 2013 that from 2015, enterprises earning more than 10 billion rubles (equivalent to 174 million US dollars) must assign 9% of their purchases to SMEs.

Russian President Putin said at the 2016 meeting of the Strategic Development and Priorities Committee that the sales of Russian SMEs were limited to regional and local markets, and even those with high quality and competitive products have few opportunities to export. Russia must establish a mechanism to find export markets for SMEs nationwide and launch products of SMEs on foreign markets. In 2017, the Russian Ministry of Industry and Trade proposed to allocate 370 million rubles (equivalent to 6.42 million US dollars) from the budget of Russian export centers to create and promote export brands "Made in Russia" overseas and include this in the government's draft resolution. The document was formulated on the basis of the SMB Development Strategy until 2030 and will help raise the visibility of Russian brands and commodities abroad.

Enterprise Incubation

Russia's Network Innovation and Development Fund has been in operation since 2013, investing 6 billion rubles (equivalent to 100 million US dollars) in about 400 start-up companies. In 2012, Russian President Putin proposed the establishment of the foundation to provide financing and professional support for Russian mass network engineering start-ups. The foundation will set up incubators for enterprises in the "pre-seed stage" (enterprise having ideas but no business plan) and "seed stage" (enterprise having basic business model and operation team). The State plans to set up 6–8 incubators in cities with IT technology foundation.

The Skolkovo Fund is part of the Skolkovo Innovation Center development program, which is supported by the Russian government. The main objective of the program is to promote the transformation of the Russian economy from a conventional energy economy to an innovative economy and accelerate the commercial application of Russian scientific and technological innovation achievements. By 2016, the fund had received more than 1500 start-up companies and created about 18,000 jobs for high-tech talents.

Communication Platform

Russia's local exhibitions are a platform for entrepreneurs and SMEs to exchange information, where they can obtain consulting services from financial institutions and organizations supporting the development of SMEs at exhibitions. At the 9th "Yamalo Small and Medium Enterprises" Inter-local Exhibition in 2016, about 260 enterprises participated in the exhibition and displayed their products and services. The "Yamalo Small and Medium Enterprises" exhibition is one of the activities organized by the Yamalo-Nenets Autonomous Region government to support the development of SMEs. The last one was held in 2014, attended by 82 enterprises.

Digital Transformation Support

In June 2019, as part of the implementation of the national entrepreneurship plan, the Russian Ministry of Economic Development cooperated with Inline Technology Co., Ltd. to establish a national digital ecosystem to support SMEs.[3]

On 22 September, 2020, Russian First Deputy Prime Minister held a meeting on updating the national project "Small and Medium-Sized Businesses and Support for Individual Entrepreneurship". The updated national project focused on digital tools that makes it easier for entrepreneurs to start and run a business. Services for SMEs and start-ups are combined in a new ecosystem based on the "one-point" digital platform with mechanisms for targeted selection and proactive approval of support tools. It is planned that the digital platform will provide access to digitized services of federal and regional authorities, SME support infrastructure organizations and development institutions, as well as a wide

---

[3] Assessment on the progress of G20 Entrepreneurship Action Plan, Entrepreneurship Research Center on G20 Economies, Oct 22, 2019.

range of commercial services through a personal account on the digital platform. It is also possible to interact with marketplaces, convenient access to banking products, training, business protection services, audit control, and business registration on electronic trading platforms.[4]

Entrepreneurship Education

Russian universities are governed by the state, in which the entrepreneurship education has embedded. The entrepreneurship education features cross-disciplinary cooperation, industry cooperation, and international cooperation. Moreover, it promotes the transfer of technology research results and development of start-ups through various entrepreneurship platforms and incubators.

Tomsk State University of Control Systems and Radioelectronics (TUSUR) is an entrepreneurial research university and one of Russia's first universities to carry out entrepreneurship education. TUSUR takes developing students' entrepreneurial spirit as one of its teaching objectives. In terms of infrastructure of entrepreneurship education, Russia has incubators providing entrepreneurship trainings for student-run enterprises, investment funds to support early projects of student entrepreneurs, R&D commercialization offices helping students or professors convert their scientific and technological achievements, and technical and commercial incubators launching small-scale product production of world-leading scientific and technological achievements. In addition, Russia has been placing a priority on special technical trainings and IP protection.

TUSUR has the UNIQ, an alumni enterprises network. It consists of more than 150 high-tech enterprises, of which products account for 80% of total high-tech products produced in Tomsk. UNIQ's member enterprises can directly use TUSUR's innovative and entrepreneurial infrastructure to promote the commercialization of TUSUR's scientific and technological achievements and the establishment and development of new enterprises. Since this organization has abundant resources and is positioned to promote some large-scale innovative projects, its member enterprises can launch joint R&D with TUSUR's scientists for a specific

---

[4] Evaluation and Prospect of G20 Members' Policies to Support Entrepreneurship in the Post-pandemic Era, Entrepreneurship Research Center on G20 Economies, Oct 22, 2020.

project. For member enterprises, they can learn the cutting-edge technology of TUSUR, have the opportunity to transform into their own products, and also have the opportunity to recruit excellent students to join their companies. For students, they have the opportunity to learn practical technology and product development skills from the industry by participating in project-based research. Some member companies are among the best companies in certain segments, which also lays a good foundation for them to improve their employability in the future. For researchers, cooperation with member enterprises will help commercialize scientific research results and even set up new enterprises and become members of the UNIQ. Therefore, the establishment of UNIQ entrepreneur network and cooperation with universities are beneficial to all parties.

In terms of teaching methods, TUSUR is a university of science and engineering and encourages interdisciplinary cooperative research. It attaches great importance to the project-based teaching method, which is implemented by the international organization—Conceive–Design–Implement-Operate (CDIO), which was joined by TUSUR as Russia's first university in 2013.

Saint-Petersburg State University (SPbU) is a comprehensive research university. It has an entrepreneurship research center, under the Graduate School of Management, which launches some entrepreneurship education campaigns. One of them is the entrepreneurship competitions organized for students, including on-campus competitions and participation in international competitions. The third entrepreneurship contest will be held in 2018, with both undergraduate and graduate students being eligible to participate in. SPbU's Donation Foundation provides the bonuses, totaling 2.5 million rubles (equivalent to 250,000 yuan) in 2018. The competition requires at least 3–5 students from 3 different majors to form a team, and requires the project to have innovative and commercial development prospects. The winning project in the first contest was the rapid and low-cost detection of lead in human biological fluids. Additionally, the Graduate School of Management also offers entrepreneurship courses, which mainly focus on the basic knowledge of entrepreneurship, development, and improvement of business plans. In terms of teaching methods, there are lectures, group discussions, case studies, and multi-participant projects. To encourage group discussion, all students need to participate in a project. The entrepreneurship research center of SPbU also undertook the Russian assignment of Global Entrepreneurship Monitor

(GEM) and the Global University Entrepreneurial Spirit Students' Survey (GUESSS).

Ural Federal University (UrFU) is one of the members formulating the entrepreneurship education standard of the Russian Association for Entrepreneurship Education (RUAEE). UrFU has the School of Public Administration and Entrepreneurship. By major, it has master program for administration major, of which the academic term is two years, containing innovation and entrepreneurship courses; it also delivers bachelor courses of trade, of which the academic term is 4 years, containing entrepreneurship courses in trade. UrFU has the Innovation System—an innovation and entrepreneurship platform, where students may complete the full process from originality to product manufacturing. There are departments responsible for the transformation of scientific research achievements and departments providing guidance on the protection of intellectual property rights, and connecting with enterprises, investment institutions, and domestic and foreign innovative organizations. A number of high-tech start-ups in the fields such as laser and LED were born here, and many specialized research and development centers in the areas such as infrared fiber technology, sports-related technology, sensor-related technology, and mechanical manufacturing were established. UrFU's innovation platform has established an incubator for IT industry, working with industry experts to help IT-based enterprises develop products, improve products, and realize sales.

Russia has entrepreneurship training programs not only for young people and women, but also for high-growth enterprises.

The G20 Youth Entrepreneurs Alliance is jointly led by two organizations in Russia, including the Center for Entrepreneurship (CFE) and the OPERA Russia. The CFE is headquartered in Moscow and focuses on three areas:

1. organizing training for those who want to start a business and have the ability to do so;
2. initiating the establishment of the RUAEE with other institutions to train teachers in entrepreneurship education and improve entrepreneurship education in Russian secondary schools and universities; and
3. promoting Russian entrepreneurial culture. The CFE has many entrepreneurship training programs. The training teachers are usually entrepreneurs and have received teaching trainings. One of

the training programs was "Startup Huddle", which pre-selected entrepreneurs, put forward problems encountered in the process of starting a business, and proposed future ideas. An expert team composed of successful entrepreneurs and investors was responsible for giving answers within 20 minutes.

The OPERA Russia is a platform for the owners and operators of SMEs to talk to government authorities and has offices in 85 regions of Russia. The Federation actively supports youth entrepreneurship and encourages technological innovation.

For young entrepreneurs, Russia has the "UMNIK" program set up by the Small Innovation Enterprise Assistance Foundation, which mainly supports young entrepreneurs aged 18–28 years and provides assistance of 400,000 rubles (equivalent to 6945 US dollars) for young entrepreneurs for two years. Since the implementation of the plan in 2008, more than 800 young scientists have participated in the competition, and a total of 150 winners have received funding to implement innovative projects.

Pskov National University holds the "You Are Entrepreneur" training program for young people who are interested in starting a business. This project is aimed at young people aged 17–30. The training is divided into five modules: (1) introduction to fundamental knowledge on entrepreneurship; (2) translation of originality into feasible plans; (3) establishment of your own business; (4) entrepreneurship funds; and (5) financial plan. The training uses the training module of the International Labor Organization (ILO) on entrepreneurship education: "Start and Improve Your Business (SIYB)" and "Generate Your Business Idea (GYB)".

Ernst & Young collaborated with the Center for Entrepreneurship and the Moscow School of Management Skolkovo to launch the EY Entrepreneurial Winning Women program in Russia. This is Ernst & Young's annual global project and the fifth competition was held in Russia in 2017. The contestants must be female entrepreneurs or executives with a certain scale of business. Through the contest, women entrepreneurs can get the chance to further study, expand their interpersonal network, enhance the popularity, and speed up the development of the enterprise.

The CFE has a "Scaleup" program. The entrepreneur acceleration program lasts for 9 months, with 15 entrepreneurs with high-growth potential being selected. The training content includes 10 parts and at least 10 networking activities. Each entrepreneur will have at least

18 opportunities for individual mentoring. The specific contents of the training include strategic planning, (Internet) marketing, sales management, leadership, asset management, and so on, because communication between entrepreneurs and successful businessmen is not only a valuable asset for high-growth entrepreneurs, but also a harvest for businessmen.

FAIR COMPETITION FOR SMEs

In June 2006, Russia enacted the Federal Law on Protection of Competition,[5,6] which finally established the current anti-monopoly system in Russia. Russian anti-trust law achieves general protection for SMEs by regulating four types of monopoly: monopoly agreement, abuse of market dominance, administrative monopoly, and concentration of operators.

Article 11 of the Law clearly stipulates that agreements, resolutions, or concerted actions of operators to restrict competition are prohibited. According to the law, the standard to judge whether a competition restriction agreement will be prohibited is whether the agreement will lead to or may lead to the consequences of restricting competition. Therefore, the consequences considered here include not only substantive consequences, but also possible consequences. This is in fact a two-tier identification standard, in which the "may-lead-to" criterion actually establishes a form of preventive regulation. It can more effectively maintain the order of market competition by cooperating with the conventional ex post relief.

For the determination of market dominance, Russian law sets different criteria for different industries, and the criteria for determining market dominance in individual industries, such as non-bank financial institutions and credit institutions, are different from those for general production and sales enterprises, and are regulated separately by governmental orders such as the Conditions for Determining Market Dominance of Financial Institutions (Excluding Credit Institutions) and the Conditions for Determining Market Dominance of Credit Institutions.

---

[5] Law of the Russian Federation on the Protection of CompetitionФедеральный законот 26 июля 2006 г. N 135-ФЗ"Озащитеконкуренции.

[6] In 1991, Russia enacted the first anti-trust law, namely the Law on Competition and Restriction of the Monopolistic Activity in the Commodity Markets.

Saudi Arabia

In 2016, the Saudi government released the new Companies Law and announced the long-term plan "Vision 2030". This vision contained various programs and plans to promote the development of SMEs. Under the framework of this vision, the Saudi Council of Economic and Development Affairs (CEDA) issued a financial development plan to support the financing of SMEs from banks. Another program named "In-Kingdom Total Value Add (IKTVA) Program of Saudi Aramco" was committed to creating job opportunities in the country. The Saudi government also introduced the Saudi Private Sector Stimulus Program, aiming at enhancing the importance of private sectors in the economy. Meanwhile, the Small and Medium Enterprises General Authority issued four detailed plans to promote SMEs, with a total amount of more than 12 billion Saudi riyals (equivalent to 3.2 billion US dollars). Besides, the Saudi Arabian Ministry of Environment, Water, and Agriculture designed the national overall agricultural products safety strategy, displaying its supports to agricultural SMEs and households.

The Saudi government has also been actively involved in the financial support for start-ups and SMEs. New enterprises established from 2016 to 2021 would be exempted from government taxes (in the form of reimbursement) during the first three years of their operations. The Saudi Public Investment Fund (PIF), the SMEs Loan Guarantee Program

(KAFALH), and the SME parallel market (NOMU) were all launched to boost SMEs.

Progress has been made in Entrepreneur Services such as technical service, enterprise incubation, and communication platform as well. The Saudi government has formulated the 2018–2020 Plan of the PIF to advance scientific research. A new city named Neom will be built as an economic special zone to lead emerging technologies and industries. Besides, while Badir Program for Technology Incubator has become a mature business incubator, universities have also set up incubators and entrepreneurship accelerators. As for the exchange platform, Saudi Arabia promotes the exchange of information between emerging industries and start-ups through various conferences and forums, such as the Future Investment Forum and Startup 100 Forum. During the outbreak of Covid-19, the Monshaat (Saudi Arab's Small and Medium Enterprises General Authority) held 10 online meetings which were attended by 1.14 million participants, to promote entrepreneurship and the digital transformation of businesses.

For special demographic groups such as youth and women, Saudi Arabia has set up specialized programs, funds, and organizations to provide entrepreneurship training services. The Prince Mohammad Bin Fahd Abdulaziz Program for Youth Development, The Centennial Fund (TCF), the Saudi Entrepreneur Program (Riyyadi), and Princess Jawaher's Mashael Al-Khair Center are remarkable examples in this area. For university entrepreneurship education, Saudi universities such as King Abdullah University of Science and Technology (KAUST) and Prince Mohammad Bin Salman College (MBSC) of Business & Entrepreneurship not only include entrepreneurship education in their curricula, but also place a priority on international exchanges and collaboration with foreign universities such as Babson College in the US.

Government Services

In 2016, the Saudi government released the new Companies Law, aiming to provide a better investment environment for investors and enhance Saudi's competitive advantages in the international market. Specifically, this new law encourages entrepreneurs from SMEs to invest in Saudi Arabia.

In 2016, the Saudi Vision 2030 was approved by the King at the Cabinet meeting and officially announced by Crown Prince Salman. The

Saudi Vision 2030 consists of three major themes: social, economic, and national development. The overall goal is to raise Saudi Arabia's ranking in the global economy from its current 19th to the top 15 by 2030. The Vision 2030 specifically calls for promoting SMEs and creating new jobs through SMEs. It targets at increasing the share of SMEs in GDP from 20 to 35%. It also attempts to strengthen vocational education in the country, reducing unemployment rate from 11.6 to 7% by 2030. Besides, the vision is dedicated to promoting women's rights, increasing the proportion of women in the labor force from 22 to 30%.

In May 2018, the Saudi CEDA issued a financial development plan under the framework of Saudi Vision 2030. This plan is committed to extending the reform in the financial sector, increasing financing for SMEs from banks. Another program to support SMEs under Saudi Vision 2030 is the "IKTVA Program of Saudi Aramco", which will provide Saudi Arabia with more than 40,000 jobs and increase GDP by about 8 billion US dollars every year.

At the end of 2017, the Saudi government launched the Saudi Private Sector Stimulus Program, which was designed to increase the contributions of Saudi private sectors to GDP to 65% by 2030. This program officially guaranteed the importance of private sectors in the country's economy. During the same period, the Small and Medium Enterprises General Authority of Saudi Arabia also issued four plans to promote SMEs, with a total amount of more than 12 billion Saudi riyals (equivalent to 3.2 billion US dollars). The plans included: first, refunding the government charges of 7 billion Saudi riyals (equivalent to 1.9 billion US dollars); second, raising 800 million Saudi riyals (equivalent to 200 million US dollars) for the KAFALH program to finance SMEs; third, providing indirect loans of 1.6 billion Saudi riyals (equivalent to 400 million US dollars) to SMEs; fourth, establishing a start-up-oriented venture fund of 2.8 billion Saudi riyals (equivalent to 750 million US dollars).

In 2017, the Saudi Arabian Ministry of Environment, Water, and Agriculture introduced the national overall agricultural products safety strategy, dedicated to support agricultural SMEs and households. The strategy aimed to ensure the safety of Saudi agricultural products, increase the output of agricultural products, and enhance agricultural capacity. In addition, it encouraged the country's sustainable agricultural production time, increased the output of agricultural products, and strived to achieve self-sufficiency.

Fiscal and Financial Support

In December 2017, the Small and Medium Enterprises General Authority announced to exempt new enterprises established from 2016 to 2021 from government taxes (in the form of reimbursement) during the first three years of their operations. The budget for this plan was 7 billion Saudi riyals (equivalent to 1.9 billion US dollars).

In 2017, the Saudi PIF announced to set up an investment fund of 4 billion Saudi riyals (equivalent to 1.06 billion US dollars) to support private SMEs. This new investment fund will contribute 400 million Saudi riyals (equivalent to 100 million US dollars) to the GDP and create 2600 jobs by the end of 2020.

The KAFALH jointly developed by the Saudi Arabian Ministry of Finance and Saudi banks provides financial supports for SMEs and is managed by the Saudi Industrial Development Fund (SIDF). Since its operation in 2006, the KAFALH program has provided 18,280 guarantees for 8933 SMEs by the end of the 2016 fiscal year, with a total guaranteed amount of 8.925 billion Saudi riyals (equivalent to 2.38 billion US dollars). Banks involved in this program included Saudi Investment Bank and Al Rajhi Bank.

The NOMU of Saudi Stock Exchange was opened in 2017. SMEs listed in NOMU must have a market value of 2.70 million US dollars and 35–50 shareholders, with no less than 20% shares being publicly traded. The Saudi Stock Exchange perceived the NOMU as a "new trading platform with relatively loosened listing requirements".

Entrepreneur Services

Technical Services

In terms of technical services, the Saudi government has formulated the 2018–2020 Plan of the PIF (which is also part of the Saudi Vision 2030), planning to invest 210 billion Saudi riyals (equivalent to 56 billion US dollars) in frontier scientific research by 2020 and create 11,000 jobs in the high-tech field in Saudi Arabia.

In addition, Saudi Arabia will build the city of Neom at the border with Egypt and Jordan near Red Sea. The Neom city will be an economic special zone of Saudi Arabia. It will have an independent tax and economic system, and will lead the world in fields such as energy and water, bioscience, food, media, entertainment, advanced manufacturing, digital science, and living quality.

Enterprise Incubation

Derived from the science development program set up in 2007 by Abdul Aziz, the king of Saudi Arabia, the Badir Program for Technology Incubator has become mature. This business incubator provides services for high-tech enterprises, including telecommunication and information technology, biotechnology, and high-tech manufacturing.

Some Saudi Arabian higher education institutions have also set up business incubators and entrepreneurship accelerators. In 2013, Saudi Arabian American Oil Company (ARAMCO) and King Fahd University of Petroleum and Minerals (KFUPM) jointly established a business incubator to provide training, financing, and other supports for entrepreneurial projects. The Accelerators Program of KAUST aims at helping students commercialize technology successfully from an early stage and forming the culture of "Made in Saudi Arabia". King Abdulaziz University cooperates with Babson College in the United States to jointly launch the King Abdulaziz University Business Accelerator, providing trainings for entrepreneurs. This program invites experts from both local and multinational enterprises.

Communication Platform

In October 2017, the Crown Prince hosted the First Future Investment Forum to discuss the trend of future industries. The Saudi Future Investment Initiative is a global initiative launched by the Saudi PIF, aiming to establish a platform for information exchange among world leaders, innovators, and investors to seek global cooperation, achieve sustainable development, and explore new industries. In December 2017, Prince Khaled al-Faisal, a consultant to Saudi King and governor of Mecca, hosted the Startup 100 Forum, which was attended by entrepreneurs, investors, incubators, and economic scholars, to advance the development of Saudi start-ups.

Digital Transformation Support

During the outbreak of Covid-19, the Monshaat (Saudi Arab's Small and Medium Enterprises General Authority), in an effort to promote entrepreneurship and the digital transformation of businesses, held 10 online meetings during the epidemic, which were attended by 1.14

million participants. The 10 online meetings covered different topics to drive digital transformation and mitigate the impact of the epidemic. Business leaders, successful entrepreneurs, and business advisors were involved, offering online guidance on topics related to the current crisis.

To finance the digital transformation of SMEs, the government provided 2 billion Saudi riyals ($5.3 billion) to provide and activate teleworking tools as an alternative to the regular work environment.[1]

Entrepreneurship Education

The Prince Mohammad Bin Fahd Abdulaziz Program for Youth Development was jointly established by Prince Mohammad Bin Fahd and College of Technology in Damman to support youth development, provide vocational training for unemployed youth groups, improve their employability, and help them start their own businesses. To date, the program has provided 40,000 jobs for the youth.

TCF is a non-government organization dedicated to helping young vulnerable groups in Saudi Arabia to set up businesses or find jobs through education and training, financial support, and other means. TCF currently has more than 2000 projects to help young people and has trained 30,000 people.

In early 2018, the Saudi Ministry of Education proposed the Riyyadi, which aimed to develop awareness and skills of entrepreneurship among young people. The program attempted to spread a culture of entrepreneurship among students. It hoped to implement entrepreneurship strategy through education and train qualified entrepreneurship coaches. Entrepreneurship contests were also encouraged and planed by this program.

The Princess Jawaher's Mashael Al-Khair Center has a special fund to train Saudi female youth, which aims to reduce the female unemployment rate and improve their living conditions. The center is committed to developing a culture of female entrepreneurship and independence. The fund has developed projects to cultivate women leadership, as well as training programs for different professional skills, such as nursing.

---

[1] Evaluation and Prospect of G20 Members' Policies to Support Entrepreneurship in the Post-pandemic Era, Entrepreneurship Research Center on G20 Economies, Oct 22, 2020.

KAUST is dedicated to building an "Innovation Ecosystem" including start-ups, entrepreneurs, and investors to turn good ideas into good businesses. The university provides entrepreneurial students with training, consulting, and financial supports, as well as patent evaluation and protection.

MBSC of Business and Entrepreneurship is a newly established private higher education institution and places a priority on entrepreneurship education. MBSC and Babson College in the United States work closely in entrepreneurship education. The pedagogy of Experiential Learning from Babson College has been introduced, focusing on the combination of learning and practice. The college also provides students with opportunities to expand their social networks and learn from mentors. MBSC lecturers are sent to Babson College for teaching training.

South Africa

The supportive policy of South African government for entrepreneurship, innovation, and SMEs can be traced back to the White Paper on SMME (Small-Medium-Micro-Enterprises) Development 1995.[1] In 2003, the National Small Business Act (1996) was amended to simplify the procedures for starting a business, lower the financing threshold and implement the preferential policy of value-added tax relief. In 2004, the Small Enterprise Development (SEDA) was legally established. In 2011, South Africa's new Companies Act came into effect, further easing the requirements for entrepreneurship.

In 2017, the South African government made SME development a priority in the National Development Plan (NDP). Since 2016, the government has increased its budget for scientific research, giving priority to research, innovation, and entrepreneurship. The South African Ministry of Science and Technology has supported 2800 SMEs in fiscal year 2017/18, and the priority areas of support include entrepreneurship and innovation.

The South African government has given special attention and support to both black entrepreneurship and black entrepreneurs. The

---

[1] In the National Small Business Amendment Act 26 of 2003, micro-business is defined as a business with five or less employees and business revenue of less than 100,000 rand (equivalent to 8.076 US dollars), very small business 6–20 employees and small business 21–51 employees, with their business revenue varies from sector to sector.

© The Author(s), under exclusive license to Springer Nature Singapore Pte Ltd. 2022
J. Gao et al., *G20 Entrepreneurship Services Report*,
https://doi.org/10.1007/978-981-16-6787-9_18

Broad-Based Black Economic Empowerment Act (2004) and the Black Economic Empowerment Act (BEE) have unleashed the black entrepreneurial and business management potential of South Africa. As South African population becomes young and youth unemployment is aggravated, the government set up the National Youth Development Agency (NYDA) to support youth entrepreneurship. As SMEs and start-ups accelerate digital transformation efforts in response to the pandemic, in Oct. 2020, South Africa Standard Bank, Mastercard and Google announced a collaboration to help them move their businesses online, accept digital payments, and attract more customers.

The South African government has continuously raised the income tax threshold for small businesses to provide preferential tax support for start-ups and SMEs. In addition to providing SMEs with subsidies and financing supports through the Development Finance Institutions (DFI), the Small Enterprise Finance Agency (SEFA) provides various supports. Credit guarantee financing is another important measure. In South Africa, the development of venture capital is mainly promoted by state-led fund projects, and many funds include projects focusing on financing women's entrepreneurship, such as the Women Empowerment Fund and The Isivande Women's Fund (IWF). In 2016, ZAR X Stock Exchange was established, which is the second stock exchange in South Africa after Johannesburg Stock Exchange (JES), and to which the first stock exchange license issued by the South African government in more than 100 years.

South Africa pays special attention to marginalized small businesses and provides technical support to women entrepreneurs and women-led enterprises. In addition, the South African government has focused on black entrepreneurs and start-ups in terms of industry encouragement.

Since the Reconstruction and Development Program (1994) called for the inclusion of entrepreneurship training in the education system, the South African government has placed a high priority on the entrepreneurship education. South Africa's entrepreneurship education highlighted multi-party cooperation, including government departments, education departments, private institutions, enterprises, non-governmental organizations, and international organizations. On the one hand, some South African government departments work together to provide entrepreneurship training for high-growth enterprises. On the other hand, in response to youth unemployment, the South African government, in cooperation with international organizations and non-governmental organizations, joined entrepreneurship education at the secondary level to improve the employment and entrepreneurship of young students. Entrepreneurship education program is also provided for disadvantaged youth groups without university diplomas. Caring about social entrepreneurship and system change is a new trend in entrepreneurship education in South African higher learning institutions. South African social promotion of entrepreneurial role models has also played a positive role in spreading entrepreneurial culture. However, as with entrepreneurship education and training, the development of entrepreneurship culture will not take place overnight, but will also take time to accumulate.

Government Services

The supportive policy of South African government for entrepreneurship, innovation, and SMEs can be traced back to the White Paper on SMME Development 1995. The South African government proposed to provide financial and non-financial supports for entrepreneurship and SMEs to expand product demand and reduce regulation. In 2003, the government amended the National Small Business Act (1996) to simplify the procedures for starting a business, lower the financing threshold and implement the preferential policy of value-added tax relief. In 2004, the SEDA was legally established. South Africa's new Companies Act came into effect in 2011, when private companies are no longer limited to 50 employees and not required to submit financial statements every year, nor do they need to release their financial statements to the public, further relaxing the requirements for starting businesses.

In 2017, the South African government made the development of SMEs a priority in South Africa's National Development Plan (NDP), including the goal of 90% employment in the SME sectors by 2030 and the promotion of innovation and entrepreneurship and the sustainable development of SMEs. Since 2016, the government has increased its budget for scientific research, giving priority to research, innovation, and entrepreneurship. According to the budget report of South African Ministry of Science and Technology for the fiscal year 2017/18, the government supported 2800 SMEs through Technology Innovation Agency (TIA) in the fiscal year 2017/18 and will support 3380 SMEs in the fiscal year 2018/19. According to the budgetary report of the South African Ministry of Science and Technology for the fiscal year 2015/16— Science and innovation: Driving forces for future growth, the annual budget of the South African Ministry of Science and Technology for the fiscal year 2015/16 was 7.482 billion rand (equivalent to 600 million US dollars), which is significantly greater than 6.48 billion rand (equivalent to 520 million US dollars) in the fiscal year 2014/15. The prioritized areas include development of human resources, creation of new knowledge, investment in research and infrastructures, and encouragement on innovation.

The South African government is committed to improving the status of blacks in the socio-economy. The Broad-Based Black Economic Empowerment Act (2004) and the BEE have increased black ownership and control of enterprises and promoted the rise of the black middle class, which not only changes the gap between the rich and the poor in South Africa and promotes sustainable economic development, but also unleashes the potential of South African blacks in entrepreneurship and business management. In May 2018, the South African government announced that it will reform government subsidy programs such as Comprehensive Agricultural Support Program (CASP), implemented since 2005, and Ilima-Letsema subsidy program to better benefit small black agricultural enterprises. The measures include supporting land reform, providing financing for farmers through agricultural financial institutions (Mafisa), establishing agricultural cooperatives, formulating agricultural logistics strategies, devising agricultural sustainable development strategies, forecasting weather, and improving agricultural marketing environment. Ilima/Letsema is a government subsidy program to help black agricultural communities develop agricultural production. The Black Industrialists Scheme (BIS) was launched in 2015, aiming to unleash the industrial potential of black people in South Africa' economy to own, operate, and manage enterprises by using state financial and non-financial interventions.

South Africa's population becomes young and youth unemployment is serious. South Africa has set up the National Youth Development Agency (NYDA) to help young people between the ages of 14 and 35 start businesses and provide financial support for start-ups.

Fiscal and Financial Support

The South African government has continuously raised the small business income tax threshold since 2015, from 73,650 rand (equivalent to 5948 US dollars) in 2015 to 78,750 rand (equivalent to 6359 US dollars) at present.

The South African government provides subsidies and financing supports to SMEs and entrepreneurs through the Development Finance Institutions (DFI). In 2016, the South African government's direct loan to SMEs was 8722 million rand (equivalent to 704 million US dollars), accounting for 1.4% of the total loan to SMEs.

The SEFA provides bridging loans, term loans, and structured finance for start-ups and SMEs. The organization is a subsidiary of Industrial Development Corporation Limited. Its products and services are mainly divided into two directions:

- Direct loans. The SEFA provides loans directly to SMEs or cooperatives. The loan amount ranged from a minimum of 50,000 rand (equivalent to 4038 US dollars) to a maximum of 5 million rand (equivalent to 400,000 US dollars). These loans include: Asset loans that help enterprises purchase new assets according to their needs, with the new assets being able to be used as collateral for loans; bridging loans that provide enterprises with short-term transitional loans to finance their operations; and term loans. South Africa has a high unemployment rate and a high poverty rate among the disabled. The Amavulandlela subsidy program of the SEFA is designed specifically for disabled entrepreneurs, providing assistance in financing, technology, procurement, and negotiations with suppliers, and will provide up to 350,000 rand (equivalent to 28,000 US dollars) for in-depth training and other business support.
- Wholesale lending. The SEFA provides funds for intermediaries, joint ventures, and special fund partners to increase access to financing for South African SMEs. The target is SMEs with financial difficulties in the market. It provides loans of 500 (equivalent to 40 US dollars) to 50,000 rand (equivalent to 4038 US dollars) for micro-business, 50,000 rand (equivalent to 4038 US dollars) to 1 million rand (equivalent to 80,000 US dollars) for small enterprises, and 1 million rand (equivalent to 80,000 US dollars) to 5

million rand (equivalent to 400,000 US dollars) for medium-sized enterprises.

Credit guarantee financing is another important way for South African government to support start-ups and SMEs. The credit guarantee provided by Industrial Development Corporation (IDC Funding) in 2016 was 234 million rand (equivalent to 18.89 million US dollars), an increase of 23 million rand (equivalent to 1.85 million US dollars) compared with that in 2015 after the significant decline in 2013 and 2014. At the same time, the government is endeavoring to set up a chattel registration system and a credit record database to reduce the risk of loans and increase the ratio of bank loans.

In South Africa, the development of venture capital is mainly promoted by state-led fund projects, and many funds include projects focusing on financing women's entrepreneurship.

The National Empowerment Fund (NEF) is a South African government-led fund to encourage black entrepreneurship, including iMbewu Fund, Rural & Community Development Fund, uMontho Fund, Strategic Projects Fund, and Women Empowerment Fund subsidizing women entrepreneurship.

The IDC Funding mainly provides support for in-operation enterprises and businessmen who are likely to develop new business, including Development Funds, Agro-Processing Competitiveness Fund, Product Process Development Scheme (PPD), Risk Capital Facility Programme, Transformation and Entrepreneurship Scheme, Green Energy Efficiency Fund.

IWF aims to promote women's entrepreneurship. Khula SME Fund mainly provides funds for start-ups in the initial stage and expansion stage. The fund was incorporated into the SEFA in 2012.

The JES is the largest stock exchange in Africa and an important financing channel for South African start-ups and SMEs. In 2016, the South African Financial Services Commission issued the first stock exchange license in the past 100 years to ZAR X, which will become the second stock exchange in South Africa.

Entrepreneur Services

South Africa pays special attention to marginalized small businesses in terms of technical support, and provides technical support to women entrepreneurs and women-led enterprises. In addition, the South African government has focused on black entrepreneurs and start-ups in terms of industry encouragement.

South African Seda Technology Programme (STP) provides profitable and non-profit technology transfer, business incubation, and quality support services to small businesses, especially those defined by the South African government as the second economy. The second economy refers to small registered and unregistered marginalized enterprises. The plan provides non-repayable financial subsidies of up to 600,000 rand (equivalent to 40,000 US dollars) per project to ensure that small businesses can successfully acquire new technologies. In addition, it provides specific technical support for small businesses with more than 50% female ownership.

The South African government announced in 2016 that it would reopen its application for the Manufacturing Competitiveness Enhancement Program (MCEP) and that each eligible manufacturer would receive a loan of up to 50 million rand (equivalent to 4.03 million US dollars) at a fixed annual interest rate of 4%. The program provides loans of up to 50 million rand (equivalent to 4.03 million US dollars) with an annual profit margin of 4% to all eligible start-up applicants and existing black industrial enterprises.

As SMEs and start-ups accelerate digital transformation efforts in response to the pandemic, in Oct. 2020, South Africa Standard Bank, Mastercard and Google announced a collaboration to help them move their businesses online, accept digital payments and attract more customers. Through the collaboration, SMEs can get free access to Standard Bank's SimplyBlu, an all-in-one e-commerce solution powered by Mastercard Payment Gateway Services, plus free Google Ads. These capabilities have been packaged as a bundled solution to help support business owners to tackle the economic challenges posed by the Covid-19 pandemic. Through this collaboration, Standard Bank's mission is to help as many SMEs with tools and support to expand their digital capabilities and take their operations to the next level. With Google Ads, SMEs can get access to a digital marketing channel that further helps them in driving increased website visits to grow online sales, bookings, or mailing list signups; more phone calls and customer interest queries; as well as more in store visits. Additionally, this collaboration bridges a gap between those who can access these online opportunities and those who can't.[2]

Entrepreneurship Education

The South African government has been attaching great importance to entrepreneurship education. The Reconstruction and Development Program (1994) emphasizes the development of citizens' awareness of entrepreneurship and requires the incorporation of entrepreneurship training into the education and training system. The White Paper on SMME Development (1995) proposed that entrepreneurship education must be included in the school curriculum. The Progress Report of the South African Human Resources Development Council (HRDC) (2013) suggested that schools should support entrepreneurship training and develop entrepreneurship education. The Coordinated Youth Employment Strategy (2013) includes "youth entrepreneurship and youth cooperative enterprises" as one of the six priority areas for the South African government.

South Africa has programs to provide entrepreneurship training to high-growth enterprises. South African Department of Small Business Development (DSBD) and the Small Enterprise Development Agency (SEDA) launched the National Gazelles Program for high-growth enterprises in 2015, selecting 40 fast-growing enterprises each year and providing financial support to 40 enterprises. In November 2017, 40 selected enterprises were announced, and 68% of the previously selected enterprises achieved 17% performance growth, indicating that the project has achieved the goal of helping the selected enterprises develop to a larger scale.

The youth unemployment issue in South Africa is serious. The population in South Africa becomes young. The youth unemployment rate in 2016 was about 30%, and about 60% of the population are aged under 35. In response to youth unemployment, the South African government, in cooperation with international organizations and non-governmental

---

[2] Evaluation and Prospect of G20 Members' Policies to Support Entrepreneurship in the Post-pandemic Era, Entrepreneurship Research Center on G20 Economies, Oct 22, 2020.

organizations, joined entrepreneurship education at the secondary level to improve the entrepreneurship of young students.

In 2013–2015, the International Labour Organization (ILO) and the South African Ministry of Economic Development, Tourism and Environmental Affairs (DETEA) jointly launched the StartUP & Go Entrepreneurship Education Project in Free State Province, where youth unemployment is high in South Africa. The project pays more attention to the cultivation of young people's entrepreneurial mindset, entrepreneurial attitude, and personal character. It is implemented in the business study courses for grades 10–12 in 62 schools in Free State Province. There are also non-governmental organizations in South Africa that provide entrepreneurship education for secondary schools, such as Foundation for Business and Development (FEBDEV), Education with Enterprise Trust (EWET), and South African Institute of Entrepreneurship (SAIE).

South African higher education institutions cooperate with each other and with industry and enterprises to provide entrepreneurship education projects, which are also provided to vulnerable youth groups without university diplomas. Concerning about Social Entrepreneurship and System Change is a new trend in entrepreneurship education in South African higher education institutions.

The VUT/Sasol Entrepreneurship Program of Vaal University of Technology in South Africa is aimed at young people aged 18–30 who do not have a university diploma and who are from vulnerable families. The training lasts for 8 months and is completely free of charge. The funds are provided by Vaal University of Technology and Sasol.

Raymond Ackerman Academy's entrepreneurship training program mainly provides entrepreneurship training courses of six months for young people aged 18–30 who do not have the opportunity to attend university. Students are required to attend on full-time basis. Raymond Ackerman Academy, co-founded by Raymond Ackerman, the Business School of the University of Cape Town, and the University of Johannesburg, is a university-level institution.[3] The academy believes that the personality, characteristics, and entrepreneurial mindset also play a critical role in entrepreneurship, so these aspects are included in the design of the curriculum system. The academy has a Gradate Entrepreneur Support Service (GESS) program to help graduate students solve their financial

---

[3] South African businessman.

problems and expand their network. The GESS program is selected in the Taillores Network Youth Economic Participation Initiative (YEPI) and the academy is one of the eight selected universities. YEPI is committed to selecting the best entrepreneurship education institutions and methods in the southern hemisphere to promote youth entrepreneurship education.

The University of Johannesburg launched its Youth entrepreneurship training program. In 2016, there were 340 small business owners graduated from the entrepreneurship training program in Johannesburg. Many participants in this program were from vulnerable families. Of these, 136 students (in 73 business categories) came from rural areas and participated in the Pfunanani Enterprise Development Project, which specifically supports the development of rural entrepreneurs. The University of Johannesburg's entrepreneurship training program was launched in response to the call of South African youth entrepreneurship. The program has received support from the university and industry community, such as Buffelshoek Trust, Sabi Sand Pfunanani Trust, Sabi Sand Wildtuin.

In 2017, the University of the Witwatersrand launched the Student Entrepreneurship Week, aiming to stimulate students' entrepreneurial awareness and using entrepreneurship as a way of employment. This activity was also launched because of the serious youth unemployment problem in South Africa and in response to the call of the Department of Higher Education and Training (DHET) for universities to actively carry out entrepreneurship education campaigns. The iEntrepreneur-themed Entrepreneurial Week mainly focuses on several aspects: information, ideas and innovations, and implementation and impact of entrepreneurship plans.

The University of Cape Town launched the training program of Social Entrepreneurship & Systems Change in 2018. Systems change refers to changing the working and living conditions of tens of millions of people, such as vaccination, women's voting rights, and free and compulsory education. This training program is aimed at senior leaders of enterprises or non-profit organizations engaged in social entrepreneurship and provides them with a new set of management tools and frameworks through short-term (5-day) training. The course explains the current situation, opportunities, and practical problems of social entrepreneurship in South Africa and around the world. The project is funded by Rockefeller Foundation, Schwab Foundation, and Motsepe Foundation.

South African social promotion of entrepreneurial role models has also played a positive role in spreading entrepreneurial culture. For example, Entrepreneur Magazine selected 27 South African richest people and shared their success stories. South Africa also has some evaluations of young entrepreneurs, such as the 2017 evaluation of 10 entrepreneurs under the age of 30. The publicity of these success stories has a positive guiding effect on young people who have ambitions to start a business. By and large, however, the development of entrepreneurial culture is not going to happen overnight, and it takes time to accumulate just like entrepreneurship education and training.

Turkey

In terms of fiscal and financial support, the Turkish government provides financial subsidies to support start-ups, such as the start-up funds provided by KOSGEB. Incentives have also been taken to reduce fees and taxes for start-ups and SMEs, with an emphasis on supporting young entrepreneurs, private institutions engaged in R&D, educational institutions, and high-tech companies. In addition, the Turkish government has set up a Credit Guarantee Fund (KGF) to expand financing channels for start-ups and SMEs, and to give special support to export, female and young entrepreneurs, and agricultural fields. Moreover, the Technology Development Foundation of Turkey (TTGV), a non-governmental organization, provides various financing channels for start-ups to solve financing problems. It launched a new Initial Market Entry Investment Program named HIT in 2017 to support health technology start-ups. Finally, the Turkish government promotes the development of venture capital through tax cut and other financing channels.

In terms of entrepreneur services, TIM-TEB Global House provides financial support and market expansion services for start-ups to help them develop overseas markets. The Turkish government standardizes the management of incubators and provides financial subsidies and tax cut for the management companies of the Technology Development Zones (TDZs), start-ups in the zones, and R&D activities in the zones. In Turkey, series of events and contests have played an important role in promoting information exchanges among entrepreneurs. Examples of such events and contests are the Business Plan Award and the Turkey Innovation and Entrepreneurship Week. In addition, the Turkish government encourages start-ups to compete for the European Enterprise Promotion Awards. In July 2020, The Union of Chambers and Commodity Exchanges of Turkey (TOBB) and Trendyol (online shopping platform) have launched the "Grow Your Business with Trendyol" SME support program, so-called "e-commerce platforms to support SMEs".

KOSGEB has been promoting entrepreneurship training courses nationwide since 2000, and plays an important role in non-school entrepreneurship education training. Besides, through the Entrepreneurial and Innovative University Index (EIUI), entrepreneurship education of higher education institutions in Turkey has been greatly improved. Entrepreneurship education has also been integrated into Turkish secondary education. Finally, Turkey pays special attention to spreading the entrepreneurial culture and raising people's awareness of entrepreneurship through the publicity of entrepreneurship contests and entrepreneurial role models, as well as entrepreneurship education.

The Turkish Law No. 7246 on Amendments to the Law on Protection of Competition (Amendment Law) with respect to SMEs is the introduction of the de minimis principle of the EU legislation in the chapter of "Conclusion on Preliminary Investigation". The revised law mainly provides a clear legal basis for making judgments on the activities of SMEs operating in very narrow geographical markets.

Government Services

Turkey's Ministry of National Education, Ministry of Science, Industry and Technology and TUBITAK signed the Developing the Entrepreneurship Protocol in early 2012 and formulated a strategic development plan for Turkish start-ups and SMEs.

KOSGEB is mainly responsible for improving the share of SMEs in Turkey's economy, as well as enhancing their efficiency and competitiveness. It set up the Entrepreneurship Development Council in 1998 and revised the Enterprise Incorporation Law in 2008. KOSGEB mainly provides support for start-ups and SMEs through entrepreneurship training, start-up funds, business incubators, and business planning awards.

The Turkish Ministry of Development provides financial support for start-ups and SMEs. From 2008 to 2016, it supported 1061 projects, totaling 243,549,507 Turkish lire (equivalent to 64.5 million US dollars). In addition to providing financial support, Turkish Ministry of Development also plans to set up a center for young entrepreneurs, which provides workplaces, training and information consulting services, as well as market expansion services.

FISCAL AND FINANCIAL SUPPORT

The Turkish government provides financial subsidies to support start-ups. KOSGEB provides capital support for entrepreneurs, including start-up grant of up to 50,000 Turkish lire (equivalent to 13,000 US dollars) and interest-free start-up loan of up to 100,000 Turkish lire (equivalent to 26,000 US dollars). Supports are provided based on the location of the start-up and whether the beneficiaries of the subsidy belong to special groups such as women or disabled people.

The Turkish government has reduced fees and taxes for start-ups and SMEs, with an emphasis on supporting young entrepreneurs, private institutions engaged in R&D, educational institutions, and high-tech companies.

Under the Law No. 6663 amended in January 2016, young entrepreneurs aged below 29 with an income lower than 75,000 Turkish lire (equivalent to 19,800 US dollars) shall be exempted from individual income tax for three years, starting from the calendar year in which they started their businesses. The Corporate Income Tax Law No. 552 stipulates that the establishment and staffing expenses of an enterprise shall be deducted from its income. Moreover, it stipulates that the venture capital investment of an enterprise may be deducted from the taxable income of the enterprise, but the amount shall not exceed 10% of the declared income.

According to Law 5746 (law supporting research, development, and design activities) issued in 2008, the Turkish government provides tax incentives for private companies engaged in R&D, including income tax deductions, insurance fee support, exemption from stamp duty, and tariff exemptions. In addition, R&D centers in private sectors that employ graduates in basic science can receive grants equivalent to the total minimum wage of two years. As of May 2018, Turkey has 906 R&D centers and 220 design centers in private sectors, with about 48,000 researchers and 4000 designers. These R&D centers have submitted more than 7000 patent applications, of which 2000 patents were approved.

For high-tech firms that transfer technology to foreign countries and firms that provide financial and legal services for technology transfer, fees prescribed by law are exempted. Fees for exporting samples, promotion materials, and participation in foreign exhibitions are exempted to support the expansion of overseas markets.

The Turkish government has set up the KGF to provide loan guarantees for SMEs, expand financing channels for start-ups and SMEs, and give special support to export, female and young entrepreneurs, as well as agricultural fields. Support is also provided to micro-businesses such as tradesmen and craftsmen for guaranteed loans.

In addition, TTGV provides financing platforms and the HIT program for start-ups to solve financing problems. Established in 1991, the TTGV is a non-governmental organization mainly supporting technology R&D and innovation in Turkey's private sectors, promoting technology commercialization, industrial innovation, venture investment, and fund management. Ideanest is one of the intermediary services of TTGV. On the Ideanest platform, experts from TTGV evaluate projects and provide consulting services for early technological innovation. Through the Ideanest platform, project owners and researchers can raise funds for their specific needs. TTGV launched the HIT program at the end of 2017 to support the commercialization of health technology start-ups. The HIT program can provide up to 50,000 US dollars for each qualified start-up to accelerate its entry into the market.

The Turkish government promotes the development of venture capital through tax cut and other financing channels. Angel investors can deduct 75% of their capital from the annual tax base for investing in SMEs. From February 2013 to June 2018, 457 angel investors received tax cut totaling 11,739,206 Turkish lire (equivalent to 3.1 million US dollars) for 34 investment projects.

The Turkish government set up a fund of funds and amended the law on the contribution of the Ministry of Finance to the fund in 2017, allowing the Turkish Ministry of Finance to directly invest in venture capital funds up to 2 billion Turkish lire (equivalent to 530 million US dollars) by the end of 2023. Previously, the amount was no more than 500 million Turkish lire (equivalent to 132 million US dollars). This move has expanded financing channels for start-ups focusing on technological innovation.

Entrepreneur Services

Market Support

The TIM-TEB Global House jointly launched by the Turkish Exporters' Assembly (TIM) and the Turkish Economy Bank (TEB) in 2015 serves as an incubator to support local innovation and start-ups with high added value and export potential. It also provides management consulting and training services for technology firms to accelerate their expansion in overseas markets. TIM-TEB Global House is currently set up in ten major cities in Turkey, including Istanbul.

Enterprise Incubation

The Turkish government standardizes the management of incubators and provides financial subsidies and tax cut for the management companies of TDZs, start-ups in the zones, and R&D activities in the zones.

KOSGEB has set standards for incubator operation. Qualified incubators can use the logo of İŞGEM®. İŞGEM® is a registered trademark of KOSGEB. A business incubator can only use the name of İŞGEM if it meets the criteria of KOSGEB and obtains the authorization.

The Turkish government provides supports such as financial subsidies and tax cut for management companies, start-ups, and activities related to R&D and design in TDZs. For example, policies for start-ups include a 50% discount on office rent. A 75% discount on office rent is possible, if the start-up's project is part of the government's R&D support program. Before 2023, the design, software, and R&D activities of companies in the zones will be exempted from income tax and corporate tax, while researchers and software developers will be exempted from any tax.

Communication Platform

Various innovation and entrepreneurship competitions are used as platforms to gather and integrate talents, technology, capital, markets, and other innovation and entrepreneurship elements. Accompanied with these platforms are services such as financial investment, technology transfer, and exhibition.

The Business Plan Award is organized once a year by higher education institutions that cooperate with the KOSGEB. Participants are students who have taken entrepreneurship courses. Students who win the first, second, and third prizes may receive 25,000 Turkish lire (equivalent to 6600 US dollars), 20,000 Turkish lire (equivalent to 5300 US dollars) and 15,000 Turkish lire (equivalent to 4000 US dollars), respectively, if they can start their own company within 24 months.

The TIM has held Turkish Innovation and Entrepreneurship Week in cities of Istanbul and Anatolia since 2012. The Innovation and Entrepreneurship Week in 2017 was attended by 200 invited speakers from more than 200 institutions in 31 countries, with a total of 60,000 participants. In these activities, universities have the opportunity to display their innovative projects at the R&D center booths. A number of group discussions, conferences, and seminars are held on topics such as technology, design, Turkish inventors, and invention history.

The Turkish government encourages start-ups to compete for the European Enterprise Promotion Awards. The European Enterprise Promotion Awards aim to award and recognize the most successful enterprises and entrepreneurial promoters in Europe. KOSGEB is the coordinator of this award program and is responsible for nominating two national candidates.

Digital Transformation Support

KOSGEB (Turkey's Small and Medium Enterprises Development Organization) provided 71.59 million lira (%12.64 million) of assistance for 258 SMEs in adopting intelligent technologies in the manufacturing process in 2019. In July 2020, The Union of Chambers and Commodity Exchanges of Turkey (TOBB) and Trendyol (online shopping platform) have launched the "Grow Your Business with Trendyol" SME support program, so-called "e-commerce platforms to support SMEs". The program aimed to grow the business by reaching millions of customers. Within the scope of the program, online trainings and tricks of e-commerce are organized to explain how to sell for SMEs in Trendyol. Additionally, this program supports the growth of SMEs and start-ups with e-commerce and ensure that they start e-commerce at zero cost in Trendyol, thus contributing to employment growth and local development. Chamber and Commodity Exchange member companies applying to take advantage of the support program are be able to market their goods on Trendyol for a month, up to 30,000TRY with zero commission. This introductory month begins after the seller has made its products available on the platform.[1]

ENTREPRENEURSHIP EDUCATION

KOSGEB has been promoting entrepreneurship training courses nationwide since 2000, and plays an important role in non-school entrepreneurship education training.

KOSGEB has established standards for trainings and trainers. Its local partners include İŞKUR (a Turkish employment agency), municipal governments, chambers of commerce, non-governmental organizations, and higher education institutions. In trainings launched by KOSGEB, trainees may receive entrepreneurship funds from KOSGEB. In January 2016, İŞKUR and KOSGEB signed the Cooperation Protocol on Applied Entrepreneurship Training. Entrepreneurship trainings under this protocol can be completed in cooperation with competent universities, private educational institutions, professional chambers of commerce, public sectors and institutions, as well as associations and foundations. While obtaining a training certificate or planning to start a business in an incubator, entrepreneurs can apply for New Entrepreneur Support, with a maximum amount of 150,000 Turkish lire (equivalent to 40,000 US dollars). In 2017, 94,016 people took entrepreneurship training courses.

TUBITAK introduced the EIUI. This index evaluates the achievements of Turkish universities in promoting entrepreneurship and innovation. The purpose of developing this index is to introduce competition among higher education institutions and quantitatively measure their performance in entrepreneurship and innovation. Through the EIUI, entrepreneurship education of higher education institutions in Turkey has been greatly improved.

The Sabanci University was ranked first in EIUI for two consecutive years in 2015 and 2016. SUCool, an entrepreneurship acceleration platform of the university, mainly supports early technology-based start-ups. SUCool provides training, counseling, office space, and legal advice. It also introduces start-ups to the international entrepreneurial ecosystems

---

[1] Evaluation and Prospect of G20 Members' Policies to Support Entrepreneurship in the Post-pandemic Era, Entrepreneurship Research Center on G20 Economies, Oct 22, 2020.

in various regions, such as Silicon Valley, London, and Berlin. SUCoolmentors start-up teams by batch, usually selecting 10 start-up teams in each batch, with the goal of designing the business model for each team. Outstanding teams have the opportunity to study in places such as Silicon Valley or London. The best team may study in Global Founders' Skill Accelerator at MIT in the US, and the second best may participate in the summer project of the Entrepreneurship Research Center at National University of Singapore. These outstanding teams may also enter the INOVENT Incubation Center for the next stage of work. Entrepreneurial mentoring is provided by experienced college lecturers or well-known experts in the industry. Through the trainings, entrepreneurs can get a better understanding of the real process from generating ideas to delivering products to the market. They can cultivate their entrepreneurial mindset and know more about product development and customer needs.

Bilkent University has a science park called Cyberpark, whose goal is to become an entrepreneurial development center that encourages technology entrepreneurs. Cyberpark has several projects for entrepreneurs, such as UTTP which provides technology transfer and commercialization training for technology entrepreneurs. The Cyberpark Accelerator Program (CAP) is a cooperative project with the Innosphere, a US entrepreneurship incubation platform, targeting Turkish start-ups whose products are sold to the US. In 2018, the CAP cooperated with the Plug and Play Innovation Platform of Silicon Valley in the United States to carry out a 14-week program in Turkey and Silicon Valley, respectively. The program was supported by KOSGEB.

The Middle East Technical University was ranked the second in EIUI in 2015 and 2016 in a row. The university has an Entrepreneurship Research and Application Center, which offers students courses in entrepreneurship and innovation. Entrepreneurship education is open to non-business school students, and some programs are for non-business school students only.

Entrepreneurship education has also been integrated into Turkish secondary education. A weekly one-hour entrepreneurship class has been added in the curriculum at junior middle schools. The course content has been updated in 2018.

Turkey pays special attention to spreading the entrepreneurial culture and raising people's awareness of entrepreneurship through the publicity of entrepreneurship contests and entrepreneurial role models, as well as entrepreneurship education. The START entrepreneurship education program initiated by the Turkish Entrepreneurship Foundation aims to create entrepreneurial culture at high schools. The program plans to provide entrepreneurship training for five public high schools and five private high schools. During the training, it will organize field visits to start-ups and meetings with entrepreneurs, with an aim to develop the entrepreneurial spirit of middle school students. In terms of entrepreneurial role models, outstanding women entrepreneurs have been widely introduced and recognized through media. There were reports about Turkey's most successful women entrepreneurs in 2017. For example, a lady used to be a Cambridge doctoral candidate before she became a restaurant owner. An entrepreneur combined the organic agriculture industry with the hotel industry, creating one of Turkey's most distinctive eco-tourism destinations. Whether these entrepreneurs were engaged in catering or wine manufacturing, they all showed to the society that women could break conventional prejudices and give full play to their talents in their own careers. Undoubtedly, these role models were good incentives for potential entrepreneurs.

Fair Competition for SMEs

The Turkish Law No. 7246 on Amendments to the Law on Protection of Competition[2] (Amendment Law) with respect to SMEs is the introduction of the de minimis principle[3] of the EU legislation in the chapter of "Conclusion on Preliminary Investigation".

The revised clause is as follows: "The Commission may decide not to conduct a full investigation into agreements, consistent practices among enterprises, and decisions of associations of enterprises that do not substantially restrict competition in the market, except for overt and core violations concerning competitors, geographical or customer allocation, and supply restrictions".[4]

Infringements involving dominant operation will serve as the minimum natural threshold demarcating de minimis rule's scope, but because the Infringement of abuse of dominant position is not clearly stipulated in

---

[2] Released on June 24, 2020.

[3] https://www.eucomplaw.com/decisionsfallout-following-t-mobile/.

[4] https://www.mondaq.com/turkey/antitrust-eu-competition-/959416/amendments-to-the-turkish-competition-legislation?type=mondaqai&score=81.

the revised bill, such Infringement may also be exempted. In sync with EU practice, clear and core breaches such as pricing, regional or customer allocations, and restrictions on supply are excluded from the exemption.

The revised law mainly provides a clear legal basis for making judgments on the activities of SMEs operating in very narrow geographical markets. In addition, it takes into account the digitalization of economic activities and the transformation of entrepreneurial ecosystem, agreements and practices that SMEs and entrepreneurial companies gain a certain share of the market but may cause negligible anti-competition are exempted, so as to promote and protect the survival and development of SMEs and entrepreneurial ecology.

United Kingdom

It is important for British start-ups and SMEs to have an improved legal environment and enhanced government efficiency. In July 2015, the British government released the Small Business, Enterprise and Employment (SBEE) Act 2015 to promote and protect SMEs' development. This is a latest development based on the promulgation of the new Companies Act 2006. In addition, the UK established the Department for Business, Energy and Industrial Strategy (BEIS) in 2016 by consolidation. It is now the specific managing agency for British SMEs.

The British government has been continuously implemented tax relief and preferential policies for SMEs. These policies mainly include: tax cut and rise of tax threshold. In November 2016, the British government announced continuing its tax cut and planned to reduce the corporation tax of SMSs to 17%. Moreover, it raised the tax threshold from 6000 pounds to 12,000 pounds at the beginning of 2017. The British government also helps SMEs solve their financing problems by providing loan guarantees and encouraging investment in start-ups.

In 2016, the British government set up the National Productivity Investment Fund (NPIF) and the Industrial Strategy Challenge Fund (ISCF) to prioritize technology innovation and transfer of research outcomes. The British government pledged to invest more in research to maintain the Britain's leading positions in technology innovation. In order to help SMEs get financed from other credit service providers through shared credit data and matched finance providers, the British government further specified a list of designated banks and financial platforms in the Small and Medium Sized Business (Finance Platform) Regulations at the end of 2016. In guiding businesses to increase research and development investment and enhance innovation capability, the British government further pledged to improve the government procurement system and give a play to the government procurement. To this effort, it released the Green Paper: Development a Modern Industrial Strategy in the beginning of 2017.

Its progress in business incubation is characteristic. The "Pitch@Palace", a program founded by Prince Andrew, Duke of York in 2014, has held a swathe of innovation and entrepreneurship competitions worldwide, with a profound significance. Several government agencies, including Intellectual Property Office, and commercial banks jointly launched the Growth Accelerator Scheme for SMEs, which provides business guidance for SMEs and start-ups and helps businesses grow quickly and stably. As to the digitalization, The UK government has issued the "Digital Economy Strategy (2015–2018)" with the primary goal of "developing the digital economy and improving the business environment". In 2020, UK government set an online learning platform for employers during the outbreak of Covid-19.

The British government has introduced initiative and entrepreneurship into the school education system and incorporated entrepreneurship education into the core curriculum system of universities, which has now formed a relatively complete entrepreneurship education system and curriculum features. Universities have set special entrepreneurship education institutions, including The United Kingdom Business Incubation (UKBI) and incubation centers, launched courses for special groups such as women and minorities, supported social organizations to champion entrepreneurship culture and education by launching featured campaigns, and provided entrepreneurship services and support for specific groups such as veterans.

The regulation on the protection of SMEs in the UK competition law is indirectly or directly reflected in two aspects: "regulation on monopoly agreements" and "regulation on abuse of market dominance". In the UK, fixed price agreements are considered to be the most harmful of all restrictive competition agreements, and the principle of illegality per se is applied.

Government Services

It is an important part of British start-ups and SMEs to have an improved legal environment and enhanced government efficiency.

The British Parliament passed the Companies Act 2006 in 2006. It is a new act after the Companies Act 1985. The UK has released a series of acts and regulations on SMEs, which aim to prevent big businesses from merging small ones, protect small businesses' patents, encourage the transfer of technology achievements to SMEs, and resolve debt issues between small businesses.

In July 2015, the British government released the Small Business, Enterprise and Employment (SBEE) Act 2015 to promote SME development regarding financial support, regulatory reform, government procurement, education, etc. In terms of financial support, specific measures are mainly taken to improve the financing channels of enterprises, such as large and listed companies are required to report their payment policies and practices to better shoulder their payment responsibility; banks are required to share their SME clients' data with other lenders through the Credit Reference Agencies (CRAs), through which all lenders must have equal access to these data; and export financing support for British exporters are increased. The main content of regulatory reform is to require the government reducing red tape and improving service efficiency, such as simplifying business registration process and improving digital registration; improve efficiency and transparency of administrative accountability of regulatory agencies; provide transparent reports on the burden imposed on businesses by the new regulations, so as to ensure that the government will continue to focus on deregulation and reducing regulatory burdens in the future, and assure businesses that all new regulations will be subject to regular review, etc. Government procurement emphasizes that the government should take measures to remove unnecessary obstacles for small businesses and make procurement practices in the public sector more streamlined and effective. In addition, the bill also proposes to provide support to the education system and training providers so as to most effectively support students in achieving positive educational and training results, including sustainable employment.

The British government has a long history of setting up special management organizations for SMEs. In the 1970s, the SME Administration of the British Department of Trade and Industry (now, the Department for Business, Energy and Industrial Strategy [BEIS]) was responsible for managing and supporting the development of SMEs. The BEIS was founded by consolidating the Department for Business, Innovation, and Skills (BIS) and the Department of Energy and Climate Change (DECC) in July 2016, having a minister in charge of relevant issues, including small businesses, consumers, and corporate responsibilities. It has the Small Business Commission (SBC), of which the offices are ubiquitous across the UK. They are mainly responsible for resolving overdue repayment and non-performing repayment of private sector and the specific work of which are carried out by small business commissioners appointed and designated by the SBC.

Fiscal and Financial Support

In the 1980s, the British government exempted SMEs from the investment income surcharge and the national insurance surcharge. Since then, the British government has continued to implement tax cut and preferential policies for SMEs. The main measures include tax cut and rise of tax threshold. In November 2016, the British government announced continuing its tax cut and planned to reduce the corporation tax of SMSs to 17%. At the beginning of 2017, the British government introduced a total of 8.9 billion pounds tax cut plan for a five-year period. The plan focuses on supporting SMEs, permanently doubling the reduction of income tax for SMEs, and adjusting the tax threshold to 12,000 pounds, which became effective from April 2017. This is a further increase since the tax threshold was adjusted to 6000 pounds in 2016. The plan will allow 600,000 SMEs in the UK to be entitled to duty-free policy.

The British government also helps SMEs solve their financing problems by providing loan guarantees and encouraging investment in start-ups.

In November 2016, the British government extended the Enterprise Finance Guarantee Scheme (EFG) for four years in the 2017 government budget, which is expected to support 2 billion pounds of SME loans. The precedent of the Enterprise Finance Guarantee (EFG) Scheme is the Small Firms Loan Guarantees (SFLG) Scheme, which was founded in 1981 and replaced by EFG in 2009. Under the EFG, more than 40 financial institutions grant loans to their SME clients. Since 2009, a total of 28,000 SMEs have been provided with financing support of 3 billion pounds.

The UK's incentive policy for venture capital is relatively comprehensive. In addition to incentive policies on direct investment of individual investors of unlisted companies, the Enterprise Investment Scheme (EIS) and the Seed Enterprise Investment Scheme (SEIS), the UK has incentive policies on indirect investment of individual investors in small unlisted companies through venture capital trusts.

The EIS mainly involves preferential policy on individual income tax and capital gains tax. Among them, the individual income tax deduction policy applies a 30% income tax deduction rate, with an investment ceiling of 1 million pounds per year and an income tax deduction ceiling of 300,000 pounds per year. If an investor loses money when disposing of his stocks, the loss can be used to offset the income in the disposal year or any previous year, thus reducing the taxable income for the individual income tax. Capital gains tax includes preferential policies on credit and deferred tax. If an investor does not get individual income tax rebate and disposes of the equity investment after 3 years, the capital gains tax will be exempted. There is no limit to the amount of deferred tax applicable to the capital gains deferred tax policy, and the policy applies to natural person investors and trustees who are related or unrelated to the invested.

The SEIS involves preferential policies on individual income tax, capital gains tax, and tax incentives for reinvestment. Investors can receive up to 50% tax relief in the tax year the investment is made, regardless of their marginal rate, the ceiling of which is 100,000 pounds a year.

The VCT involves preferential policies on corporate income tax, individual income tax, and capital gains tax. Gains attained by a VCT from investors may be exempted from corporate income tax. An individual investor is entitled to preferential individual income tax, dividend and bonus income tax rebate, capital gains tax rebate, and preferential deferred capital gains tax when subscribing for new shares.

In order to encourage and support young people to start businesses, the British government launched the Start Up Loan Scheme and set up Start Up Loans Company in 2012. At the very beginning, it targeted people aged 18–24, providing loans within 5000 pounds for their feasible business plan. At present, the amount has been increased to 25,000 pounds. In addition to providing loans, Start Up Loans Company also provides counseling and entrepreneurship mentoring services. By August 2016, Start Up Loans Company had offered a total of 250 million pounds loans, creating 45,000 jobs.

Entrepreneur Services

Technical Services

The British government places a high priority on the role of technology innovation in promoting start-ups and SMEs. At the end of 2016, the British government pledged to increase 2 billion pounds of research and development investment every year by 2020, and also proposed to set up the NPIF in the next five years, with a total amount of 23 billion pounds, giving priority to the development of technology innovation and infrastructure. In addition, the NPIF will provide a total of 4.7 billion pounds of additional research and development funds between 2020 and 2021 to maintain UK's advantages in research and development and innovation after the Brexit. The British government will also set up the ISCF to accelerate the translation of scientific research achievements and encourage businesses to innovate by tax incentives and other means.

With the development and popularization of the Internet, network knowledge and skills are increasingly important for the development of start-ups and SMEs. In 2013, the British government launched a total of 100 million pounds Broadband Connection Vouchers Scheme to provide 3000 pounds of broadband installation subsidies to small businesses. The SME Digital Capability Program run by GO ON UK helps small businesses acquire Internet-related skills.

Information Services

In the British SME credit market, the information conducive to credit risk assessment, including financing needs of SMEs, credit records, settlement accounts, are only shared among conventional financial institutions. New financial institutions that are not conventional financial institutions cannot effectively fill the financing needs gap of SMEs due to lack of access to such information.

In 2015, the British government released the Small and Medium Sized Business (Credit Information) Regulations, stipulating that designated banks must submit basic information of businesses, loans, settlement accounts, and other information to designated credit institutions, including Experian, Equifax, and Credit Safe, after the approval of SMEs. This compulsory information sharing measure can help new financial institutions obtain customer information of SMEs and provide financing support.

In 2015, the British government also released the Small and Medium Sized Business (Finance Platform) Regulations. In November 2016, it specified the list of designated banks and designated finance platforms in the Regulation, requiring the nine banks[1] to push the information of SMEs that they refuse to lend to the three financing platforms,[2] including business information and financing information, to help SMEs get financed from other credit service providers by matching up them with finance providers.

Market Support

The British government gives limited preference to SMEs through government procurement. It increases its support for SMEs by setting up a single procurement marketplace—Contracts Finder and improving efficiency of public tenderers.

In January 2017, the UK released the Developing a Modern Industrial Strategy: Green Paper, proposing to improve the government procurement system and giving full play to the government procurement in guiding business to increase research and development investment and enhancing innovation capability. In early 2015, the British government promulgated the Public Contracts Regulations 2015 (PCRS 2015), the revised government procurement regulations, which requires government tenderers to disclose detailed bidding information on the Contracts Finder portal website. Subsequently, the British government relaunched the Contracts Finder portal website, which is the only portal for public tender. It allows suppliers to inquire about bidding projects and details of bidding contract based on factors such as industry, geographical location, and price, without any cost.

At the same time, the British government also issued a new version of the Pre-Qualification Questionnaires (PQQS) to simplify the public tender and improve efficiency. For example, suppliers' self-declaration is adopted to assess their qualifications and only the bid winner is required

---

[1] Nine banks: Allied Irish Bank, Bank of Ireland, Barclays Bank, Clydesdale Bank, Northern Bank, HSBC Bank, Lloyds Banking Group, the Royal Bank of Scotland and Santander UK.

[2] Three major finance platforms: Funding Xchange, Funding Options, and Business Finance Compared.

to provide relevant supporting documents to reduce the burden on businesses. In July 2016, the British government released the Procurement Policy Note—Legal Requirement to Publish on Contracts Finder (PPN), requiring public tender to publish low-threshold procurement opportunities and contract information on the Contracts Finder portal website to enable micro, small, and medium-sized business to access government procurement orders in a convenient way.

Enterprise Incubation

Pitch@Palace means "reported at the palace", which is a public welfare platform for business incubation founded by Prince Andrew, Duke of York in 2014. The program aims to bring together the most influential industry leaders in various fields and provide strong entrepreneurial support for entrepreneurs. Since its foundation, Pitch@Palace has supported more than 300 entrepreneurial projects worldwide and established more than 5850 effective value links. A number of entrepreneurial projects were successfully acquired by internationally renowned companies such as Apple and Twitter, and received a total investment of more than 500 million pounds. Since 2015, the Pitch@Palace Global Innovation and Entrepreneurship Competition has been held in countries and regions such as Malaysia, Africa, Estonia, and Latin America.

Several government agencies, including Intellectual Property Office, and commercial banks jointly launched the Growth Accelerator Scheme for SMEs, which provides business guidance for SMEs and start-ups and helps businesses grow quickly and stably. This Scheme is jointly managed by the British Intellectual Property Office, the Design Council, UK Trade and Investment (UKTI), and the UK Export Finance (UKEF) in cooperation with British commercial banks. By providing SMEs with tailor-made business guidance and development strategies and equipping them with specialized mentors, the Growth Accelerator Scheme helps enterprises remove obstacles in financing, leadership and management capabilities, commercial innovation, strategic development and implementation, and helps enterprises achieve the goal of accelerated growth.

Communication Platform

Some private activities carried out with the support of the government are distinctive in promoting exchanges between businessmen and entrepreneurs and in encouraging the public to start businesses. StartUp Britain is a national campaign initiated by several entrepreneurs and started in 2011. This campaign includes a national program called StartUp Britain Bus, which aims to promote exchanges between businessmen and entrepreneurs and provide support and services for entrepreneurs in starting and developing businesses. Business in You is to use the story of successful businessmen to inspire entrepreneurs and potential entrepreneurs to realize their business ideas.

Digital Transformation Support

As to the digitalization, the UK government has issued the "Digital Economy Strategy (2015–2018)" with the primary goal of "developing the digital economy and improving the business environment" to develop the UK into the country most suitable for digital entrepreneurship.[3]

In 2020, UK government set an online learning platform for employers to share free, high-quality digital, numeracy and soft skill courses with their staff to boost team productivity and motivation during the outbreak of Covid-19.[4]

ENTREPRENEURSHIP EDUCATION

The British government introduced initiative and entrepreneurship into the school education system in the Education Reform Act 1988, and has now formed a relatively complete entrepreneurship education system and characteristic curricula.

The Council for Science and Technology experts wrote a letter to the British Prime Minister in October 2016 advising universities to include entrepreneurship education in the core curriculum system of universities, especially for students majoring in Science Technology Engineering Mathematics (STEM), which has been confirmed by the British Prime Minister. The British Higher Education Quality Assurance Agency

---

[3] Assessment on the progress of G20 Entrepreneurship Action Plan, Entrepreneurship Research Center on G20 Economies, Oct 22, 2019.

[4] Evaluation and Prospect of G20 Members' Policies to Support Entrepreneurship in the Post-pandemic Era, Entrepreneurship Research Center on G20 Economies, Oct 22, 2020.

(QAA) published a report entitled "Entrepreneurship and Entrepreneurship Education" and argued that the goal of entrepreneurship education is to produce entrepreneurial effectiveness, namely entrepreneurial awareness, entrepreneurial thinking, and entrepreneurial ability (QAA, 2012). Under the guidance of the report, the entrepreneurship education curriculum in British universities is divided into two types of "About Courses" and "For Courses" to help students understand entrepreneurship in depth and improve their insight and practical ability to become entrepreneurs in the future. So far, British universities have established a three-level entrepreneurship curriculum system including "entrepreneurship awareness", "entrepreneurship knowledge" and "entrepreneurship career", and universities also have specialized entrepreneurship education institutions such as the United Kingdom Business Incubation (UKBI) and entrepreneurship centers.

Oxford University has an Entrepreneurship Center, which provides entrepreneurship education and support for Oxford's students, alumni, and faculty. The Entrepreneurial Center will bring together people from universities, industry, and government to discuss and analyze the current hot issues of entrepreneurship. In addition, the Entrepreneurship Center organizes entrepreneurship education and training programs, such as the Venture Idea Exploration Workshop (VIEW), which teaches students some entrepreneurship theories and exercises some skills needed for entrepreneurship, such as public speech, market research, and business planning. The center has also set up Oxford Entrepreneurs, an alumni network platform for entrepreneurs, to provide various support for entrepreneurs from setting up enterprises to making them bigger and stronger.

The goal of the Cambridge University Entrepreneurship Center is to cultivate students' entrepreneurial spirit and skills and to provide students with various resources. "Enterprise Tuesday" is a free program, which will invite entrepreneurs and investors to attend school lectures every Tuesday night to let students know the real business world and develop personal networks. "Accelerate Cambridge" of Cambridge University is an accelerator established in 2012. It provides three months of training for the settled teams, so that the teams can avoid making some common mistakes, access to various resources, and accelerate the establishment and development of businesses.